W9-BDA-921

REFERENCE.

5 Court House ........ 15 National Theatre
6 Merchants Exchange 16 Museum
& Post Office ........ 17 Tremont House
7 Faneuil Hall ........ 18 U. S. Hotel
8 ............ Market 19 American House
9 Boylston " ...... 20 Marlboro Hotel
10 Athenæum ......... Churches

21. Dickinson's Printing Establishment &
Type & Stereotype
Foundry.

# SARAH'S LONG WALK

# SARAH'S LONG WALK

## *The Free Blacks of Boston and How Their Struggle for Equality Changed America*

STEPHEN KENDRICK

AND

PAUL KENDRICK

BEACON
150

BEACON PRESS, BOSTON

BEACON PRESS
25 Beacon Street
Boston, Massachusetts 02108-2892
www.beacon.org

Beacon Press books
are published under the auspices of
the Unitarian Universalist Association of Congregations.

07 06 05 04 8 7 6 5 4 3 2 1

This book is printed on acid-free paper that meets the uncoated paper ANSI/NISO
specifications for permanence as revised in 1992.

Text design by Patricia Duque Campos
Composition by Wilsted & Taylor Publishing Services

Library of Congress Cataloging-in-Publication Data

Kendrick, Stephen, 1954–
Sarah's long walk : the free Blacks of Boston and how their struggle for
equality changed America / Stephen Kendrick and Paul Kendrick.
p. cm.
Includes bibliographical references and index.
ISBN 0-8070-5018-0 (alk. paper)
1. Free African Americans—Civil rights—Massachusetts—Boston—History.
2. African Americans—Segregation—Massachusetts—Boston—History.
3. Segregation in education—Massachusetts—Boston—History. 4. Boston (Mass.)—
Race relations. 5. Roberts, Sarah C., b. 1844—Trials, litigation, etc. 6. Free African
Americans—Massachusetts—Boston—Biography. 7. African American girls—
Massachusetts—Boston—Biography. 8. Boston (Mass.)—Biography. 9. Beacon Hill
(Boston, Mass.)—Biography. 10. Beacon Hill (Boston, Mass.)—History.
I. Kendrick, Paul, 1983– II. Title.

F73.9.N4K46 2004
305.896'073074461—dc22
2004015085

*For Liz, Anna, and Elizabeth*

*Well, race . . . it's always something you don't want to do.*
*And it's always about confronting yourself, always tailor-made*
*for you to fail in dealing with it. And the question*
*of your heroism and of your courage in dealing with this trial*
*is the measure of your success. Can you confront it with honesty?*
*And do you have the energy to sustain an attack on it?*

WYNTON MARSALIS

*This town of Boston has a history. It is not an accident,*
*not a windmill, or a railway station, or a cross-roads tavern, or an*
*army barracks grown up by time and luck to a place of wealth; but*
*a seat of humanity, of men of principle, obeying a sentiment*
*and marching loyally whither that shall lead them; so that its annals*
*are great historical lines, inextricably national.*

RALPH WALDO EMERSON

# CONTENTS

# INTRODUCTION

## *Brown* and Before

On December 9, 1952, a tall, burly man rose, ready to make his argument but knowing, in good Supreme Court tradition, that he would quickly be interrupted by inquiries and peppered with hard questioning. Thurgood Marshall, longtime chief legal counsel for the NAACP, had worked for this moment for a decade. His broad, handsome features, with his normally genial smile under a trim mustache now set and stern, betrayed little anxiety. The lawyer settled himself in the well of this venerated place and leaned forward, hovering commandingly over the lectern, respectful and calm, addressing the justices with an informal ease. Looking up to the highly polished wooden podium of the United States Supreme Court, with nine impassive faces staring down at him, Marshall knew he represented more than a hundred years of black lawyers determined to dismantle segregation in America.

Before the high court that day, five cases were yoked together. Each concerned young children across the nation who were excluded from local public schools simply because they were black. All five cases had been carefully nursed during a long and twisting judicial process until, together, they combined to form a kind of battering ram against the imposing and seemingly impenetrable fortress of America's racial division. Although small and encouraging legal victories concerning higher education over the previous decade had been slowly chipping away at segregation, Thurgood

Marshall and his legal team had resolved to lay siege to the citadel itself through the total desegregation of all public schools in the nation.

This radical effort, daunting and emotionally draining, was an endeavor that might well prove, in the end, impossible. All custom, social order, history, and legal precedence lay against it, but the fact that Chief Justice Fred Vinson was now about to respond to the NAACP legal team's painstakingly precise written briefs with the official beginning of an oral argument could be seen as a great victory in itself.

Some could say that, but Marshall intended to win, no matter how long it might take or how many more cases they had to bring —there was no sign of a shortage of fresh outrages to choose from. Yet to come so far and then hit the unexpected buzz saw of Felix Frankfurter!

No one on the NAACP Legal Defense team ever dreamed that any of these justices would be warmly responsive to their challenge of one of the most powerful impulses of American life—namely, the racial separation of school-age children. However, it was assumed that Frankfurter, a Vienna-born Jewish immigrant, an old Harvard Law School liberal, and a consultant to the NAACP in pre–Supreme Court days, would be their ally in this difficult moment. Instead, he peppered Robert Carter, the first NAACP lawyer who spoke for the interests of the child Linda Brown of Topeka, Kansas, with sharp and needling questions. Carter survived the morning's opening cross-examination, but barely.

Now as the afternoon session proceeded, it was Marshall's turn, and he faced the justices with a sense that his team needed, somehow, to regain the initiative. Their chief problem was the 1896 Supreme Court decision *Plessy v. Ferguson,* the primary legal undergirding for segregation in all areas of life in the United States. Somehow, the defense team had to get around this infamous decision justifying the doctrine of "separate but equal."

In this turn-of-the-century Louisiana case, a New Orleans black man named Homer Plessy deliberately had himself arrested by insisting on riding in the "whites only" train car to nearby Lake

Pontchartrain. The Supreme Court decided that transportation for blacks and whites could legitimately be kept entirely separate, just as long as it could be demonstrated that such modes of travel were roughly equal. From this decision on, segregation in all areas of American life was deemed acceptable, upheld in multiple legal judgments concerning restaurants, water fountains, streetcars, theaters, and most of all public schools. *Plessy* was a vast problem they had to somehow get around.

*Brown v. Board of Education* was a complex set of cases, but at its heart, it was about somehow reversing this monumental decision, and Associate Justice Felix Frankfurter, no matter how quietly sympathetic he might be to their goals, was not about to let Marshall and his lawyers think that they could somehow dance around *Plessy* as if the prior ruling did not matter. Too many state and federal legal decisions were now based on *Plessy*, and too much of the texture of life, not just in the South, was also subtly imbued with this rigid subtext of daily affairs being kept racially separate.

In these 1952 Supreme Court oral arguments, a duel developed between Marshall and Frankfurter. Marshall, respectful even to legal adversaries passionately defending segregation, was finding it hard to resist lashing back at the small, owl-faced justice. Marshall later said of his ordeal under the justice's probing questioning, "Frankfurter was a smart aleck, you know." He even thought seriously of saying in defense of his people, "May it please the Court, I wish to mention the fact that we have not come as far as some people think. For example, if this involved Jewish kids, I don't think we'd have this problem." The black lawyer had expected that as a Jew, Associate Justice Frankfurter would understand the true nature of discrimination.

The whole basis of the NAACP case was simple, that this kind of separation could never be equated with anything remotely called equality. Marshall stated as clearly as he could, over and over, that living under segregation was a sustained humiliation. Black children suffered not from some theoretical injustice but, as they phrased it, an "actual injury."

The intellectually agile associate justice was known for asking interesting and provocative questions, and yet he could also be simply perverse in his wide-ranging and at times abstract oral arguments. In the course of the questioning, Frankfurter asked Marshall if overturning *Plessy* would not allow South Carolina school boards the right to separate out blue-eyed students. Was there anything wrong with the idea of allowing "all blue-eyed children to go to separate schools"?

Marshall shot back instantly the terse "No, sir, because the blue eyed people in the United States never had the badge of slavery which was perpetuated in the statutes."

Part of Frankfurter's insistent questioning centered on an obscure Massachusetts state court case—more than a hundred years old—called *Roberts*, a case Justice Frankfurter had already raised with Robert Carter in the morning's arguments. Thurgood Marshall wanted to avoid talking about such past cases if he possibly could, since that past contained far too many difficult decisions upholding and sustaining segregation, so he jabbed and covered himself as best he could. He especially wanted to avoid a difficult case brought by a black Beacon Hill parent on behalf of his five-year-old daughter, Sarah, which would give him nothing but trouble. Instead, Marshall wanted to focus the Court's thoughts on the meaning of the Fourteenth Amendment if he could, passed in 1868 after the Civil War and the dissolution of slavery. That amendment used the phrase "nor shall any state deprive any person of life, liberty, or property, without due process of law; nor deny to any person within its jurisdiction the equal protection of the laws."

Chief Justice Vinson, not inclined to overturn precedents, wondered why the lone dissenter in the *Plessy* decision, Justice John Marshall Harlan, had not mentioned public schools in his impassioned plea against the concept of "separate but equal." Marshall replied that Harlan had been chiefly concerned with what the *Plessy* case was actually about, namely, the narrow issue of transportation. Then Marshall speculated that "the public school system was in such bad shape...but on the other hand, in the majority opinion, the significant thing, the case they relied on, was the *Roberts* case which was decided before the Fourteenth Amendment was even passed."

Frankfurter shot in. "But that does not do away with a consideration of the *Roberts* case, does it?"

"No, sir, it does not."

The Boston-trained lawyer bore in. "The significance of the *Roberts* case is that that should be considered by the Supreme Court at a time when that issue was rampant in the United States."

The diminutive justice soon had Marshall on the ropes. Marshall's reply was fumbling and disjointed. This bothersome 1849 *Roberts* case was not where he wanted to be.

> Well, sir, I do not know about those days. But I cannot conceive of the *Roberts* case being good for anything except that the legislatures of the states at those times were trying to work out their problems as they best could understand. And it could be that up in Massachusetts at that time they thought that Negroes—some of them escaping from slavery, and all—but I still say that the considerations for the passage of any legislation before the Civil War and up to 1900, certainly, could not apply at the present time. I think that every race has made progress, but I do not believe that those considerations have any bearing at this time. The question today is—

Frankfurter cut him off curtly. He knew, as well as the NAACP legal team did, that *Plessy* had been largely based on this Boston school-desegregation case, and that one of the great legal minds of American history, Chief Justice Lemuel Shaw of the Massachusetts Supreme Judiciary Court, had written this influential decision. Indeed, Judge Shaw created, from his fertile and teeming legal genius, the whole idea of "separate but equal." Frankfurter interjected, "They do not study these cases. But may I call your attention to what Mr. Justice Holmes said about the Fourteenth Amendment? 'The Fourteenth Amendment itself as an historical product did not destroy history for the state and substitute mechanical departments of law.'"

Marshall was being forcibly told that getting the justices to use the Fourteenth Amendment as a way of nullifying the towering influence of the *Plessy* decision was just not going to happen.

Forced into a corner, Marshall backed down, conceding, "I agree, sir."

After two days of further argument, John W. Davis, the opposing counsel, was heard to say of the vexing case of *Brown v. Board of Education* that those representing the status quo had the majority on their side, five to four, or perhaps even six to three. It was hard for Marshall to disagree.

Then the justices surprised everyone by issuing not a decision but a pause in the proceedings. The Supreme Court asked both sides to consider five questions concerning the history and intent of the Fourteenth Amendment (and on how overturning *Plessy* could possibly be implemented), fully research them, and then return within a year with new arguments. This unusual move, largely interpreted then and now as a delaying tactic for the Court, forced Marshall to regroup, assemble a new team of investigative historians, and look anew at what the men born and legally trained before the cataclysm of the Civil War actually meant by the phrase "equal protection under the law."

It also forced him to figure out how to turn back this ghost of Judge Lemuel Shaw and the *Roberts* case, which was about a five-year-old black Boston girl forced to walk past five white schools to reach the black school she was ordered to attend.

To win *Brown v. Board of Education* and allow twelve-year-old Linda Brown of Topeka, Kansas, to attend an integrated school, Thurgood Marshall had to overturn not only social custom, overt prejudice, and the *Plessy* decision, but also that troublesome 103-year-old case initiated by a Boston parent who was angry that his child, Sarah, had to walk so far.

. . .

Over the crest and then down Joy Street, it is a chilly January night of sleet on Beacon Hill. It requires no effort at all to believe this is still antebellum Boston, reflected in the shining brick sidewalks and the rows of glazed streetlights, each flickering with a yellow gas flame. Tonight, it is only the iced cars tightly lining this crowded street that betray that the century has turned twice from when these towering Greek Revival red brick homes were in an area called Nigger Hill.

The steep descent increases once you walk past the infamous cross street of Pinckney, long ago designed effectively to separate the elite side of Beacon Hill from the north slope, where the poor servants and tradespeople lived, which before the Civil War was one of the largest free black communities in America. Today the homes of black leaders Lewis Hayden, John Hilton, and William Cooper Nell are occupied by a far different kind of Beacon Hill resident. Nearing Cambridge Street, the sharp bay water winds still sweep in, though the water no longer laps up to the very edge of this neighborhood as it did then.

Warm lights from Smith Court spill out into the dark street, the old center of black Boston. Here stands the old black Smith School, restored now as the Museum of Afro-American History, as well as the African Meeting House, the oldest black house of worship in America still in public use. Tonight there is a meeting of local white and black researchers and activists hosted by National Park Service rangers who work at the historical site, along with a public presentation on the history of the neighborhood.

A tiny man in his late seventies named Horace Seldon, dressed in a light green ranger uniform, looks over the hundred of us seated in a great circle. His booming voice startles us. "Look about you," he cries, gesturing around him to the plain yellow brick sanctuary. "You cannot work here and not be aware that in this room Frederick Douglass and Lewis Hayden spoke about their days in slavery. Here are the echoes of William Lloyd Garrison speaking on a winter night like this in 1832 creating the New England Anti-Slavery Society. Garrison said he was *a man all on fire*. He needed to be, because he had a mountain of ice to melt in the America of his day." He then dares us to live up to the men and women who worshiped and gathered in this sanctuary to dream, to organize, to fight back.

Then a ranger named Bernadette Williams rises to tell us about how the *Roberts* case began here. "One father, and a lawyer named Robert Morris, helped change American history," she said.

. . .

Two years previously, we happened to be in Memphis. We walked along Beale Street and luxuriated in soul food and blues, and Paul saw for himself where his favorite Stax records had been recorded. He also insisted we go to the old Lorraine Motel, where Rev. Martin Luther King had been assassinated, which was now the new National Civil Rights Museum. The museum was crowded, and the good-natured joshing and children's laughter died away as we wound our way through the exhibits and got closer to the sobering end of the tour. We will always remember the absolute silence in that motel hallway. We could simultaneously look into King's room and clearly see the line of fire from the boardinghouse across the way to the spot on the balcony where he died, slammed back so hard by the bullets that his shoes flew off his feet and were later found twenty yards away in the parking lot below.

This was not the only powerful moment we experienced that remarkable day. At the start of the tour, there is a great room with a timeline designed to orient you to the broad sweep of the story of civil rights, from the infamous Middle Passage to today. Stephen noticed and was intrigued by a small caption telling of a young girl in antebellum Boston named Sarah Roberts and how her startling case had gone all the way to the Massachusetts Supreme Judicial Court. We wondered why we had never heard her story before. The idea stayed with us, even when it seemed nearly impossible to find out more about her.

When, years later, we found ourselves living in Boston, we resolved to discover whatever we could about this largely forgotten case, and how America had been changed by this intriguing interaction of white and black in this one small neighborhood. More than 150 years ago, the small geographical area of Beacon Hill, about ten blocks by ten, contained within its boundaries two worlds, one poor and black, the other white and wealthy. Yet as separate as these worlds seemed, each contained within itself certain brave individuals who decided to cross the line of Pinckney Street to work together.

The result of our quest is the book you hold. However inspiring the story of *Sarah's Long Walk* may be, it remains not a particularly sentimental or comfortable story. It is difficult to envision just how powerful the forces of racism were for this generation of Boston blacks and how they affected even their abolitionist allies. Louis Agassiz, a Harvard scientist, told a Charlestown (Massachusetts) audience in 1847, exactly the time period of this book, "The brain of the Negro is that of the imperfect brain of a seven months infant in the womb of a white." In the end, this struggle concerns how an essentially white abolitionist movement was transformed into a black-led and -inspired protest movement resembling nothing so much as the civil rights movement of the early 1960s.

This is the story of civil rights born in the age of abolitionism. If one wants to understand racial attitudes in modern-day Boston, there is perhaps no better way to begin than by reading the Pulitzer Prize–winning book *Common Ground,* J. Anthony Lukas's marvelous intertwining of the lives of three Boston families during the racial disputes of the early 1970s. These compelling stories center around the angry explosion the city experienced over busing and school desegregation, and the reader is quickly brought up to speed to the fact that racism does not seem to bear a sectional stamp or carry any expiration date. Boston was then, and is now, still a harsh city where its people are, if not strictly segregated, at the very least still encouraged to be segmented and separate if possible. The high ideals and the imposing saga of liberty that are the city's natural legacy remain quite real, and noble, but so does the painful struggle, across far too many generations, to achieve a fraternity between white and black.

In *Common Ground,* we did begin to find Sarah Roberts, though she is mentioned only in a brief passage. There we also first encountered Charles Sumner's ringing words before Judge Shaw so many years ago, that a "school, exclusively devoted to one class, must differ essentially, in its spirit and character, from the public school known to the law. . . . It is a mockery to call it an equivalent." Lukas summed up the meaning of Justice Shaw's denial of equal protection in this way: "the separate but equal doctrine was to have a profound effect on the nation's history. . . the genesis of the legal principle which was to govern the country's race relations until 1954."

Lukas had the luxury of interviewing in depth the ordinary people he was writing about. We obviously did not have that opportunity; indeed, to bring to full life their struggles and successes proved our most daunting challenge, since so many of their records are lost or were never considered important enough to preserve in the first place.

Yet within these humbling limits, we thought it was an essential story to recover.

Our focus over two years of research broadened from one family's experience into that of a whole society living in that geographically small area called Beacon Hill. It is hard to believe how closely packed together the characters we will encounter in our story truly were. In one half-hour walk, you can visit the homes of Charles Sumner (located in the former black section of the north slope); the birthplace and later the home of Wendell Phillips; the home of George Hillard, Sumner's law partner and a man who signed the warrants returning fugitive slaves to the South (meanwhile his wife was harboring escaped slaves in a hidden room in their home); and the Mount Vernon Street homes of Lemuel Shaw and Ellis Gray Loring. As the white protagonists of this story, it is perhaps not surprising that they lived in such close and seemingly cozy proximity to one another—Boston has always been a small world for its elite.

Yet the same short walk also includes the former homes of African American leaders such as David Walker, Maria Stewart, John Hilton, Robert Roberts, and Lewis Hayden, a man who stood on the front steps of his Beacon Hill home and promised to explode two kegs of gunpowder if slave catchers who were threatening his hidden fugitives moved one step closer. Across the way from the African Meeting House, there still stands the home of William Cooper Nell, the printer whose dogged determination drove the school desegregation boycott and protest movement for more than fifteen years.

After a short walk over the Boston Common, and then down Summer Street and toward Government Center along Downtown

Crossing, one can easily visit the former sites of William Lloyd Garrison's *Liberator* office, the printing shop of Sarah's father, Benjamin Roberts, and the law offices of Robert Morris, the twenty-four-year-old lawyer who took Sarah's case and in doing so galvanized this remarkable community.

The *Roberts* case, now seldom recalled except as a minor incident in the white-led abolitionist movement of Boston's William Lloyd Garrison or relegated to a footnote in Supreme Court legal records, is in fact a key moment in our history, the precise moment when one black community realized it was free in more than name. Arguing before Judge Shaw, Sumner said, "On one side is the city of Boston, strong in its wealth, in its influence, in its character; on the other side is a little child, of a degraded color, of humble parents, still within the period of natural infancy, but strong from her very weakness.... This little child asks at your hands her personal rights."

The deeper we went into this story, the more we realized that the "great man" tradition of historical writing was too small, too confining, for the wealth of courage and creative social protest that this generation of free black activists displayed. Though *Roberts v. the City of Boston* was lost in the courts, on the streets of Boston it proved to be a different matter.

This black community won complete victory within five years, through boycotts, protests, the creation of new outlets for their message, and, yes, the effective use of white allies, with Boston becoming the first major city in America to open its public schools to African Americans. For, as the battle for open schools went forward, this small, vulnerable Beacon Hill community of fewer than three thousand free blacks discovered within itself the resolve and determination to force the opening up of theaters and railway cars, the legalization of interracial marriage, the opening of government jobs for blacks, and, by fighting for a memorial to Boston Massacre martyr Crispus Attucks, the first formation of African American Union regiments to fight for the end of slavery itself.

One of the most important movements in historical writing today is an emerging emphasis on the experience of common people in extraordinary circumstances. We have been much influenced by Alfred Young's recent *The Shoemaker and the Tea Party,* in which the author's research was guided by the question, "How does an ordinary person win a place in history?" Young admits, "Until quite recently, professional historians have rarely opened the gates to ordinary people." But this is not a recent question only. In 1856 Frederick Law Olmsted noted that those who record history have been tied to the elite and self-perceived leadership class, and the "dumb masses have often been so lost in this shadow of egotism that, in later days, it has been impossible to discern the very real influences their character and conditions has had on the fortune and fate of nations."

Thurgood Marshall would often tell his fellow Supreme Court justices that his function was to constantly remind them of the law's effect on humble people, "all those John Doakes," as he called them. Looking back on the long years of work and litigation leading to *Brown,* Marshall said he was not the hero of the tale. In a speech in 1969, he said change had come because of the courage of forgotten people: "The citizen who believed that equal protection meant just that—the citizen who, with the assistance of those lawyers who still believed in the promise of justice and equality, never gave up the fight against the relics of slavery."

When reporters turned their attention away, and all the hired lawyers left town, what remained was the bravery of local people who stayed on, facing hatred and community resentment, people who had put themselves and their children on the line, and this awed Thurgood Marshall. The saga of civil rights did not start in his time, and he was acutely aware of this truth. Former NAACP Legal Defense Fund lawyer William Taylor echoed this sentiment when he told us that school-desegregation cases always had a better chance of success with a galvanized community behind the legal action. This was never demonstrated better than by the bravery of these long-ago citizens of Beacon Hill and the movement that crystallized in a hugely influential lawsuit. Now that we know their story at last, it allows us to see just how long this struggle to define equality has been going on, and how change actually happens, fueled by the uncommon courage of average women and men.

In the midst of the long Smith School boycott in antebellum Boston a turning point came, and no one at the time recognized it —nor did they recognize it when a century later Rosa Parks's aching feet made her refuse to sit in the back of the bus. Robert Morris cried out after the campaign's eventual victory in 1858, "Let us be bold, and they will have to yield to us!" This is the story not of the famous but of great things achieved by ordinary people with the genius of boldness.

# PART 1

# A Star in the East

*The position of the colored citizens of Boston
is in many features a peculiar one.*

WILLIAM COOPER NELL

# O N E

# The Lawyer

Long years after becoming a renowned and wealthy advocate for his people, attorney Robert Morris still remembered that painful spring day in 1847. All lawyers face intense pressure in their first case before a judge, but this opening case was different. On the very next day, Morris, trained to be a table servant like his father before him, would become the first black lawyer in America to argue a jury case.

On that spring day, Morris sat despondently in his new office on State Street, located at the very center of Boston's banking and legal district. Mere steps away was the site of the Boston Massacre, where, only seventy years earlier, a black sailor named Crispus Attucks had, in the words of Morris, spilled "the first blood that crimsoned the pavement" during the desperate and deadly confusion of that night's melee. Morris later remembered feeling more than just the raw nerves of a young attorney. His anxiety was so intense that he felt nearly overwhelmed. Yes, he was now an attorney trained under the respected Brahmin Ellis Gray Loring, his kindly legal mentor and friend, a man who proclaimed Morris surely the equal of any other newly minted lawyer. Yet the quiet and nearly reclusive Loring, though brave and often mocked for his shockingly radical abolitionist leanings, had never faced a moment remotely like this one.

This trial's eve came at the very beginning of a notable forty-year career. At every turn—from the fifteen-year struggle to open

Boston schools to African Americans; to the desegregation of trains, theaters, churches, and the halls of the gold-domed State House itself; to finding himself accused of federal treason for his role in liberating a fugitive slave; to the creation of black regiments to fight for an end to slavery—Robert Morris was there. However, like so many characters in this long, unfolding legal and social drama, his name is obscure and rarely remembered today.

There are no statues of Morris along present-day Commonwealth Avenue and no biographies. More astonishingly, when the case *Sarah Roberts v. the City of Boston* is written about, his name is often ignored or noted erroneously. In a basic collection of historic documents concerning the destruction of Jim Crow laws in Boston annotated by Leonard Levy, the foremost legal scholar of our time, Morris's name is repeatedly written as Robert E. Davis, a staggering error. It is one thing to have one's historical influence devalued; it is quite another to be stripped of one's name.

Any consideration of fame would have seemed quite impossible to the unnerved and heavyhearted young lawyer contemplating his first jury case. He wrote, "I sat down, and I cried."

In an era when even prominent white figures might go through the painfully slow process of being photographed only a few times in their lives (after being asked to hold a pose for nearly a minute, usually with a grim and unsmiling countenance in dim daguerreotypes), it is hardly surprising that few photographic records of individual free blacks exist. Yet surprisingly, two photographs of Morris do exist. In one, the prominent attorney is shown standing, tired and worn, gazing at the camera with a world-weary directness. He is short and slight, with a sharply trimmed mustache and beard that are beginning to gray. The other is of the young Morris, a nattily dressed young man, head slightly cocked, eyes sympathetically alert and the expression gentle. He appears to be a man on the make, ready to confront anything. That confidence would be indispensable in the crowded years ahead.

Though Morris came from humble origins, one would not know it from his meticulous dress and gentlemanly manner. Morris was becoming a fixture on the Boston legal scene alongside his legal

Robert Morris as a young lawyer.
*(Courtesy of Moorland-Spingarn Research
Center, Howard University)*

teacher, Ellis Gray Loring, when this first jury case presented itself.
It came Morris's way because he was already known and well respected, already the object of the *Liberator*'s comment that many
could "rejoice that it fell to the lot of one so well fitted to make the
first experiment." There was widespread anticipation that the
young man would hold up admirably. The faith invested in him was
the result of nearly a decade of his political and activist leadership
among the blacks of Beacon Hill, along with his engaging personality. A man who did not often show his burdens in public, Morris
presented himself to the world in an elegant, calm, and steady
manner. He was renowned for his quick wit and disarming ability to
make others laugh.

In the decade before the Civil War, roughly nine out of ten
African Americans were slaves, and only about 2 percent attended

any kind of school, so Morris, as a trained black legal professional living in freedom, was already a man of distinction. If he could but conquer his fear now, he would enter into an almost unfathomable role. In 1850 there were 23,939 lawyers in America. Of those, Robert Morris was one of only two blacks to pass the bar.

By coincidence, the only other known black lawyer in America had tried some years before to make Boston his adopted home. Macon Allen, an Indiana native, had traveled east to enter the vocation that Alexis de Tocqueville called the "aristocracy" of this young nation. The handsome twenty-nine-year-old originally passed the Maine bar exam but set his sights on Massachusetts. However, Allen quickly discovered that in the Bay State, passing the bar might be easier than actually managing to get to the testing site. He was so poor he could not afford transportation from Boston to the examination, which was held in Worcester. On a May day in 1845, Allen was forced to walk an excruciating fifty miles simply to sit the exam. Somehow, he overcame his fatigue and passed the test, but more difficulties lay ahead.

Once back in Boston, he found that prejudice kept him from gaining his footing in the bustling Boston legal scene. Henry Bowditch, a white abolitionist, somberly wrote of Allen's prospects that "there is a method of exclusion more terrible than merely a formal one . . . the gentleman alluded to would starve in that profession."

There is also no evidence that Allen became in any way incorporated into the black leadership class of the city. Only a few months after his pioneering feat, he was dejectedly writing to white New York abolitionist John Jay about relocating to New York, to escape the "peculiar custom of the New England people." That custom was, of course, New England's brand of racism. So it fell to young Robert Morris to take Allen's breakthrough a step farther, to stand before a jury, to go up against a white opponent and make a persuasive case—not just for his client, but for the very idea that a black lawyer could possibly sustain a practice. Allen's inauspicious entrance into the legal world was probably a factor in the pressure that overtook Morris, though we have no direct knowledge that they ever met. Yet it seems unlikely that Allen's struggle would not have been common knowledge to the watchful eyes of the black leaders of Boston.

The trigger for Morris's distress, though, came in a more direct fashion, in the form of opposing counsel John C. Park. Morris had just returned from visiting the mercurial Park, and whatever professional privilege and courtesy Morris had become accustomed to in Loring's office now came under rude attack. Morris's first case as a lawyer came from a black man claiming he had not been paid for services rendered. The day before the action was to be heard, the eager Morris decided to call upon the opposing counsel to ensure that there would be no occasions for delay.

Morris walked into Park's office with what he later recalled was his "usual happy way." However, it did not take long for Morris to realize that here was hostility that had little to do with the legal conflict at hand. He stood awkwardly, with Park mockingly refusing to offer him a seat in the office. It was not long before the opposing counsel sprang out of his chair. However, instead of offering his seat, he belligerently shook his fist near Morris's face and bellowed, "Are you going to try this case?" When Morris replied that he would indeed be trying the litigation, Park exploded, "Then I will give you the devil!"

One imagines that Morris might have prepared himself to meet the inevitable resistance to his groundbreaking role, yet it seems he never expected the ferocity of this first encounter with Park. Walking back to his office on State Street, he wondered whether this was really how he would be treated by fellow members of the bar. His recollections of the incident imply that somewhere deep inside himself, he thought the achievement of passing the bar would somehow protect him. When Morris found this was not so, and that perhaps he would be the target of concentrated anger because he represented a changing social norm, he doubted his "ability to face the storm."

With tears, and emotions revealed in a way he had not expected, he displayed the indomitable spirit that would characterize his whole life. He said simply, "I thought of the mighty odds against which I had to contend, and then it was that I made the vow that I have never broken. It was this: I would prove myself to be a man and a gentleman, and succeed in the practice of the law, or I would die."

With newfound resolve, Morris walked into the courtroom the next day to find two surprises. The first was a packed courtroom. Wherever he turned, he saw the room filled with black faces, silent and expectant. As he gazed around this magnificent sight, he saw etched into their faces, many of them strangers, "a wish that I might win the first case that had ever been tried before a jury by a colored attorney in this country." He also noticed that his tormentor of the previous day was nowhere to be found.

Morris soon learned that Attorney Park had been replaced, and the defendant was proceeding with a new lawyer. He sat down to wait for his case to be called, and when the time came, "I went to work." Even before speaking a word, "something in the courtroom that morning...made me feel like a giant."

Using all that he had learned in his long training, Morris laid out the evidence with his characteristic energy and quick gestures. He made his arguments to the judge and, in his words, "spared no pains to win." Soon the judge had given the jury their charge, and they left the courtroom to deliberate. In almost no time, they trailed back into the courtroom with their decision delivered to the foreman. When the clerk asked for the verdict, the foreman shouted, "Not guilty." Morris wrote that his "heart bounded up, and my people in the court room acted as if they would shout for joy."

· · ·

Only one generation separated Robert Morris from a young boy who had survived the Middle Passage in bondage. His grandfather, known as Cumono, endured the horrific transatlantic transport and finally arrived in Ipswich, Massachusetts, sometime in the mid-1700s. The boy grew to be a man of short stature, like his grandson Robert, but with a thicker build. Some remembered him as having a noticeably round head, which in his later years would be crowned with "snow white" hair. Sometime after his arrival in the English colonies, he trained as a carpenter and was remembered most notably for helping build the town's first church. Over time, he seemed to have also created a recognized position in the New England town, as a byway would be named Cumono Lane in his honor.

Although the first of Morris's legacies was well remembered, it was not due to the particular admiration of white citizens. Despite his labors for the town, Cumono was recalled mostly for a story that has become long associated with him, though it makes for uncomfortable reading today. Even after his grandson had lived a life of distinction and acclaim, upon Robert Morris's death in 1882, the *Ipswich Chronicle* did not recount the Boston lawyer's achievements; instead, it returned to a humiliating story about "Old Quonomo," who died "some seventy years or more ago."

The newspaper narrated that Cumono had just finished a day at work at a local distillery owned by John Heard. It was said that the carpenter would often linger until well past dark, drinking after the labors of the day. He left the distillery with a bottle full of rum and started toward home. Along the way he went past a large pond where "at certain seasons of the year, the sheet of water...resounded with croaking life." The paper portrayed the inebriated Morris, with "excited imagination," thinking that the noisy splashes of the water were somehow talking to him, saying over and over, "Quomono! Jug o' rum." In his terror at the sight of a talking body of water, "Quomono" promptly threw his alcohol into the pond and took off, dashing away from the menacing pond. The reporter then notes how the members of the town gleefully repeated the story for "many years at Quomono's expense." Although there is no way of knowing if this drunken night at the pond ever occurred, the story certainly reeks of the kind of minstrel characteristics and racist caricatures that Cumono Morris's grandson would spend a lifetime dispelling.

The fact that his life had become linked to this demeaning tale was not the only distressing aspect of Cumono Morris's life. After marrying Kate Wallis in Ipswich's South Church on November 1778, he went on to have at least three children. Sadly, one drowned in October 1795, and another daughter, named Kate, died in September 1799. Cumono's wife died eight years later. He survived for eleven more years, expiring alone in a poorhouse in Ipswich on March 10, 1818.

Fortunately, one of his children, Yorkshire, born in 1786, survived and carried on the family name. As a young man, Yorkshire left Ipswich and traveled twelve miles south to find employment in Salem, Massachusetts. Salem, which was founded well before Boston and had always been proudly aware of its status as one of the first settled communities in the Massachusetts Bay Colony, was a wealthy and prospering maritime shipping center. Most of the black community there found work related to the local shipping industry. Black residents lived around the area on the turnpike leading to the port center, in muddy huts, most of which were cramped, some barely ten feet wide. There was a knoll at the center of this community where, according to local legend, early-eighteenth-century settlers cooked oxen. For this reason, the heart of the Salem black community came to be known as Roast-Meat Hill.

Yorkshire Morris's son Robert would by no means be the first famous African American to emerge from Salem. One hundred and thirty-one years before Robert's birth, a West Indian slave named Tituba allegedly taught local girls witchcraft, thus setting off perhaps the most infamous (and deadly) series of trials in American history. The central role of a black in this shameful episode may well have resonated with Salem residents long after 1692, as racial tension was very much a part of life for the town's black population.

When Yorkshire Morris relocated to Salem, the memory of vicious white mobs attacking Roast-Meat Hill, wanting to clear it of "disagreeable inhabitants," was still fresh. And when blacks attempted to move into the town, their efforts were often met with fierce resistance. Thus, the small and embattled community around Roast-Meat Hill remained within its confined limits.

In 1813 York Morris married a young woman named Mercy Thomas from nearby Marblehead. Mercy eventually bore York eleven children, one of whom, born on June 8, 1823, was named Robert. By this time, York had become the most sought after waiter in Salem. He took great pride in his appearance; Salem residents fondly remembered him as resplendent in his blue coat and brass buttons.

York may have looked majestic, but one frigid winter day, this finery created an uncomfortable situation for the waiter. He was attending to the visiting judges of the Supreme Judicial Court of Massachusetts. As he moved around their table, one of his gleaming buttons accidentally snagged the wig of Chief Justice Parsons. As he scuttled around the dining room, Morris was completely unaware that the wig of a famous jurist was attached to his coat. However, the judges around the table certainly noticed the bald head of the chief justice and his hair "flying around the table" on Morris's outfit. The mortified judge exclaimed, "You black rascal, bring me back my wig."

Although Yorkshire's son, the young Robert, was exposed to the heights of the Massachusetts legal world from a very young age, he also experienced primitive prejudice. In Salem's churches, as was common practice in all of Massachusetts's cities, blacks were forced to sit in "Nigger heaven," the term used for the elevated balcony seating where they were obliged to go. More importantly in terms of Morris's future, Salem had recently established a segregated school for blacks, but the school was discontinued in the year of his birth.

Thus Morris was born into a community wrestling with the notion of integrated schools. The closing of the black school forced parents to enroll their children in other schools, a move that was met with protest in the white community. The African Writing School reopened in 1827, but closed again after one year, during which one teacher taught seventy students of all ages in a single room. By the time another school for African American children opened in 1837, Robert Morris had already left Salem. Thus, he received almost no formal schooling in his formative years. His childhood experiences, however, acquainted him well with the brutal realities of a community's struggles for equal school rights.

A final crucial element of Morris's childhood in Salem was his growing acquaintance with the political process. Before the Revolutionary War, the slaves of Salem were allowed a time of revelry on the annual Election Day. Dating back to British colonial practices, this election celebration was an important introduction to the democratic process for the disenfranchised, but whites primarily viewed it as a harmless way to relieve slave frustration so that it would not manifest itself violently. These late May days were filled with dancing, drinking, fiddling, and the customary parade of drums, swords, and banners.

Although originally conceived by whites as a benign celebration, once blacks were enfranchised under the state constitution, this day took on an elevated meaning in their community. Both major parties, Federalists and Democrats, were now forced to seek black support vigorously. York Morris and John Remond, father of the famed and effective abolitionist Charles Lenox Remond, became the leading champions of the Federalist Party in the black community. These men were loyal to the cause, perhaps overzealously so; once they were accused of dressing up black women as men and sending them to the polls to vote Federalist. Regardless of their questionable tactics, these two leaders had an impact, as both would raise sons who would become strong advocates of political rights for blacks.

The year 1834 marked the last election York Morris would see. He died in October at the age of forty-eight. Robert was only eleven at the time, but he had already internalized his father's teaching that he was never to believe "the idea of inferiority of any person." Now, with the added responsibilities of helping support his family, Morris waited on tables, as his father had, and struggled to achieve some semblance of an education. Fortunately for Robert, by this time he was already the favorite "table-boy" among the wealthy of Salem. For the next two years he would find employment with the affluent and kindly King family.

The genial lawyer John King had long been considered one of the most prominent men in Salem. King's house stood along Salem's picturesque Essex Street, the town's main thoroughfare, far from Roast-Meat Hill. The "dignified and imposing" houses that line Essex Street must have been a constant reminder to the young Morris of the possibilities that social mobility could offer. John King was a Harvard graduate and served as a state senator, representative, and the first president of Salem's Common Council. Like his father before him, Morris's precise domestic skills and pleasing manner allowed him to be in a position where, though in a menial profession, he was also serving men highly represented in the Bay State's fraternal order of lawyers. This placement would be crucial for his future.

It was at the Kings' house, on Thanksgiving Day in 1836, that life would change dramatically for thirteen-year-old Morris. Typically, the Ellis Gray Loring family of Boston would visit the Kings and dine with them for the holiday. Loring was one of the most prominent of Boston names, tracing a lineage back to thirteenth-century England. But though the family was now among the aristocracy of Boston, with a family structure replete with socially connected and conservative legal minds, they nursed among them one very quietly rebellious young man.

Ellis Gray Loring, remembered today, if at all, as Ralph Waldo Emerson's personal lawyer and friend, followed family tradition and matriculated at Harvard. Though he became a member of the distinguished Phi Beta Kappa fraternity, he was eventually dismissed from the school for resisting school authority. All appeals for his degree were denied, and though there is no record of his offense, this episode revealed at least one Loring who henceforth might not strictly follow the Brahmin line.

Despite his debacle at Harvard, he entered the law profession in 1827 and received a position as solicitor for the Western Railroad Company; Loring, however, was looking for something more rewarding than simply transportation law. It was in the growing struggle against slavery that he would find his passion.

This would be the defining stand of Loring's life. As his obituary pointed out many years later, the twenty-seven-year-old lawyer fully realized that becoming associated with this unpopular cause meant forfeiting his chances for "a highly respectable place in society," a natural role a family like his expected him to fulfill.

A writer for the *Boston Commercial Gazette* in 1836 pondered what it would be like to have an abolitionist in the family, concluding, "It is quite a satisfaction to me that I find none in all my family to be of that sect, and if there be any such, severed be that connection hence forth and forever."

Ralph Waldo Emerson, Loring's classmate at Boston Latin

School and at Harvard, wrote in his early journal that these strange and annoying radicals were an "altogether odious set of people," and worse, "the worst of bores and canters." Nevertheless, Loring cast his lot with this new brand of reformers when he became one of the twelve signers of the constitution of the newly formed New England Anti-Slavery Society in 1832. He lost connections, friends, and clients but remained steadfast in his belief that "nothing is to be conceded to comity towards the slave-holding states." He was soon known as the most prominent lawyer in the early New England abolitionist circles.

Despite Loring's radical associations, his bond with the King family remained strong. The King children called him Uncle Ellis and always eagerly awaited his arrival for Thanksgiving. That November in 1836, Loring had just finished the most important case of his life. He had gone to trial to defend the interests of a six-year-old slave girl named Med.

Mary Slater, Med's owner, had come to Boston to visit her father, Thomas Aves, thereby bringing the little girl into the free state of Massachusetts. Arguing the writ of *habeas corpus* ("produce the body") before the girl could be returned to Louisiana as a slave, Loring, on behalf of the Boston Female Anti-Slavery Society, used the trial to painstakingly trace the history of abolition in Massachusetts.

Loring then had to show how this evolution of black freedom dictated the present justification for freeing the girl. This was not to be a case of dry and finicky minor points of law. Loring seized the opportunity to interject forceful abolitionist rhetoric into his summation. He declared, "Slavery then is contrary to good morals; a violation of the law of nature, and of the revealed will of God."

This case was important beyond the understandable interests of the young slave girl, becoming a key legal marker in the struggle to protect simple legal rights for black citizens—if one could yet assert this term at all, for America was far from reaching a consensus on whether blacks could be classified as citizens.

Loring's words would also be important for the future of Robert Morris. Representing Mary Slater was another increasingly prominent young Boston lawyer, Benjamin R. Curtis. In the years to come, Curtis would find himself whipsawed back and forth in the turbulent forces surrounding slavery. His instincts were to follow the conservative mercantile interests of Boston's State Street banking connections to the cotton trade, and as a judge, he would be no friend to abolitionist lawyers. Yet two decades later, sitting on the United States Supreme Court as a justice faced with the crucial slave case *Dred Scott v. Sanford* (a decision that may well have made the Civil War inevitable), Benjamin Curtis wrote a surprisingly scathing dissent in favor of the former slave Dred Scott's right to freedom. Once again, as in the case of Med twenty years earlier, the legal issue was simple: was a slave still a slave when on free soil?

Loring and Curtis were squaring off in front of another character crucial in this narrative, the fearsomely homely yet brilliant new chief justice of the Massachusetts Supreme Court, Lemuel Shaw. While only beginning to form his intimidating judicial impact in the mid-1830s, Judge Shaw was already a national force to be reckoned with, an imposing legal mind whose opinions were composed with stark clarity and cold certainty.

Curtis and Loring were young lawyers receiving their first national publicity, particularly in the southern press, where the *Med* case was watched with increasing trepidation. This nervous interest erupted into towering rage when Loring achieved one of the great legal triumphs of the abolitionist period. The conservative Shaw finally determined that any slave owner who voluntarily brought a slave into a free state had "no authority to detain him against his will, or to carry him out of the State against his consent, for the purpose of being held in slavery." This judgment was not wholly unexpected, as Shaw, a New Englander, would not be a judge inclined to defend southern institutions blindly. Yet there was an unusual sting in his further declaration: "Bond slavery cannot exist because it is contrary to natural right and repugnant to numerous provisions of the Constitution and laws, designed to secure the liberty and personal rights of all persons within its limits and entitled to the protection of the laws."

Loring's arguments had clearly found favor with Judge Shaw, and the decision could not have been more tailored to the young abolitionist's fervent hopes. When the elderly John Quincy Adams prepared his famous defense in the *Amistad* case two years later, the former president consulted Loring with inquiries about the young man's celebrated argument.

As Loring enjoyed an entertaining Thanksgiving dinner with old friends, he found himself being particularly impressed by the quick wit of the thirteen-year-old boy waiting on the family's table. It occurred to Loring that he needed someone about the age of this young servant to take care of housecleaning chores around his house in Boston. Based on his brief observation of the bright young man, he noted that Robert Morris would fit the bill perfectly. Loring met Morris's mother, Mercy, and talked his proposition over with her. With her permission, Morris set off with the Lorings the following day for a new life in Boston.

Winter wasted no time in arriving in full force that year, and the day after Thanksgiving was a frigid one. A stagecoach arrived at the King residence to take the Lorings and Morris to Boston. Unfortunately for Morris, segregation in transportation was rigidly enforced, regardless of the weather. The route from Salem to Boston was roughly thirty miles south along the rocky Massachusetts coast. The man who would devote much of his adult life to fighting segregation in Boston entered the city nearly frozen, forced to sit the whole way on the outside of the coach.

The Boston that Robert Morris first saw under the cover of snow that evening in 1836 was a place undergoing a titanic change. The small city of the American Revolution, then measuring only about six hundred acres, was nearly an island, attached to the mainland only by a narrow causeway, which is the present-day Beacon Street. The vast wharves in the north of the city, with hundreds of ships and their forest of bristling masts, dominated the city still, but the size of the city had nearly doubled, with the filling in of marsh tidal areas and the extension of the port. Boston was no longer an isolated peninsula, and new bridges, railways, and new causeways were being constructed in every direction. The rural areas to the west, beyond the Common, were quickly being built up with elegant new

Ellis Gray Loring (1803–1858), abolitionist lawyer and mentor to Robert Morris. *(Charcoal and white chalk on paper by Eastman Johnson, ca. 1848; courtesy of the Massachusetts Historical Society)*

Federal-style town houses. At the same time, the high hills behind Charles Bulfinch's new State House were being dug down and used to fill in the low areas, extending the city into the sea waters. The population of the city had more than quadrupled, from 18,000 people in 1790 to 93,000.

Ellis and Louisa Loring lived at 671 Washington Street, an area now choked with commercial properties, but back then a graceful section of narrow streets with clapboard houses and English-style gardens. Situated close to the venerated sites associated with freedom, it was a short stroll to Faneuil Hall, a huge three-story building that was a kind of holy place in the political and civic life of the city, called affectionately the Cradle of Liberty. Haunted by the echoes of Revolutionary fervor, Bostonians loved the spare second-floor chamber with its classic Doric columns and rows of straight-backed chairs. Atop the cupola was the beloved golden grasshopper. Also close by was the South Church, equally filled with the old voices of Adams, Otis, and Hancock.

However, there would have been few blacks living near the Loring home, where, for a decade, Morris lived, worked, and studied. Yet the young servant boy received more than a place to live. He also got a warm, liberal environment where he was encouraged to learn and to closely observe and absorb the richness of the city called the Athens of America.

Ellis Gray Loring's life in Boston epitomized the "bubbling cauldron of religion and politics" that John Adams had long ago called Boston. Loring was a counselor for the Massachusetts Anti-Slavery Society, and his wife, Louisa, was a steadfast organizer of its annual fair, which the women of the movement sponsored. During these years as Loring's servant, Morris was to meet a wide circle of Loring's famous friends, including Emerson, Sumner, Longfellow, the fiery Unitarian minister Theodore Parker, former mayor and noted reformer Josiah Quincy, and abolitionist and woman's rights advocate Lydia Maria Child, the latter so delighted with the young Morris that she thoughtfully purchased a copy of Olaudah Equiano's slave narrative for him.

Boston has never been very humble about itself and its purpose, with its curious combination of stern moral conscience and a liberal self-conscious yearning for learning, culture, and liberty. As Oliver Wendell Holmes said, "All I claim for Boston is that it is the thinking centre of the continent, and therefore, the planet."

After a few years of Morris's table service, Loring noted that a white boy he employed as a copyist in his office was inattentive to his duties. Loring began sending Morris off in the early Boston mornings to take care of the neglected work. Still responsible for his domestic chores, Morris would often have to take the copying work home and work into the night. Despite this mounting burden of tasks, Morris showed good penmanship, intelligence, and the diligence that his predecessor lacked. While in the Loring residence, Morris was often found reading from the sheepskin-covered books that were laid out on the baize-clothed tables of the living room. Seeing Morris's interest in books, Loring told him, "When you get through with your work, spend your time in a useful way; go down to the office and study."

Morris took his advice, and Loring was further impressed by the young man's concentrated learning habits. One day Loring called the adolescent boy into his office, making Morris an offer that transformed his life. "Robert, you are capable of making something of yourself. Now I want you to tell me what you want to do, and I will secure for you the opportunity to make the trail. Do you wish to learn a trade, or do you wish to study law?"

Morris quickly answered the law. Morris's gratitude for this opportunity never wavered. He remembered later, "At a time when it was dangerous for a white man to utter a word of sympathy for a brother with a skin not colored like his own, this good man showed his firm adhesion to principle by placing a colored boy in his office, to fit him for those pursuits from which public opinion had proscribed him." There would be times that this odd duo would be laughed and sneered at as they walked in and out of courts, but this deterred neither Morris's determination to be a lawyer nor Loring's resolve to see Morris's ambitions realized.

Over time Morris and Loring grew closer. Morris's father was gone, and Loring had no son; one newspaper commented on how the two did indeed seem to be almost like father and son. Although Loring and Morris developed an exceptional relationship, they were very different men. Aside from obvious dissimilarities, Loring filled his letters with poetry and tidbits about Florentine art, and Morris, in the words of one contemporary, "made no pretense to the elegant culture of a man of letters." Morris never shied away from conflict and was aggressive when he felt it was necessary. His comfort level in the public sphere was quite unlike his mentor's. As a young boy, Loring shrank from the fierce competition instilled at the Boston Latin School. In many ways these traits never changed.

Especially as he grew older, Loring took little pleasure from public attention and disliked open controversy. He had resisted these impulses in taking the famous *Med* case only because it was such a vital matter. But after the period of Morris's training, Loring was rarely seen in court again. He remained a vital chamber counselor, but his famous abolitionist friends noticed a "peculiar" withdrawal from "conspicuous service and a distrust of himself as a public speaker."

Morris, by contrast, would become a nationally known figure by the time he was out of his twenties, and he never looked back. Gladly taking upon himself the tasks and burdens of a very public leadership, he was always "aggressive and assertive." Though Loring's name and calm counsel would be quietly threaded through the daily record of the abolitionist movement for years to come, it is almost as if the older lawyer had handed the mantle to Morris.

In this regard, Robert Morris, passing the Massachusetts bar on February 2, 1847, and astonishing Boston as victor in his first court case, seemed at last ready to take the lessons learned from Loring and advance them in a way his gentle friend could not.

# The Slopes of Beacon Hill

They called it Nigger Hill.

The other Boston that Robert Morris would have seen when he entered the growing city was not noble, enchanting, or cultured. Free black citizens lived gathered along the steep north slope of Beacon Hill, where the waters of the Charles River flowing into the harbor lapped up along present-day Charles and Cambridge Streets. In winter the wind on the hill was cold, and the smell from the tidal salt flats at low tide was noxious and nauseating. Powerful tar smells from the long rope walks were none too delightful either, but the walks were at least being torn down to be replaced by packed-in housing and crowded town-house tenements. Here were the bleak charity buildings, the wayfarers' lodge, crowded hospitals, the county jail, and the city morgue. The back side of the Hill was now being laced with streets of "tortuous intricacy," as well as narrow alleys and passageways that arched and snaked between houses and apartments. City authorities would call this crowded, teeming area a breeding ground for vice, but the residents realized early on that when slave catchers and federal marshals roamed the streets, these same foul passageways were ideal for escape and cover.

Blacks in the antebellum North were relegated to the most menial jobs. In Boston in the 1830s, not only were they almost completely blocked from professional roles in law or medicine, but there were few black plumbers, carvers, roofers, chandlers, caulkers (the job Frederick Douglass had as a fugitive slave when he reached Massachusetts), cabinetmakers, upholsterers, polishers, mechanics, or workers in heavy industry. This almost total economic discrimination is why Douglass observed that while in the South blacks were slaves of individuals, in the North they were, in effect, slaves of the whole community. Instead, they found work as they could as sailors, barbers, coachmen, waiters, hairdressers, dealers of new and used clothes, tailors, musicians, wood sawyers, and teamsters.

Drawing on his early life in Salem and then his adolescent life in Boston, Robert Morris later remembered that "almost all over New England [blacks] were despised, and neglected, and debarred the common privilege of riding in our public conveyance, denied the right to send their children to our common schools and of frequent public places of amusement." Boston life was hard for its black population, a group of fewer than three thousand souls that by the 1830s was concentrated as a community on the north side of Beacon Hill. Their home was the windy, undesirable steep rise. This was land that the wealthy merchants now located on Mount Vernon or Chestnut Streets did not want.

Known first as Trimountain because of three high peaks marking this remarkable topographical structure, Beacon Hill was a sparsely settled area for many decades. Hardly a fixture of early Puritan Boston, this steep grassy area was used primarily as grazing pasture for animals and was braved by only a few eccentric builders. In fact, the arching hill was notable mainly for the sixty-foot-high tower with a beacon built at its peaking crown as a warning light to alert the city's residents of impending danger.

By 1730, a hundred years after the city's founding, the streets that compose today's Beacon Hill had been mostly laid out. But the end of Beacon Hill as a rural area came when it was selected as the future location of the Massachusetts State House. The renowned architect Charles Bulfinch, an instinctively brilliant and determined shaper of the city, designed the majestic, gold-domed State House to tower over Boston, evoking a sense of awe and classical Republican virtue. To make the Hill more conducive to residential development, between 1799 and 1802 it was lowered and leveled.

Mansion houses began to spring up, built by ambitious developers. From this point on, the south side of Beacon Hill became home to Boston's most patrician population. By the mid-nineteenth century, this small neighborhood, "home to philosophers and poets, abolitionists and transcendentalists, . . . was witness to and participant in the Flowering of New England." As George Santayana remembered from his childhood on the south slope, "The corner of Beacon and Charles streets was central and respectable. Indeed it formed a sort of isthmus, leaving the flood of niggerdom to the north and of paddydom to the south."

So one half of Beacon Hill was home to the wealthy and cultured, as represented by Daniel Webster, Edwin Booth, the Adams family, the James family, Julia Ward Howe, and Louisa May Alcott, among other national luminaries. Yet the famous names remembered today tell only part of the story of the sunny side of Beacon Hill. Wealthy proprietors, as they parceled out narrow plots of land, ensured that these new residences would be bought by people such as Nathan Appleton, the inventive and agile textile factory owner. Appleton built more than just his lovely Beacon Street town house; he also built whole manufacturing towns beyond Boston, which helped propel a burgeoning industrial revolution. These homes were owned by a tightly knit group of interlocked families, bound by common bonds of marriage, as well as their economic and civic life. If one was part of their world, it was a whole world, and if not, then it was easy to say, as Lydia Maria Child did after visiting one too many parlors on the Hill, that she longed to escape the "constrained elegancies of Beacon Street."

These homes, virtually unchanged today, remain a precious architectural heritage, reflecting the lovely vision of Bulfinch's neoclassicism, long, flowing rows of red brick town houses, each marked with subtle variations of bowfront windows, ornamented glass above painted doors, and black railing ornaments. Inside these houses, one crossed black-and-white marble tiles to view the sweeping vista of Persian-carpeted stairways leading up to parlors decorated with French wallpaper, Chinese silk hangings, fine English furniture, and gilded portraits of proud New England forebears whose stern expressions revealed a certain unease with the luxury that surrounded them. This world was not completely closed to the Bostonians on the other side of the Hill, for without their considerable labor, it would be inconceivable. In Appleton's home, in fact, the door would have been answered by the masterly houseman Robert Roberts, elegant and dapper in black manservant attire. Grandfather to Sarah Roberts, Roberts's skills were so in demand that in 1825 he was hired away from Appleton by the former governor Christopher Gore.

These two worlds were tightly held together, and in fact they occupied such a small area that today one can walk around the full circumference of Beacon Hill in forty minutes. The poet Robert Lowell, whose ancestry was firmly rooted in old Beacon Hill aristocracy, once reflected on this uncomfortable proximity when his parents, poor and down on their luck, were forced to buy a home on Revere Street near the "unbottomed" section. His mother complained, "We are barely perched on the outer rim of the hub of decency." In fact, they were only fifty feet from exclusive Louisburg Square, "the old historic cynosure of Boston's plain-spoken, cold-roast elite—the Hub of the Hub of the Universe." One major street cutting from Beacon Street through the whole of Beacon Hill all the way to Cambridge Street was once called Belknap, but the well-to-do at the top of the Hill near the State House wanted a comforting sense of separation from the blacks, so they renamed their portion of the street Joy. Soon, the middle section followed suit, and at last, to avoid the insult, the residents from the bottom section of the street insisted that they be made "Joy" as well.

The poor workers' side of Beacon Hill housed more than half of the black community of Boston. By 1850 it contained more than 70 percent of the black population. From Myrtle Street to Cambridge Street, and then from Charles Street to Belknap Street, there lived about one thousand blacks, with over a thousand more distributed nearby within the fifth city ward, in what is now called the West End. Eighty-four percent of them lived on four streets: Southac (now Phillips), Belknap (now Joy), May (now Revere), and West Cedar.

This intense concentration of the community was due to residential racial segregation and a lack of economic opportunity.

In colonial days, slave women working for the Boston elite were the first to live on the hill. After the Revolution, when Massachusetts had washed its hands of slavery, the majority of the black population shifted from the North End (an area facetiously called New Guinea), near the docks and the shipping industry, to the area around Beacon Hill in the West End. Whatever work was available to blacks was concentrated in this central business area of the city. Public transportation cost about twelve cents a day, so for a laborer, who might earn a dollar a day, it was an unrealistic expenditure. They needed to live near their work.

Furthermore, the strict segregation of residential housing was enforced to the point of violence. In the early 1830s, a black family tried to break the status quo by moving into a white residential area. White neighbors let this family know their house would be torn down before they would permit blacks to live there. Robert Morris, too, would personally experience these entrenched patterns later in his life.

The families of black Beacon Hill were both traditional and unique. There was a high percentage of two-parent families. As historians James Horton and Lois Horton note, "Not only was the black family a strong antebellum institution in Boston, but families formed the foundation for the community against slavery and for civil rights." One feature distinguishing these households from many of those on the wealthy side of the Hill was the high number of paying boarders. Because of most blacks' financially precarious position, as well as the fact that Boston was a transitional place for those who had just escaped slavery in the South, boarding with other families was the only realistic option for many. Most families, somewhere between 30 and 40 percent, were more than willing to take in paying guests.

Beacon Hill's northern slope was particularly ill suited for the kind of concentrated poverty found in the black community. The devastating effects of bad air around filthy houses in an overcrowded area, aggravated by the tight lanes, alleys, and courts, resulted in a high mortality rate. In 1790 a Boston doctor walking through this area was appalled at the "horrid stink of pollution," and the succeeding decades only made matters worse. The teeming streets were filled with bars, sailors' dance halls, and cheap boardinghouses that were described as "damp unwholesome lodging."

Prostitution became a hallmark of what proper Boston labeled "Mount Whoredom." At the "witching hour of night" several black women were known to provide entertainment for the price of twenty-five cents. Many of their clientele were white men from various parts of Boston and of various political affiliations, causing one observer to remark that there were "Know-nothings and Know-somethings." This caused resentment among blacks and their allies, as they bemoaned how these white men "will not marry our colored women, nor be seen with them in the day time; but at night they are to be found at all the corners and in all the lanes of the city. The darkness of night covers all distinctions." Southac Street, with more blacks than any other street in the city, was known for being the site of much of this activity, as there were sixteen "widows" who, though claiming no occupation, were well known for their source of income. In fact, one observer called Southac Street "the most wretched part of the city, where idleness and drunkenness abound."

While to some whites of Boston the north slope of Beacon Hill represented the fulfillment of many desires and indulgences, to others, in a city descended from Puritan stock, it seemed the embodiment of evil. One white preacher said, "It consists principally of drunkards, harlots, spendthrifts and outcasts from the country: in the truth; Beelzebub holds a court there." In 1818 the Reverend James Davis gave a perhaps exaggerated description to the Female Anti-Slavery Society that illustrates how "Nigger Hill" was viewed by white Boston.

> Without impropriety it may be said, there is the place where Satan's seat is. There awful impieties prevail; all conveyable abominations are practiced; there the depravity of the human heart is acted out; and from this sink of sin, the seeds of corruption are carried into every part of town. Five and twenty or thirty shops are opened on

Lord's days from morning to evening and ardent spirits are retailed without restraint, while hundreds are intoxicated and spend the holy Sabbath in frolicking and gambling, in fighting and blaspheming; and in many scenes of inequity and debauchery too dreadful to be named. . . . Here in one compact section of the town, it is confidently affirmed that fully believed, there are three hundred females wholly devoid of shame and modesty.

While some decried the conditions of lower Beacon Hill due to well-intentioned, reform-minded impulses, for others the conditions only strengthened their prejudice toward Boston's black population. In 1822 the legislature went so far as to have a commission consider the prospect of excluding blacks from the state, though they soon conceded its impossibility. But the biases that fueled the Lyman Commission were passed on to the children in the form of local lore. It was said that a Bostonian was passing through an attractive Boston street when he overheard a child crying. Moving closer, he saw that the child was very frightened, with his caretaker menacingly saying, "Henry, if you don't be still crying, I will carry you down to Belknap-street, and give you to the *old black man*." When the youngster could not stop, the nurse then added, "Now, if you don't stop, I *will certainly* give you to the *old black man*."

In the face of these dispiriting living conditions and staunch prejudices, it was crucial to set up institutions of mutual strength within the black community. Early local leadership emerged in the remarkable person of Prince Hall, remembered as a small, almost effeminate man, born to a mulatto woman and an English father. Hall became the first effective leader of a community actively trying to separate itself from the white supremacist culture that surrounded it. One need only hear Hall's description of what it was like to be black in Boston in 1797 to understand the need for community strength. He asserted,

We could not bear up under the daily insults we meet in the streets of Boston, much more on public displays of recreation. How at such times are we shamefully abused, and that to such a degree, that we may truly be said to carry our lives in our hands, and the arrows of death are flying about our heads. Helpless women have their clothes torn from their backs. . . . I was told by a gentleman who saw the filthy behavior in the Common, that, in all places that he had been in, he never saw so cruel behavior in all his life; and that a slave in the West Indies, on Sundays or holidays, enjoys himself and friends without molestation.

One of the most notorious examples of the "molestation" on the Boston Common occurred on the day the black community assembled there for their annual celebration of the end of America's role in the Atlantic slave trade. White boys consistently enjoyed disrupting the celebration, and one year they decided to try to drive away the blacks from the Common. Abolitionist Lydia Marie Child recalled watching hundreds of whites chase a smaller number of blacks through the Common, onto the south side of Beacon Hill, and north toward their homes. Unexpectedly, as they chased over the cusp of the hill, the rowdy young whites found themselves calmly faced down by George Middleton, a black Revolutionary War veteran, holding a loaded musket pointed and ready to fire. The day ended without any further violence, but such was not always the case. On July 14, 1826, blacks in Boston's West End were subject to a riot at the hands of vitriolic whites dressed in blackface and carrying pitchforks.

Wendell Phillips, who was born on the corner of Walnut and Beacon Streets, the wealthy son of the mayor and scion of Beacon Hill, grew up facing the Boston Common and remembered, "There were two ways to get rid of arrogant young Negroes, you stoned them, or if that failed, you simply kicked the Negro in the shin and waited for his nose to bleed."

. . .

The first recorded African slaves to reach New England arrived on a ship called the *Desire* in 1638, only eight years after the founding of Boston. By 1700 only a thousand blacks lived in New England, a third of them in Massachusetts. Five hundred blacks, enslaved and free, lived in Boston. Many of their children would fight in the war against England to create a new nation.

This Revolutionary War generation chose to realize commonalities instead of racial differences. Crispus Attucks's role in the Boston Massacre was often pointed to as the best example of shared class frustration vented by interracial groups at a common oppressor. In 1783 the Massachusetts Supreme Court abolished slavery, claiming it was clearly incompatible with the new state constitution of 1780, as Charles Sumner would later note in the *Roberts* case. In fact, the economic climate of the northern states was inhospitable to the "peculiar Institution" of slavery, and by 1830 all states above Maryland were free states. But the early decades of the nineteenth century saw a lessening of these alliances, with the nation hitting its first labor surplus in the 1820s. This was the beginning of an economic crisis for Boston blacks, which manifested itself particularly in the 1840s and 1850s.

The abolitionist movement arose at a time when blacks felt increasingly under siege, economically and politically. In fact, even their allies, as we will see, had considerable disdain for them. Julia Ward Howe, who later wrote *The Battle Hymn of the Republic* to display her abolitionist fervor, said of the men and women surrounding her on the Hill that they were "coarse, grinning, flat footed thick skulled creatures, ugly as Caliban, lazy as the laziest brutes, chiefly ambitious to be of no use to any in the world." She added, however, that black children "must go to school with the white race."

In addition to the fears of mob action and violence at the hands of the larger community, blacks also had to be constantly on guard for slave catchers. Frederick Douglass explained the feelings of an escapee: "There is no city of refuge for him. There is no valley so deep and secluded, no mountain so high—no plain so extended, no spot so sacred, throughout that broad land as to enable a man having a skin like mine, to enjoy in safety the right to his own heart and hands." Like Douglass himself, many black Bostonians were escaped slaves. One recent arrival to Boston said that the scores of recent escapees from the South made him feel that he was back in the "old country."

Yet free black Peter Randolph remembered, "The name of Boston always had a musical and joyous sound to the colored people of the South." Although there was no racial equality there, black Bostonians could not help but compare life in the South to their new life. Boston held an undeniable allure as a beacon to African Americans, a place of opportunity and liberty. Fugitives could find education, some employment, and community in Boston. Unfortunately, their realistic fear of slave catchers gave a nervous, guarded, and constantly uneasy tone to their lives. Former fugitives were not the only ones who had to be vigilant; each and every resident had good reason always to be on guard. No one was completely safe, and no one, despite his or her color, could be truly trusted.

The specter of slavery not only pursued people but also haunted others unable to forget family and friends left in bondage. A black Bostonian named Moses Grandy was a typical example, having been a slave in North Carolina before purchasing his freedom and migrating north. In a quest to buy the rest of his family, he sawed wood, labored in a coal yard, and was a stevedore and a sailor on boats bound for Puerto Rico. He spent an entire life accumulating the money to free his family members one by one. By the end of his life, he had paid a total of $3,060 for his wife and nine of his eleven children; two of his daughters had already bought their own manumission.

But to those who lived with these threats in black Boston, there was also hope, provided by various institutions of support such as churches, educational societies, businesses, and political groups. The women of the community could often be found around William Johnson's grocery at 13 Southac Street. Aside from the store's provisions, information, news, and gossip about the families of the Hill and the larger community were widely consumed. For the black men of Beacon Hill the place for this type of socializing was Howard's Barbershop, located at the foot of the hill on Cambridge Street. Many who had not received a formal education in their youth or knew little about politics, obtained their political education there. Aside from this pedagogical aspect, those seeking employment might stop in to check the job opportunities posted, along with other community information. Tickets to local events— for instance, concerts of the children's choir or an antislavery fair—

would be on sale there too. J. J. Smith's barbershop was similar, but it was more noted for its explicit antislavery discussions. J. J. Smith's was also the place where one might have glimpsed a young white lawyer named Charles Sumner, known to stop in for an impassioned discussion.

Most important, there was the church, the center of the community's growing self-assertion. In their attempts to attend white churches, blacks had been greeted with humiliation and segregation. Black abolitionist George Downing said of these experiences, "The man whose devotions are disturbed by having a family of well behaved and decently dressed colored persons in the pew next to him, may know much of the doctrines of Christianity but is very little imbued with its spirit." This treatment led to blacks' beginning to hold services in private homes and then at Faneuil Hall, and finally forming the African Baptist Church in the African Meeting House on Belknap Street.

Baptists would not long have a monopoly on the religion of the community, however; the African Methodist Episcopal Church was formed in 1818 and the African Methodist Episcopal Zion Church in 1838. Nevertheless, the African Meeting House occupied a unique position on Beacon Hill as a center for much community activity. Built by black laborers, the Meeting House was a three-story building in the Federal style. Still standing today, it is the oldest African American church building in the United States.

The Reverend Thomas Paul organized this first church and went on to be its minister for two and a half decades. Born in New Hampshire, he began preaching in Boston at the age of sixteen. Most days he could be found performing baptisms in Boston Harbor or helping new residents of Boston with social contacts and employment opportunities. The church's membership rolls blossomed under his leadership; the twenty-four-member church he established in 1806 had quadrupled by 1820. His preaching was renowned, and some whites even defied contemporary social norms by attending and participating in his church. Before his resignation in 1829 and death in 1831, he also helped to establish the Abyssinian Baptist Church in New York City, later the pulpit of Adam Clayton Powell.

The First Independent Baptist Church, later the African Meeting House, Smith Court, Boston, 1843. (*Courtesy of the Boston Athenaeum*)

Paul's death came at a significant time in the formation of the Beacon Hill community. His health had begun to fail him in the 1820s, but his final resignation led to much dissension in the church. Eleven years later, these arguments culminated in the splintering of the congregation. Some historians suggest the church's controversy centered on the extent to which the church should participate in the burgeoning activism of the black community. In antebellum times and beyond, leadership in the black community came primarily from the ministry. Yet in the future struggle for equality in Boston, its primary leadership would come from outside the church.

Still, Rev. Paul, along with Prince Hall of the African Masonic Lodge, was an essential part of a generation that worked to form a strong black community. The two men helped form organizations such as the African Society and the Massachusetts General Colored Association, both of which provided services for a community struggling against huge odds in Boston.

By 1831 the most prominent characters of this post–Revolutionary War generation, Thomas Paul and Prince Hall, were dead, and the stage was set for two people who would radicalize the next generation of blacks in the city. Though not much celebrated today, even by people familiar with the story of black empowerment, their efforts were unprecedented in American history. The course of the *Roberts* case is impossible to imagine without them.

· · ·

A tall, slender, and dark-skinned man named David Walker arrived in Boston in the mid-1820s. He was not a native of Boston, but one of the many black Bostonians born in the South. However, unlike many refugees from Dixie, he was not born a slave. In 1789, the year that Boston schools became officially established, he was born free in the slave-holding state of North Carolina. In his early adulthood, Walker moved to Charleston, South Carolina, one of the few places in the South where the free black population was sizable enough to establish, as he would later find in Boston, successful associations of communal aid. He lived in Charleston exactly at the time of Denmark Vesey's planned slave rebellion and may well have assisted in its planning. This audacious and potentially bloody uprising unraveled before it could be undertaken. Vesey was betrayed by a fellow black and was subsequently executed, with thirty-six others, for a plot that involved up to four hundred people and four years of planning.

Vesey profoundly influenced Walker's ideas of a great slave uprising. Writing of slaveholders, Walker asserted,

We must remember that humanity, kindness and the fear of the lord, does not consist in protecting devils. . . . Are they not the Lord's enemies? Ought they not to be destroyed? Any person who will save such wretches from destruction, is fighting against the Lord, and will receive his just recompense.

After watching Charleston deal with the fear and growing mistrust in the wake of Vesey's death, David Walker traveled widely along the East Coast before finally settling in Boston. He opened a used-clothing store in Dock Square, then called a slop shop. Quickly, Walker became popular in the black community, known as a generous man who burned with intense Methodism and fiery ideas. He had first rented a room on Southac Street, but soon moved into a brick house on the perpendicular Belknap Street in the heart of the black community. Aside from running his own business, he worked as an agent for the first black paper in America, New York's *Freedom's Journal,* inviting people over to his house to sell subscriptions to the financially vulnerable paper. But it was for his writing that he would be remembered.

Having grown up surrounded by slavery, Walker found the poverty and discrimination that blacks in Boston experienced deplorable. One day he encountered a black man on the streets with shoes strung over his shoulder, and his conversation with this man would become a centerpiece in his famous *Appeal to the Colored Citizens of the World.* Walker found himself railing against "what a miserable set of people we are!" because "we cannot obtain the comforts of life, but by cleaning their boots and shoes, old clothes, waiting on them, shaving them."

The other man could not understand Walker's wrath, answering, "I am completely happy!!! I never want to live better or happier than when I can get a plenty of boots and shoes to clean!!!"

Walker wondered whether men like this thought "our greatest glory is centered in such mean and low objects." This experience drove his 1829 *Appeal,* a powerful early document of African American liberation. Walker's biographer Peter Hinks writes that the psychological and social effects this short document had on black America can be equated only with "the impact that Thomas Paine's *Common Sense* had on the white patriots of revolutionary America." This comparison is particularly apt because of Walker's mastery of the radical values of the Revolutionary era, be they his natural-rights ideology or his emphasis on economic self-determination. He also wrote in a larger world context of Greek revolutionaries fighting the Turks, Polish liberators fighting the Russians, and slavery in Latin America, which was ended by Spain with the bloody Haitian slave rebellion.

In this radical climate, Walker produced a document composed of four articles centering on those who were physically and mentally enslaved. He cried, "Are we MEN!!—I ask you, my brethren! Are we MEN? Did our creator make us to be slaves to dust and ashes like ourselves?" Walker believed there would be no equality anywhere in America until slavery was overthrown, by whatever means possible.

It appears that great efforts were made to disseminate these astonishing words in the southern states, but such labors were repelled at every point by frightened whites who took extreme precautions to thwart their distribution. Nothing like this had ever appeared in the new nation, and Walker's familiarity with the South meant he was not powerless to use ingenious and covert methods to have the incendiary pamphlet make its way into slaves' hands. The ships leaving Boston Harbor, for example, were often manned by associates of Walker buying and trading clothes in his Dock Street shop. After some sixty copies had been carried by a mariner to a black minister in Savannah, Georgia, the legislature of that state quarantined all black sailors entering the state, a move that was quickly copied by other states.

Governors throughout the South sent angry letters to Harrison Gray Otis, the mayor of Boston, who expressed his powerlessness to stop free speech. The legislature of Virginia called a special closed-door session to deal with Walker's *Appeal.* In time, numerous southern blacks died for the simple crime of reading or distributing the *Appeal,* and others were imprisoned and sold. Walker may never have known that in his native North Carolina, a group of runaways were caught with the *Appeal* in their possession. They paid for this offense with their lives.

It was more than the institution of slavery that was the subject of Walker's fury; he closed his second section of the *Appeal* with a scathing critique of the segregated schools of Boston. In a nation where nine out of ten blacks lived in areas in which learning to read was an illegal act, it was a bold declaration that here, even where they could freely learn, the segregated schools of the North were not giving black children the proper education that they desperately needed. Walker must have known that he was offending more than the white patrons of these struggling schools. He was also disturbing some local black leaders who were protective, if not proud, of their schools. He pointed out not only the marked inferiority of the facilities but also the lagging knowledge of basics such as arithmetic, accounting, and composition in prose or verse.

A line of demarcation can be seen after the release of this pamphlet in Boston. The *Boston Evening Transcript* observed how this document changed the black community:

> We have noticed a marked difference in the deportment of our colored population. It is evidence they have read this pamphlet, nay, we know that the larger portion of them have read it, or heard it read, and that they glory in its principles, as if it were a star in the east, guiding them to freedom and emancipation.

Walker's writing was radicalizing Boston's black community, but he would not be the person to lead them. On June 28, 1830, as the uproar over his writings still continued, he was found slumped over, dead in a doorway in the North End. Rumors immediately began circulating that he must have been killed, in part because it was widely known that there were bounties as large as $10,000 on his head in the South. To his community at the time, and even to some recent writers, it was an understandable suspicion, yet it appears more likely that consumption was the actual cause of death. He left behind one son, who would become a friend and ad-

mirer of Robert Morris. In fact, Edwin Garrison Walker would follow Morris into the legal profession and would one day movingly
eulogize his predecessor.

In the immediate shadow of Walker, there emerged another fiery
activist who deserves to be better remembered today, not only as
one of the first black writers but as the first woman, black or white,
to forge an identity as a public speaker. As David Walker was ready-
ing to leave his dwelling on Belknap Street, in moved a beautiful
woman named Maria Stewart. She and her husband knew and
greatly admired Walker, and she captured in her public addresses
something of the fiery pamphleteer's religious fervor and visionary
quality.

The young Maria Stewart, described as boldly assertive, was
widowed soon after her marriage. But being alone was not new to
Stewart, who had been orphaned at a young age in Hartford, Connecticut, and then bound to a minister's family as a servant. In her
early years, she experienced the drudgery that characterized the
lives of northern blacks. When Maria reached Boston, she was married by Rev. Paul in 1826 to James Stewart, a former sailor and shipping agent who warmly supported his new wife's interests. James
died three years later, but soon after the deaths of her husband and
David Walker, she embarked on a career that included four public
lectures, the publication of a political pamphlet, and a collection of
religious meditations.

Particularly significant about Stewart is that, like Walker, she
concentrated on the issues of northern blacks and their struggle for
equality, as much as on the state of slavery in the South. Speaking in
Boston's Franklin Hall, she boldly declared,

> Tell us no more of southern slavery; for with few exceptions, al-
> though I may be very erroneous in my opinion, yet I consider our
> condition but little better than that. Yet, after all, methinks there are
> no chains so galling as those that bind the soul, and exclude it from
> the vast field of useful and scientific knowledge. O, had I received
> the advantages of an early education, my ideas would, ere now, have
> expanded far and wide; but, alas! I possess nothing but moral capa-
> bilities—no teaching of the Holy Spirit.

It was not enough for her to be told that her life was favorable to others of her race, because she knew only one existence. She would not be satisfied because she knew that whites, unlike blacks, would not be "willing to spend their lives and bury their talents in performing mean, servile labor." Like Walker, she had grown tired of watching those in her community "spending their lives as house-domestics, washing windows, shaking carpets, brushing boots, or tending upon gentleman's tables."

Many people, including most abolitionists, resisted open protest of the conditions of their lives in the North for fear that southerners might seize on it and use it to their advantage. In 1837 the *New Orleans Paper* wrote of Boston abolitionists, "Are they not well convinced from the statements of their own travelers and observers, that the condition of the Southern slave is ten-fold better than that of the Northern free negro, better for himself?"

Similarly, in 1830, during one of the most famous debates in Senate history, South Carolina's Robert Y. Hayne disputed Massachusetts's Daniel Webster after the famed orator rejected the idea that any state could nullify federal legislation. Put on the defensive by Webster, Hayne declared, "There does not exist on the face of the earth, a population so poor, so wretched, so vile, so loathsome, so utterly destitute of all the comforts, conveniences and decencies of life, as the unfortunate blacks of . . . Boston." While this was politically motivated hyperbole, the fact that this quote was carried in newspapers across the country illustrates how the fate of free northern blacks was tied to sectional arguments. Their poverty always stood as a talking point for slavery's defenders.

The result was that Maria Stewart could be an avowed enemy of slavery while still rigorously speaking against the injustices of the North. Stewart also held a radical view of gender. Speaking to black women of Boston, she cried, "Ye daughters of Africa, awake! Arise! . . . distinguish yourselves. Show forth to the world that ye are endowed with noble and exalted faculties." Most black women of Beacon Hill were live-in or day domestics. Others found work washing or sewing at home. Another possible option was trying to make money by taking in boarders. Stewart not only challenged racial

ideas but also spoke these words with a feminist edge that articu-
lated the possibilities of greater things for her fellow women.

Stewart, like Walker, would be gone from the Boston scene almost as quickly as she appeared. Her direct challenge to black men
to change was received as hostile by the leadership class of black
Boston. She stepped into the center of this controversy when she
spoke in the Masonic Hall, a place of black male pride in Boston.
When Prince Hall established the Masonic Hall in 1784, it was the
first white or black lodge founded in the United States from a
charter obtained from a Masonic body in England. This was the beginning of Masonry in America and a forerunner of the twentieth-
century black fraternity movement. It was in this setting that
Stewart asked, "Have the sons of Africa no souls? Feel they no ambitious desires?" She demanded, "Show me our fearless and brave,
our noble and gallant ones . . . that has distinguished himself in
these modern days by acting wholly in the defense of African rights
and liberty." Instead, she saw "gross neglect, on your part."

This was more than enough for many in the community to decide that she should not be part of its future. Seven months later,
discouraged and dejected, Stewart determined to leave Boston. "It
was contempt for my moral and religious opinions in private that
drove me thus before a public. Had experience more plainly shown
me that it was the nature of man to crush his fellow, I should not
have thought it so hard."

By the time Stewart left for a new life in New York in 1834, another radical was establishing himself firmly in Boston. Unlike
Walker and Stewart, he would stay on to fight, affecting the lives of
every soul on Beacon Hill, white and black. His friendship with and
support of William Lloyd Garrison would profoundly affect every
aspect of the abolitionist movement as it struggled to gain a
foothold in Boston and beyond.

What has seldom been written, however, is how the reviled and
beleaguered Garrison could have survived to become the influential leader he later became without the examples of Walker, Stewart,
and, most important, his thirty-five-year association with his productive partner in protest, William Cooper Nell.

# THREE

# Through the Vestry Window

Smith Court, the very heart of old black Boston, has hardly changed in 180 years. In a small alley that juts off Joy Street near the bottom of the hill, sputtering yellow gas lamps still illuminate the small groups bustling to and forth to meetings and special events held at the present-day Museum of African American History, long ago the segregated Abiel Smith School, and then, also along the left side of the court, at the African Meeting House. Most nights, the church's clear windows are ablaze, as the National Park Service keeps a busy schedule of events going. After extensive historical renovation, the church has nearly been returned to its earlier, historic condition, when almost every important event in the life of the black community took place there.

The Meeting House building functioned as a town hall, school, and church all in one. It remains a simple, solid, three-story red brick building with four arched doorways leading to an upper-level sanctuary. This is the room where the voice of virtually every major participant in this era's ferment and toil resounded, including Frederick Douglass, Robert Morris, Harriet Tubman, Wendell Phillips, and, perhaps the most incongruous one of all, a seemingly mild-mannered small man named William Lloyd Garrison. He was to be, despite his milquetoast demeanor, the very center of trouble and turmoil in the city of Boston for nearly forty years, until, with the victory of the Union armies in 1865, he declared his life's work over with the freeing of all slaves.

On January 6, 1832, a twenty-year-old black man was standing outside the church, stubbornly enduring the evening's snow, hail, and icy rainstorm. William Cooper Nell was fixated by what he could see through a vestry window of the Belknap Street Church. He could just make out that the embattled abolitionist newspaper editor William Lloyd Garrison was leading an unusual meeting, for white men, particularly men like these—lawyers and community leaders such as Ellis Gray Loring—did not often frequent this side of the hill. And this was exactly Garrison's idea: forcing his reluctant, though idealistic, associates to brave the signing of their names to a document they knew would cause them all a great deal of trouble. The editor thought, correctly, that being in the basement of this black church would crystallize for them what exactly was at stake that night.

Though Nell did not know it at the time, he was witnessing the first meeting of the New England Anti-Slavery Society. The small group of abolitionist sympathizers had braved the terrible storm to climb down Beacon Hill to Smith Court for their fateful meeting. The men were gathering not in one of their more accustomed locations off State Street but in this church basement, which doubled as the crowded school for the West End's black children. Though the men whose signatures created the New England Anti-Slavery Society that night were all white, black observers and sympathizers were present as well.

Walking back out into the snowy street after the contentious yet historically groundbreaking meeting, Garrison glanced back at the humble church, then pointed up the slope toward the State House and beyond, promising, "Friends, we have met tonight in this obscure school-house, but before many years we will rock Faneuil Hall."

William Nell always remembered that night and what he had witnessed. It marked the beginning of his idolization of and love for Garrison, which would continue his whole life. It is impossible, even in a narrative centering closely on what black abolitionists accomplished for themselves, to deny or diminish the powerful role Garrison played in their saga for more than thirty-five years. Yet it is important, even as his unique influence is acknowledged and celebrated, to begin to see Garrison as one character among many.

William Lloyd Garrison in 1835 at the age of thirty. The *Liberator*
was in its fourth year at the time of this mezzotint. *(Courtesy of the
Boston Public Library/Rare Books Department)*

His commanding image, whether seen positively or negatively (and
few characters in American history have created such fierce division, from his own era stretching to today's historical evaluations),
has so long dominated any evaluation of the abolitionist movement
that at times the Boston of his day seems to have been solely his
domain. As we will see, this narrow focus does serious discredit to
many other abolitionists, white and black, and distorts what really
happened in the city.

For Boston, the Garrison saga really began at a July Fourth celebration when the relatively obscure, twenty-four-year-old printer climbed into the pulpit of the grand Park Street Church, a conservative religious bastion whose white steeple prodded the sky and towered over the Boston Common. The young Garrison, already balding and bespectacled, nervously proceeded to deliver a blistering sermon against slavery that belied his meek appearance. He was not a clergyman, but he did speak in the strong dissenting Puritan tradition of Anne Hutchinson and Roger Williams, for whom there was a necessity of expressing one's conscience on the moral laws of the world. Antislavery supporter Abby Kelly wrote, "Abolitionism is Christianity applied to slavery," and Garrison embodied this belief in his speech, beseeching a moral awakening and seeking immediate repentance of America's soul before God's terrible reckoning could come.

A plaque commemorating that talk is proudly displayed outside the Park Street Church today, but his first listeners were not so pleased upon its delivery. The truth is that Boston took a good long time to decide that this argumentative, high-minded scold was truly a moral hero. While a calm and noble statue of Garrison watches over Commonwealth Avenue today, in his own time he was nearly lynched by an angry Boston mob, not more than a mile from this statue. In 1835, in seeking to disrupt a female antislavery meeting and an appearance by British abolitionist George Thompson, a throng of hundreds of Boston men grabbed Garrison, dragged him through the streets with a noose around his neck, and nearly killed him. The "gentlemen" of the city, from the mayor on down, stood by and let the troublemaker meet his fate in the streets, but Garrison was tougher than they, and for another quarter of a century, he managed to remain true to his vow to "lift up the standard of freedom in the eyes of the nation, within sight of Bunker Hill and the birthplace of liberty."

William Lloyd Garrison was born in Newburyport, Massachusetts, to a poor mother who had been abandoned by her husband. Even fellow reformers of the time such as Emerson felt uncomfortable with someone from an impoverished, and evangelical, background. But Garrison's mother, an intensely religious woman, instilled in Garrison before her early death the strong religious impulse that he would apply to social reform. His desire to write for the improvement of society, as well as his skill as a printer, took him from Massachusetts to Vermont to Baltimore. It was in slave-holding Maryland, where he first lived and socialized among free blacks denied civil rights, that he grew to believe that the question of slavery was inseparable from the status of free blacks in the country. As his principles became more radical, he steadily attracted more attention. While working on a newspaper with Quaker abolitionist Benjamin Lundy, Garrison was accused of libel and forced to serve forty-nine days in a Baltimore jail.

It was while he was in Baltimore that David Walker's *Appeal* arrived like a shot in the night. Whereas the pacifist Lundy found this unprecedented account of black rage disturbing, its "impassioned and determined spirit" intrigued Garrison, who called it a "remarkable production." He would never condone violence, but he did share principles with Walker, specifically Walker's use of the American Revolution's ideologies for abolitionist purposes. Like Walker, Garrison drew from the nation's early ideas of natural rights that, when violated, required the dissolution of that government. To him, slavery was clearly a violation of God-given rights, and thus the Constitution itself was a pact condoning, even upholding, such oppression. While against violence, Garrison outraged his opponents by calling for northern secession from the slave-holding South. He declared that the Constitution must be voided or rewritten, and if not, then he would not mind the rupture of the Union. He called his new philosophy "passive resistance."

Garrison came to Boston to start a newspaper because he felt its intellectual and reformist climate was more suited to what he was trying to accomplish than Baltimore's. From the beginning, he knew that he needed black support for his paper to survive. Initially his readers assumed he was black because his tone was so reminiscent of Walker, and it was unthinkable that a white man would write what he did.

All this made some blacks initially skeptical, but their doubt soon gave way to something close to adoration. In 1830 blacks as well as whites would have been shocked to hear a white man say that he was ashamed of his color. Rev. Thomas Paul, ailing and near death in 1830, heard Garrison speak and could not help but embrace the young man afterward. Garrison returned the support by hiring his son, Thomas Paul Jr., as an apprentice for the new newspaper. Paul's son would grow to be a controversial figure in the struggle for equal school rights.

To further drum up black support for the *Liberator*, Garrison toured New England and met with as many leaders as possible. Many people, upon first seeing him, had a reaction not unlike Frederick Douglass's a few years later. Once the altogether austere-looking man began to speak, out came "holy fire," and he seemed to transform into a "Moses raised up by God to deliver his modern Israel from bondage." His relationship with the black community would grow more complex in later years, but the situation in these early years of Garrison's reign in Boston was summed up by a black New York physician, James McCune Smith, who found it difficult to judge, between Garrison and the black populace, who loved whom more.

For $2 a year, a subscription could be purchased to his four-page paper, which came out at the end of every week. Both he and the black community knew that the success of this enterprise depended on their subscriptions. Of the first four hundred subscribers to the *Liberator*, three-fourths were black. Thus, in his first issue he declared to them:

> Your moral and intellectual elevation, the advancement of your rights, and the defense of your character, will be the leading object of our paper. We know that you are now struggling against wind and tide, and that adversity "has marked you for his own"; yet among three hundred thousand of your number, some patronage maybe given. We ask, and expect, but little that may save the life of *"The Liberator."*

To ensure the publication's success in Boston, Garrison aimed to make it into the paper of the black community. This meant publishing pieces on social events, achievements by members of the community, obituaries, employment opportunities, and warnings when certain kidnappers were said to be in Boston. He also welcomed submissions of articles by blacks so that their voices could be expressed. Those whites reading the *Liberator* obtained a glimpse into a world that most knew little about. And for a neglected, ignored, and ill-treated black community, someone from the outside was finally listening. Garrison seemed to understand that "no tyrannical masters domineer over your persons.... But still you remain under many unjust and grievous disabilities... as an inferior caste, hardly superior in your attainments and circumstances to the slaves." His first issues featured a running column called "To the Free People of Color of the United States," in which he discussed prejudice in all its manifestations in the North.

Garrison was radical, but he believed blacks could obtain their rights through legal means. He wrote, "The fact, that you have been treated, by common consent and common usage, as aliens and brutes, is no proof that such treatment is legal, but only shows the strength, the bitterness, and the blindness of prejudice." Soon the Garrison Juvenile Choir, the Garrison Independent Society, and the Juvenile Garrison Independent Society were formed on Beacon Hill. Garrison's brand of radicalism had picked up where Walker's and Stewart's had left off, and he was ready to help form the ideologies of young black reformers who were coming to power in the community. Whereas Stewart and Walker had signaled an increase in radicalism, Garrison's coming showed something different. His ideas ushered in a new era in which there was a shift from a community that strove to form stronger separatist institutions to a community that would work in coalitions with white reformers for equality through integration. The essential connection for this to happen was none other than his assistant, William Nell.

In the year Garrison began producing his paper, Nat Turner, a mystic slave preacher in Southampton, Virginia, had seen the sky turn blood red. Turner responded to this alleged sign from God by leading a group of fellow insurgents through the predawn shadows, indiscriminately slaughtering sixty unsuspecting whites. Turner carried out what the South Carolinian rebel Vesey had failed to do and what Walker predicted was inevitable: a horrific slave rebellion that terrified the South. This fear meant that Garrison's northern paper was viewed with even more panic in the South. Like Walker's *Appeal*, Garrison's *Liberator* was banned in most slave-holding states, and enormous bounties were placed on the editor's life.

The governor of Virginia was so convinced that this new anti-slavery newspaper had incited Nat Turner's bloody uprising that he sent a demand to Boston's mayor that he force Garrison to cease publishing. It apparently took some time for the city authorities to find Garrison's small printing office, but when they did, Mayor Harrison Grey Otis wrote back to Virginia that he should lay aside his fears, for "the only visible auxiliary of Mr. Garrison was a Negro boy."

Unbeknownst to the mayor, this boy was William Nell, who was rapidly becoming a politically minded radical himself. Though Garrison was considerably older than Nell, Nell still referred to him as "my best friend and benefactor," and once he called it a "religious duty to defend Mr. Garrison."

William Nell began his career as a social activist by following not Garrison but the example of his own father, tailor William Guion Nell. While in his late teens, Nell gained a place as the secretary of the Juvenile Garrison Independent Society and began to work for Garrison in the *Liberator*'s office. Though Rev. Thomas Paul's son had already claimed the position of apprentice, Nell eagerly did any chores around the office that needed to be done and, in the process, acquired the useful skill of printing. No one earned any money, least of all the editor. One friend later described the place where the two men worked together for so long.

> Everything around it had an aspect of slovenly decay. The dingy walls; the small windows, bespotted with printer's ink, the press standing to one corner, the composing stands opposite; the long editorial and mailing table, covered with newspaper; the bed of the editor and publisher on the floor—all these made a picture never to be forgotten.

William Nell had been a very sensitive boy, particularly with regard to his race. Once, when he was a small child, his Sunday school teacher asked him what he wanted to be when he grew up. Nell may have been young at the time, but he had deeply internalized the notion of how blacks were treated in Boston and reportedly replied, "What is the use of trying to be somebody? I can never be anything but a Nigger anyway." His fatalistic view of the world started to change, however, as he grew older.

Nell's acute sense of history was an important component of his development. This interest was nurtured by stories of his father, a community leader and founding member of the Massachusetts General Colored Association. Though a dedicated integrationist, Nell would always be skeptical of these types of organizations. As a boy growing up on Beacon Hill, some days Nell would stroll over to the State House and wander in the east wing, which was filled with mosaics, murals, and monuments to United States history. He loved collecting stories from the black veterans of America's first two wars, and these tales began to instill in him more pride in his race and his forebears. His father was one such man, as he had been born in David Walker's free black community of Charleston, South Carolina, but left to become a ship steward. In the War of 1812, he fought on General Gadsden's ship and was captured by the British. Nonetheless, he survived the war and arrived in Boston in 1817 to seek work as a tailor. He eventually established a business on Court Street, in today's financial district, and lived on Beacon Hill.

The other important factor that influenced young Nell's outlook on the world was Garrison's arrival in Boston. After watching him silently from outside the vestry window, Nell would throw himself into a life of unflinching activism and writing. Nell was a slim, light-skinned young man whose thin face contained strong, chiseled features, and he was known to be "chaste in conversation." Seemingly always moving made his body appear almost elastic at times. Though he was always a better writer than a speaker, his first public speech had a great impact. The *New England Telegraph* wrote after seeing him, "We believe that there is not one white lad in a thousand at that age and having enjoyed no better advantages for education, who could have done as well."

This speech was also crucial because it laid out a personal ideology from which he would never stray far. Looking out on the Garrison Independent Society, he told them that "prejudice is the cause of slavery." He thus viewed his fights against discrimination in Boston as part of the struggle against slavery. Black self-help work was interchangeable with antislavery work. His fight against prejudice on the "school question" was particularly important for him because "*Colorphobia* is not exhibited by children."

Throughout the 1830s it was said that no public meeting of black Boston was complete without Nell there diligently taking notes. A consummate journalist, he had a notebook on him at all times, and he would wake up at night to scribble down thoughts, putting a line under each one. These writing and recording skills were well utilized as he documented countless events for the *Liberator*. Though his mother had died in 1834 and he was responsible for the care of four younger sisters, he seldom missed an event. The Adelphic Union Library Association was one of these improvement groups that were so dear to Nell. The Adelphic Union was organized in 1838 to bring weekly lectures and debates to the black community of Boston. These talks were held in the Smith School room on Belknap Street during the fall and winter on every Tuesday night for the price of fifty cents each or seventy-five cents for the season. Topics included "The Air—to be Illustrated by a Series of Experiments," "The British Corn Laws," "The Antiquities of the Palencians of Central America," "Pneumatics," and "The Philosophy of Reform." While some of these topics were in the vein of general education, many were shaping the community's political views, as they considered questions such as whether women should have equal rights, what accounted for prejudice, and what forms of education were best for the community.

An affiliate of the Adelphic Union was the Young Men's Literary Society. While Nell made his mark coordinating the Adelphic Union, Robert Morris became a prominent member of the Literary

Society. This group was known to comprise "the most promising young colored men of the city of Boston."

Since his arrival in Boston, Robert Morris had wasted no time in becoming a community leader. It was inevitable that Nell and Morris would begin to know each other. Morris attended the Adelphic Union lectures that the young Nell arranged and reported on. Nell, however, had little in common with the younger Morris.

Though Morris had not been raised in the Boston black community as had Nell, he seemed far more comfortable in it. Nell's letters are filled with gossip and tidbits about the white abolitionists he so greatly admired and from whom he craved attention and affirmation. He often wrote of "Friend Mr. Garrison," boyishly reminding Wendell Phillips that "he allows me to call him that." This is not to say he did not work wholeheartedly for the betterment of the black community, as rarely would a copy of the *Liberator* pass without a notice—placed by him—for a fellow black citizen of Boston looking for employment or a place to live.

Whereas Nell spent much of his time with white abolitionists, Morris's political contacts were far more rooted in the black community. Morris worked and was friends with white abolitionists, particularly Ellis Gray Loring, yet he never idolized them the way Nell did. He also made a point of stressing to those blacks who had achieved higher levels of education or professional advancement that they should not forget those on the lower social rungs of Beacon Hill. Though David Walker's death prevented his watching his son Edwin's admittance to the bar, Morris was there on that important day, smiling proudly at the prospect of another black lawyer in Boston. But after Edwin took the oath, Morris grabbed him and said, "Don't ever try to run from our people. Do you ever wear gloves? If you do, take them off and go down among our people." Not surprisingly—unlike Nell, whose hero was the pacifist Garrison —Morris reserved his reverence for the fierce Denmark Vesey and Nat Turner.

Despite their differences, Morris and Nell were fast friends in Morris's first years in Boston. They worked together constantly and wrote each other monthly when one was out of Boston. Morris even thought highly enough of Nell to introduce him to his sister, at a time when many of Nell's friends were trying to set him up with the ladies of Boston. Nell called her "my little friend" and said he thought of her with great respect, though there is no evidence that a romance ever blossomed. However, despite these favorable aspects to their relationship, they did retain a certain unease with each other. In a letter Nell wrote to another friend, he urged him not to mention the letter because Morris "will think I mean to slight him." They were both men of strong personalities, as demonstrated at a Young Men's Literary Society meeting in 1843. They got into an argument, though Nell immediately regretted the severity with which he responded to Morris, since Morris had only been defending someone else who had more greatly offended Nell. This would not be the last time they would fight because of alliances with other people, but for now Morris did not demand an apology. Nell, however, felt civilly obligated to send one anyway. Despite these rough patches in their friendship, Nell clearly admired Morris, demonstrated by the fact that he repeatedly wrote to white abolitionist Wendell Phillips about Morris's achievements. In 1843, when Morris began his quest toward the bar, Nell affirmed, "May his path be brilliant with success."

During Nell's and Morris's maturation, a Revolutionary War veteran named John Telemachus Hilton was the primary leader of the community. Hilton was thirty years older than the young, ambitious duo, but together, they formed an interesting leadership trio for the black community of the 1840s. Hilton came to Boston from Pennsylvania in the era of Prince Hall and Thomas Paul. A major organizer at the Masonic lodge, he worked first as a clothier, then as a barber. With Nell's father and other leaders such as Walker, he formed the General Colored Association of Massachusetts in 1826, a vital group that strove to uphold and support West End community life in an increasingly stressful and difficult time—and in so doing, created a black abolitionist group working on the streets of Boston four years before Garrison's white association. Historians have rightly credited Garrison for courage, steadfastness, and fierce and unrelenting idealism, but few have correctly or graciously noted, as Garrison himself did, that only the support of the free blacks of Boston saved his paper and gave him his platform to radicalize the whole movement of abolitionism. He stood with others, and when it counted, they stood by him.

# FOUR

# First Class

One hundred and fourteen years before Rosa Parks took her seat in the front of a Montgomery, Alabama, bus, a fugitive slave from Maryland who had just been hired as a speaking agent for the Massachusetts Anti-Slavery Society deliberately sat himself in an elegant Eastern Railway carriage. With the train ready to embark for Newburyport from Lynn, the conductor informed the man that he would have to leave for the caste car, reserved for Negro passengers.

Refusing, Frederick Douglass ignored the order.

> I was soon waited on by half a dozen fellows of the baser sort (just such as would volunteer to take a bull-dog out of a meeting house in time of public worship) and told that I must move out of that seat, and if I did not, they would drag me out. I refused to move, and they clutched me, head, neck, and shoulders.... I had interwoven myself among the seats. In dragging me out, it must have cost the company twenty five or thirty dollars, for I tore up seats and all.

Wrenching up the bolted railway car seats—and then enduring a beating—was the only response Douglass offered that day, but his protest was repeated so often that for a week Eastern Railway trains refused to stop in Lynn, a cap to what Douglass called "this ridiculous farce."

This scene helps us begin to understand the world in which black activists and white abolitionists operated, and why the Roberts case

Frederick Douglass in 1854. *(Courtesy of the Boston Athenaeum)*

would later galvanize free blacks. A man like Frederick Douglass, and the challenge he embodied, came as a profound shock to a nation that saw itself as a bastion of freedom and hope. Less than seventy years after the Declaration of Independence, the new nation in the 1840s was optimistic, confident, and a burgeoning example to the rest of a tired ancient world. Alexis de Tocqueville observed that Americans were optimistic by nature, with an "indefinite faculty for improvement." From the time of the Revolution, when Tom Paine declared America to be "a birthday of the new world," this open vista of noble change had sustained the people.

The era from 1845 to the abyss of the Civil War is one of the few periods that can compare to the swirling change and sense of dislocation of the 1960s in its ferment, social chaos, and vibrancy. What may seem in old tinted photographs and yellowed etchings to have been a quaint and quiet time was anything but, with the advent of quick-paced and unrelenting technological innovation. Boston found itself in the heart of this change. Henry Adams, at the end of the century, recalled his Beacon Hill childhood as having been lived between old Revolutionary verities and a new sense that the "old universe was thrown into the ash-heap and a new one created."

The invention of the rotary printing press, the laying of the transatlantic cable, Morse's telegraph, Whitney's cotton gin, Fulton's steamboat, the quickening pace of the laying of railroad track, increasing locomotive engine power, Cunard Steamers, Singer's sewing machine, and even the advent of the iron plow—all these made the pace of daily life seem to teem with exhilarating transformation. Daniel Webster concluded, "Society is full of excitement."

There was also a sense that any and all aspects of culture and politics could be changed as well. It was called the Newness. There was a tidal wave of reform movements: the call for universal peace, the women's rights campaign, the temperance movement, prison reform, the elimination of the death penalty, care for the mentally ill, treatment for the blind, and the creation of public schools. Emerson called the cascade of crusaders, utopians, and cranks the "Daemon" of reform.

There is always a shadow side to the fever for change. The most controversial and disquieting of all these movements to Americans was the abolitionist movement. This confident land was being forced to confront its ugliest and most telling rejection of the promise of the Declaration of Independence, and few Americans relished embracing such a disturbing challenge. It was becoming increasingly hard to square their optimistic confidence with sharply rising partisan hatreds, conflict between North and South, the nativist movement against immigrants, the hunting of fugitive slaves, rising violence—verbal and physical, even, as we will see, on the floor of the Senate. In all the growing chaos of this era, it would be the abolitionist struggle—though borne by a very few and at some danger to themselves—that would ultimately define this time of reform.

It is impossible to understand the story of the *Roberts* case and equal school rights in Boston without first dealing with the underlying tensions, and great hopes, that the abolitionist movement fueled. The great fifteen-year effort to desegregate the Boston schools is an amazingly complex story, beginning in fierce campaigns against segregation in transportation and interracial marriage bans. These victorious battles gave the black community of Boston a sense of its own power. The only difference between these campaigns and the school campaign that followed—and this distinction is crucial—is that the fight for school desegregation would ultimately be under black leadership.

One historian rightly observes, "The campaign to integrate the schools was itself a school for politics," and the battle to desegregate the railways and to open the definition of marriage was the opening salvo for the long battle of the schools.

White abolitionists did not come easily to an acceptance of black civil rights. Black abolitionists viewed the end of slavery and civil rights together in a way that was foreign to many white reformers. One black activist, James McCune Smith, noted that nowhere did the constitution of the American Anti-Slavery Society mention any goals of social equality for blacks. In fact, it is hard to imagine that whites would be energized to fight against segregation when some were known to segregate even abolitionist meetings.

A black woman named Charlotte Coleman discovered this when she attended an 1841 Boston Female Anti-Slavery Society meeting. Exasperated with what she perceived to be the hypocrisy of these reformers, she sat in the "white" section of the meeting, much to the consternation of many of the women. One of these disapproving abolitionists sent Coleman a letter maintaining her commitment to abolitionist work but stating her belief that "colored people were very well in their place." These views led black abolitionist Samuel Ward to conclude that most white activists "best loved the colored man at a distance."

For other abolitionists, a lack of concern for black civil rights was a matter of perceived pragmatism. They felt that expending energy on these rights would not only distract them from the slavery ques-

tion but also unnecessarily antagonize people who could potentially be brought to like-minded views. One such white abolitionist,
Charles Follen, speaking to a Massachusetts Anti-Slavery Society
meeting in 1836, thought that they should not needlessly "shock the
feelings, though they were but prejudices, of the white people, by
admitting colored persons to our anti-slavery meetings and societies." However, he could not help but note that these words "give
the lie to our own most solemn professions."

It would be a long struggle even within the abolitionist movement to help reformers understand that they could not ignore the
rights of free northern blacks to simple equality. William Lloyd Garrison would do much in this regard, and his sensitivity went far in
explaining why he had such sway and influence with early black
abolitionists. Within the first year of the publication of the *Liberator,*
Garrison was writing about the unfairness of the law prohibiting interracial marriage. This became a major issue for Garrison, and he
would mention it in almost every issue. The prohibition against the
marriage of blacks and whites dated back to the slave codes of the
colony. When slavery was officially abolished in the state of Massachusetts in 1780, this was the only aspect of the slave code that survived. In 1836 a law making such marriages void, even if they had
been performed legally in another state before the couple moved
to Massachusetts, expanded this injustice. To many observers, such
as school advocate and abolitionist Lydia Maria Child, the most draconian aspect of the current situation was the state of illegitimacy
this threw over the children of such marriages.

Garrison was not a popular man in Boston, but of all his detested
ideas, the repeal of the marriage law ranked at the top. More than
the integration of the church, theater, or railway car, it was the institution of marriage that evoked ideas of amalgamation, thus provoking more intense hostility. Garrison paraphrased and then
answered his critics when he wrote, " 'What would you have us do?
Would you have us invite Negroes to our parties, and give them our
daughters in marriage?'—Give if you can a good reason why a vir-
tuous, well-educated black should not be invited!...In a word, we
would have them judged by character, not by color." This consti-

tuted a revolutionary statement for 1831, and the mob that attacked Garrison four years later would have these words in mind.

There had been intermittent petitions to the legislature on the marriage question during the 1830s, but no one took much notice until 1839, when a group of white women from Lynn, Massachusetts, decided to make their opinions on the issue known. Caroline Augusta Chase and 735 other white women signed a petition to end all laws that made a distinction based on race. Soon other petitions came in from various Massachusetts towns with similar sentiments, until the legislature had received 1,300 names. Boston newspapers poured scorn on the idea, and the women were subjected to dogged ridicule. The *Boston Post* characterized their aims as "the privilege of marrying black husbands," adding, "This is rather a cut at the white Lynn beaux—or perhaps some of these ladies despair of having a white offer, and so are willing to try *de colored race.*"

George Bradburn, a Nantucket Whig, went against his party's conventional attitudes toward race when he argued that the law was unfair to the children of these marriages and to the clergy, who were fined for performing the services joining the two parties. Bradburn was not prudent with his words, and when one of his opponents finished railing against Bradburn's cause, he none too subtly wondered why that man's complexion was about as dark as a black man, nearly causing a brawl on the floor of the legislature. It seemed that Bradburn had not endeared himself to his colleagues or the press. The *Boston Phoenix* mockingly wrote, "If any fair daughter of Ethiopia for whom he feels a tender passion, we hope a special act of the Legislature will enable him to say—'Hail, wedded love.' " But in fact, Bradburn and the abolitionists had made progress, as the law just barely survived a close vote to repeal it in 1840.

Throughout this increasingly heated debate, black activists remained silent. Perhaps because historically so much white racism has been intertwined with fears of black male sexuality, Boston blacks fighting for other fundamental rights decided that it would be unwise to press too hard on this one. While certain white abolitionists pressed for the repeal of the marriage law, blacks concentrated their protests more on segregation in all forms of public transportation.

Douglass's explosive railway protest was not an isolated incident. To be sure, the line between protest and daily practical desperation was hard to discern when it came to transportation. On a wet and freezing day, Rev. T. S. Wright's wife was forced on the deck of a boat on a trip from Philadelphia to New York. Mrs. Wright begged to be let inside because she was unwell. At one point, she desperately offered to pay double the fare, but the captain of the boat callously rejected her pleas. Soon after the boat came to shore, she died of pneumonia.

Segregation on the railways particularly bothered blacks because of the necessity of this form of transportation. Between 1840 and 1855, the railroad industry in Massachusetts grew quickly, with the railroad mileage expanding from 318 to 1,264 miles. Every mile seemed marked by humiliation and inconvenience for those kept in separate compartments (by contrast, as many embittered northern blacks noted, southern slaves could sit in the white carriages along with their masters). Unlike the marriage issue, there was no specific legislation guiding transportation.

Even as the legislature mulled over the marriage question in 1840, William Nell traveled with his mentor William Lloyd Garrison to deliver antislavery lectures in Salem. After staying the night, they boarded the train back to Boston the following morning. They were seated next to each other when a perturbed train conductor noticed the light-skinned Nell. As early as 1834, Garrison's paper had written on the unfairness of the treatment of blacks, but now his actions would have to live up to his editorial protests. Words were exchanged, but it soon became clear to Nell and Garrison that the only way back to Boston would be to sit in segregated seating. At that point, Garrison realized he could protest these arbitrary distinctions by getting up and seating himself in the filthy section reserved for blacks, as well as those passengers deemed drunken or ragged. Making light of the situation, Garrison remarked to Nell as they sat down in the black section that perhaps this was the right place for him, because he had gotten pretty tan on a speaking tour of Europe and "might perhaps be taken for a color'd man." Nell assured him that though he did not think his friend could pass for a black man, he "always knew how to feel as one."

These fierce customs had remained unchanged since Robert Morris took the same route from Salem to Boston four years earlier. The difference was that now a white abolitionist was willing to share the burden to protest the distinction. Garrison's friend and fellow abolitionist Wendell Phillips followed suit whenever he traveled with Nell. Though the wealthy Phillips, a Boston grandee if there ever was one and the son of the mayor, was uncomfortable sharing a room with Frederick Douglass as they traveled together on the abolitionist lecture circuit, he nevertheless realized that his principles had to be placed above his social comfort. Boarding a train at the Eastern Railroad station months later with Phillips, Nell tried to sit where he had been forbidden to sit months earlier, but when this effort was thwarted again, Phillips took his place with Nell in the segregated section.

Robert Morris, training for the law at this time, decided to join these progenitors of the modern "sit-in." He took every opportunity, as he said, to "annoy the railroad companies" by sitting where he was forbidden to sit to test their zeal for enforcing an unjust policy. This kind of action was a revelation to Morris, who began extending these forms of protest to many places around Boston, buying tickets to theaters and lecture rooms or attending a white church. He would not leave until the whites around him were forced to eject him from the premises, demonstrating to all who were watching what discrimination really looked like. He would then use what he was learning in Loring's law books to defend his actions when confronted by Boston authorities.

Men were not the only ones protesting the trains' policies. A black abolitionist woman named Mary Newhall Green was boarding a train with her child when she was asked to move to the "dirty car," which she would not do. They were both thrown off the train, causing injury to the small child. Before her husband was also thrown off, he was beaten ruthlessly as punishment for the family's activism. There seemed to be no decent limits to the reach of segregation.

The West End community, along with Garrison and his small but growing band of white abolitionists, was now at fever pitch. The *Liberator* was becoming a creative forum for discussing ways to defeat the segregation in railcars, with a sense that with such a victory, others would naturally follow. A regular feature of the paper was the "Traveler's Directory," where the different attitudes of various companies were rated based on the experiences of Massachusetts blacks. Some companies, like the Boston and Lowell Railroad and the Boston and Worcester Railroad, got marks such as "humanity respected" or "equally free for all" and their schedules were listed. In contrast, lines like the Boston, New Bedford, and Providence Railroads were classified with appraisals such as "a vile distinction enforced by brutal assaults." For the prime enemy, the Eastern Railroad, the guide read that there was "an odious distinction on account of color." Just to make sure that the protests would be personal, the *Liberator* also listed the names of all the supervisors of discriminating railroads.

The traveler's directory allowed black customers to know how to avoid railroads that might cause them injury. The printed directions also represented how protests were evolving. In an article entitled "Eastern Railroad," the *Liberator* wrote that "the corporation had proved, beyond dispute or cavil, that neither convenience, accommodation, nor improvement is the ruling principle with them, but monopoly and profit."

After trying numerous times to appeal to the owner's higher moral sentiments in their "ride-ins," the activists decided to boycott, thinking the pocketbook would pinch even if the conscience remained numb. Above all, people had to be made to realize that there was no official authorization for any railroad to continue these injustices.

Meanwhile, on the state legislative side, Bradburn watched the repeal of the marriage law again being turned down in 1841. Furious at the second failure of the bill, he decided to pour his frustrated energy into the railroad matter. He obstructed Eastern Railroad's plans to expand and tried to make them lose their charter altogether. By getting behind both issues, he was effectively linking them in a mutual movement against Jim Crow distinctions. Both causes would benefit from this framework. For the marriage issue, it made it a more legitimate cause, de-emphasizing amalgamation fears.

The growing agitation was not powerful enough to save Bradburn's job, however. Near the end of 1841, he discovered that conservative Whigs, predictably disagreeing with his progressive advocacy for blacks, refused to renominate him for another term. Not only had the black community lost an ally, but this was a warning to other politicians considering sticking their necks out for equal rights. Nevertheless, a committee was appointed to study the two matters that were in place, despite Bradburn's untimely exit from the fight. By 1842, the head of the committee, Charles Francis Adams, guided a repeal of the marriage law through the state Senate, but it faltered in the House. In the railroad matter, the committee brought in abolitionists to testify to the current situation's injustices. Wendell Phillips and Robert Morris's mentor Ellis Gray Loring appeared before the committee detailing the violence that blacks had been subjected to. They argued that legislators could intervene because railroads were not typical companies but entities that relied on funds, protections, and privileges made possible by the state.

Phillips and Loring tried to impart to the legislators how vital an issue this was for blacks, but what was needed was the authenticity of an argument by someone who was directly affected by the injustice. The dramatic appearance by Salem activist Charles Lenox Remond was a first in American history. Remond, born in Curaçao, had been raised in Salem, Massachusetts, where his father and Robert Morris's father were community leaders. While the younger Morris was busy establishing himself in legal Boston, Remond's passionate speaking skills and considerable courage allowed him to become one of the most famous black abolitionists, and one generally seen as the first professional antislavery lecturer. A striking man, with hair that shot up at least a half foot above his head, he was a fixture at Boston events, having recently returned from addressing packed crowds all over Europe. He had suffered firsthand experiences with the railways' malevolence, often forced out of the common area on trains, as well as once nearly freezing to death on a steamboat.

Despite whatever pressure Remond may have felt, he calmly began pointing out the absurdities of racism by reflecting on his recent European tour, where he was "received, treated and recognized, in public society, without any regard to my complexion." He then contrasted this with treatment he received upon returning to his native state, where "the rights, privileges and immunities of its citizens are measured by complexion." Finishing forcefully, he asserted that if whites chose not to socialize with him, that was their choice, "but, in civil rights, one man has not the prerogative to define the rights of another."

The black community soon found that Remond, Phillips, and Loring delivered more than anyone could have expected. Surprisingly, the committee agreed that the railroad companies were indeed violating people's rights, "on the broad principle that the constitution allows no distinction in public privileges among different classes of citizens of this commonwealth." These were important seedbed words, because the fight for equal schools would center on exactly this point—one that this legislative committee upheld in 1842. The committee unanimously stated that distinctions among citizens were unconstitutional, and further, that these rights could not be subjected to individual tastes.

By 1842, with the concurrent battles over marriage and transportation at crucial stages, the nation was starting to pay attention to the ongoing agitation in the Bay State. An article in the *Washington Globe* epitomized much of America's puzzlement at this progress of the abolitionists when it complained, "It is only necessary now to pass an act to compel the tavern keepers to put the two races in the same bed, without 'any distinction of descent, sect... or color.'"

Close to home, on the floor of the state legislature, the marriage bill was still provoking similar antipathy. Yet new legislators were also starting to espouse rhetoric similar to that of the abolitionists. One Worcester representative declared, "No man is responsible for his color—God makes no distinction. As long as they are recognized as citizens, this law is an arbitrary one, and makes a distinction between one class of citizens to the degradation of the other." Progress was being made.

While the Boston black community had protested forcefully against segregation on the railways, they had largely let their white abolitionist allies deal with the marriage issue. This changed at the beginning of 1843, four years since the repeal of the marriage bill had first been proposed at the State House. Now, gathering in their neighborhood just blocks from the State House's great gold dome, the West End community, in a heated meeting, at last passed resolutions advocating the repeal of all laws that distinguished people by race. This time, they had absolutely no hesitancy in including the marriage law, for they believed that the time had come for this insult to be "wiped away."

It turns out that their political instincts were right. The year 1843 would finally see victory on both fronts. In February, the state Senate passed both the repeal of the marriage law and a statute forbidding segregation on the railways, but corresponding bills still needed to pass in the House. Again opposition was fierce, politicians citing the creation of the Smith School and the various black churches as proof that blacks wanted to be separate. But in a close vote, the reformers at last carried the day. It was a stunning victory for the abolitionists. The marriage bill's repeal was all the more remarkable when one considers it would take the United States until 1967, more than one hundred years, to make all interracial marriage prohibitions illegal.

With the less popular marriage ban passed, it seemed that the train act would also pass, but some representatives were still holding out. Opponents argued that while the marriage repeal did not force whites to marry blacks, a transportation desegregation bill would force them to sit next to blacks. A new technique of the bill's adversaries was to make the proposal even more far-reaching, thinking a more general desegregation law would attract greater opposition.

Train reformers in the House began to pressure the companies in question to bring the matter to resolution. In a tribute to the earlier instincts of the abolitionist community to go after the money, it finally took the nervous action of stockholders, not the legislature, to desegregate the trains. A majority of the stockholders in Eastern Railroad were now tired of being associated with a company with such biased practices. This was affecting business, after all. With the railroads ending their discriminating policies at last, the legislature dropped its efforts to pass a law to that end, no doubt with relief.

The marriage repeal and train reforms created not just important practical changes in the fabric of life of the free black citizens of Boston but, more important, gave them a sense of their own potential power and the capacity for future victories. These direct actions, boycotts, petitions, legislative pressures, legal actions, and mass meetings were all part of the lessons taken by this community, to be effectively used in the upcoming assault on segregated schools.

It was true that most of the leaders in these early battles were dedicated white abolitionists, but this would not be the case in the school battle to come, at least after the first year's efforts. To be sure, the free blacks would still need and retain their white allies, but agency over the campaign would be theirs.

Despite these considerable victories, few Boston blacks were fooled or deluded into thinking their situation was still anything but desperate. In an official report of the city, statistician Jesse Chickering's dispassionate depiction of the state of Boston broke for a moment when he noted, "Where ever they go, a sneer is passed upon them, as if this sportive inhumanity were an act of merit... though their legal rights are the same as those of whites, their condition is one of degradation and dependence."

This chapter began with the fugitive slave turned activist Frederick Douglass on the railway lines. In a moving letter, he wrote what life was really like in the midst of these campaigns for equality. Standing on the Boston Common, he decided to buy a ticket to a menagerie, something he would never have dared to do as a slave. "I went, and as I approached the entrance to gain admission, I was met and told by the doorkeeper, in a harsh and contemptuous tone, *'We don't allow n——rs in here.'*" Then in church at a revival meeting, "a good deacon, . . . told me, in a pious tone, '*We don't allow n——rs in here.*'" Then on the steamer *Massachusetts,* the eating house, the omnibus, all the same, "*We don't allow n——rs in here.*"

Where this hurt the most, and most ruinously, was the denial of entrance to schools. De Tocqueville, in his American travels, once encountered Sam Houston on a steamboat bound for New Orleans, and they fell into conversation. Houston, who had fought against the Indians, commented on their considerable intelligence, and then added, "The difference one notices between the Indian and the Negro seems to be the result solely from the different education they have received." The Indians were, in the end, still free in their souls and hearts and could act free. "The ordinary Negro has been a slave before he was born and had to be taught to live as a free man."

This was the urgency fueling the larger struggle beyond the victorious railway and marriage battles. Short of the abolition of slavery itself, the key to freedom lay in the coming siege on the schoolhouse door.

# FIVE

# "Mr. Prejudice"

William Cooper Nell was a shy, serious boy of twelve and one of the most promising young pupils in the small, cramped basement school at the African Meeting House. When it came time for the annual examination of the school, Boston mayor Harrison Gray Otis accompanied school board member Samuel T. Armstrong to the building. The tradition was to examine not only the whole school but each pupil as well. Those who scored highest were awarded the Franklin medal, feted, and celebrated at a medal ceremony at Faneuil Hall. It was a great honor in Boston life to become a Franklin scholar.

After scoring in the top three in his class, young Nell awaited his invitation for the medal ceremony, but because he was black, none came. Instead he was given a biography of Benjamin Franklin. Though only twelve, Nell understood that something rightfully his had been denied him, and he resolved to do something about it.

As the night of the grand dinner at Faneuil Hall approached, Nell made his plans. He asked a waiter he knew if he could join the waitstaff for that special night. When the ceremonies began, Nell's curiosity turned into acute pain as he watched a train of white students being lauded for achievements that were no greater than his. As he was serving the students, their parents, and community leaders, someone noticed who he was, breaking through the waiter's

William Cooper Nell (1816–1874), dedicated activist, staunch integrationist. *(Unidentified photographer; courtesy of the Massachusetts Historical Society)*

normal invisibility. Samuel T. Armstrong, who had inspected Nell's school, recognized the increasingly despondent boy. When a suitable time came, he leaned over to Nell and whispered, "You ought to be here with the other boys."

Nell made no response. Instead he bitterly thought to himself, "If you think so, why have you not taken steps to bring it about?"

That evening was the beginning of the epic struggle for black students to be granted equal rights. The refusal to grant the Franklin medal to Nell did more than galvanize just one man, because it was Nell's pain and fierce resolve that, in turn, kept this community's struggle alive for so many years. Whenever it sputtered and nearly died, as it did many times, Nell somehow managed to stir the ashes and bring the flame back. He swore to himself, remembering that twelve-year-old boy in a waiter's dress in Faneuil Hall that night, that he would "do my best to hasten the day when the color of the skin would be no barrier to equal school rights."

Eleven years later, Nell was living in a Federal-style clapboard house across the street from the segregated Smith School. From windows overlooking the school, he saw schoolchildren arrive every morning, a constant reminder of his promise to end such schools. In 1840 he resolved to begin, at last, a campaign to make that vow a reality. Though it would be years before another printer, Benjamin Franklin Roberts, would come forward to transform a wide-ranging boycott campaign into an epic legal battle, it was Nell who consistently kept the faith, redirected misplaced energies, and refused to surrender when it seemed easier to resign oneself to the old ways.

The campaign for integrated schools began during the rise and definition of mass popular education. For Bostonians, public schools ensured "social stability in a time of change." In 1820 Boston was a city of 43,000 people, 12 percent of whom were born overseas. Forty years later, Boston exploded into a packed and overflowing city of 178,000 people, more than half of whom were of foreign birth. In 1840, the year that agitation over segregated schools commenced, Massachusetts had 18 high schools. Twenty years later, there were 108.

It was a time of more than statistical growth, however. There was also a revolution in educational reform, with one reformer, Horace Mann, presiding over a Massachusetts struggle that would define for the whole nation what free public schooling could mean to its potential as a free society. The reforms would be staggering, with the establishment of the first public high school in 1821, the founding of the first teacher training school in 1839 and the passage of the compulsory school attendance law in 1852.

In these years the black population was growing, but its growth could never compare with the levels of Irish immigration to Boston. According to Mann, the architect of Boston schools,

A foreign people, born and bred and dwarfed under the despotism of the old world, cannot be transformed into full stature of America merely by a voyage across the Atlantic. . . . They remain unfitted until they have become morally acclimated to our institutions.

For those who came from cultures outside of the American one, public schools would become the chief Americanizing institutions.

The Revolutionary generation of Boston would have found it hard to fathom the growth of Boston's populations, but they did believe primary education was an effective brand of social control, imparting "piety, sobriety, frugality and industry" to all children. In this age of Emersonian optimism, Horace Mann felt that the common school movement in Massachusetts constituted "the greatest discovery ever made by man . . . other social organizations are curative and remedial; this is preventative and an antidote."

Thus it is surprising that those in power in Boston resisted so forcefully, and for so long, the inclusion of blacks in schools, which were seen as vital for training and transforming young souls into future citizens. Yet the primal power of racism can never be underestimated as a motivational force, especially for a school committee that declared in 1846, "The less the colored and white people become intermingled, the better it will be for both races." An outsider like de Tocqueville, who did not understand the depths of racial separation in America, was shocked to find during his tour of Boston that "in Massachusetts the blacks have the rights of citizenship, they may vote in elections, but the prejudice is so strong that it is impossible to receive their children in the schools."

It did not help matters that in 1787 black leaders had led a campaign for segregated schools. In the context of other events at the time, this request made sense to the black community of Prince Hall and Thomas Paul, as they were busy building many essential institutions of community support at the time. Furthermore, the treatment of young blacks in the public schools was distressing, with one common disciplinary measure being to send a student to the "Nigger seat." The students were then told that they were "worse than . . . little nigger[s]," and then, if needed, came the additional admonition that "they will be poor or ignorant as a nigger, or have no more credit than a nigger." Black children also endured constant bullying and harassment. Parents understandably did not want their children to be exposed to this chronic discrimination and thus petitioned for a separate school in 1787, and again in 1798. In reply to the second petition, the School Committee told them that they could not fund such an effort but that parents were free to establish such a school on their own. There exists no evidence of any protest within the black community to the move toward segregated schools.

Black schools in Boston began in the home of Primus Hall, conveniently situated in the hub of the community at 63 West Cedar Street. Hall was a strong and revered leader of the black community, being the son of Prince Hall. Prince Hall had been a free man when courting Primus's mother while she was still a slave for a family on Beacon Street. Their son Primus had also been a slave as a child, but after distinguishing himself as a soldier in the Revolution, he was freed.

Back in Boston in 1798, Primus Hall turned his house into a makeshift school. However, after three months of classes, a yellow fever epidemic swept through Boston and the school was closed. A black school did not open again for three years, during which time the community again unsuccessfully petitioned the School Committee for funding. When the school reopened, taught by two Harvard students, its benefactors were wealthy whites. Schooling then moved from private residences to a carpenter's shop for three years, until 1806.

The African Meeting House was completed in that year with financial help from white philanthropists, who instructed that the basement should be the permanent home of the school. Now came the task of getting enough money to fully fund a school in the completed church. With a remarkable effort showing the commitment to education that all members of the black community shared, $500 was raised and a new schoolroom was outfitted. The donors included black sailors who managed to raise $200 and poorer members of Beacon Hill who contributed another $88. Local black families also donated their labors and craftsmanship to help outfit the room properly. In addition, parents were asked to pay twenty-five cents a month to support their children's school, though this would prove to be too much for many residents. The African School was now, in effect, a private school, since the School Board would not officially acknowledge or administer it. However, this began to change by 1812, with the School Board beginning to make annual contributions to the school. Noticing the increasing success of the school, the School Board considered extending its control over it.

In 1815, still struggling to support the school on a shoestring budget, the black community got a large gift from Abiel Smith. Smith was a wealthy and wily businessman known as a merchant prince because of his vast fortune. During the American Revolution alone, he acquired $20,000 in gold, and he was not above having his wife and sister smuggle goods to increase his wealth. Smith knew Prince Saunders, a black man from Vermont who, with the help of the Reverend William Ellery Channing, had gone to Boston to teach black children. Saunders persuaded Smith to leave an endowment for his humble school. When Smith died in 1815, it was found that he had responded to Saunders's lobbying quite generously by leaving a trust amounting to about $5,000 per year for the education of black children.

Now that there was money allocated specifically for the school, the School Board had no qualms about absorbing the African School, as it was now commonly called, into their jurisdiction. One of their first moves was to fire the black teacher without any explanation. The sad process of realization would be a slow one for the black community, but this firing was the first of many incidents demonstrating that the school's absorption by the School Committee had resulted in a loss of control over a key component of the emerging community. The friction created in the wake of School Board's decisions would provide the anger that would later fuel an integration movement.

By this time the School Committee was composed of a Primary and a Grammar School Committee. There were two elected officials from each ward, though later the Grammar School Committee began appointing the Primary School Committee. As for the African School, the Primary Committee was responsible for four-to-seven-year-olds, who were taught in a separate room of the African Meeting House basement. The Grammar School Committee was accountable for older elementary-school children; there was no high school option for blacks.

In 1821 the school got an interesting new teacher with the arrival of John Russworm. He taught through 1824, at which point he was accepted by Bowdoin College, making him the first African American admitted to an institution of higher learning. After college he did not return to Boston but instead went to New York, where he costarted *Freedom's Journal*, the first African American newspaper. In fact, it was hard to get any teacher to stay for long, as the pay was low and, because of the School Committee, the position was now insecure. Since many children did not live with their parents, teachers would be called on for extra responsibilities, such as appearing in police court for indigent children. When the African School opened, there were forty-seven pupils, although attendance would fluctuate to a high of eighty, which put a tremendous burden on teachers, especially in such a small space. The basement would get "hot and stifled and unbearably cold in the winter." Despite these drawbacks, teaching was more attractive for blacks than most career options.

As the 1830s dawned, Beacon Hill parents on the northern slope were becoming more and more frustrated with their schooling situation. They no longer had control over their school. Instead, it was subject to an indifferent school board, which kept it inferior in terms of the building, grounds, appropriations, teacher staffing, supervision, salaries, curriculum, location, and maintenance. David Walker's *Appeal*, when it became a national phenomenon, openly lamented these contrasts and told the story of a black child who spent nine years in the school learning only rudimentary grammar.

The first whites to protest on behalf of the African School were David and Lydia Maria Child. Lydia was a popular novelist, and David a lawyer for and one of the founders of the New England Anti-Slavery Society. (Today Lydia is mostly remembered for writ-

ing the Thanksgiving song "Over the River and through the Wood.")
In 1832 the couple provided a two-pronged attack on substandard
schools. David, a member of the School Committee, produced a
strong report condemning the treatment of blacks in the school system, and Lydia, employing her literary standing, published her *Appeal in Favor of That Class of Americans Called Africans.* Like Walker's
*Appeal,* she dealt with multiple forms of discrimination, highlighting the particularly callous exclusion of blind black students from
the New England Institution for the Education of the Blind. Her
prime target, though, was the segregation and discrimination maintained by the School Committee. She described the school: "The
apartment is close and uncomfortable, and many pupils stay away
who would gladly attend under more convenient circumstances."
Both Childs displayed a reasoning that was a forerunner of affirmative action arguments, maintaining that since society hurt blacks
in so many ways, any educational differences, if there must be any
at all, should be in favor of African Americans. David Child even
suggested taking funds away from white schools to improve the
African School, a breathtakingly radical proposal for the early
nineteenth century.

While this couple pounded away at the School Committee, the
black community was up in arms over a more specific controversy.
After John Russworm left the school in 1824, the School Committee
appointed the white Reverend William Bascom to be the next
teacher. In the same year that the Childs wrote their protests, James
Barbados, a hairdresser and leader of the black community, watched
the teacher enter a brothel during school hours. The accusation of
Barbados carried additional weight because four girls at the school
also maintained that their teacher had taken "improper familiari-
ties." While the black community was outraged, the School Committee defended their appointee, claiming that the girls were of low
moral character.

These initial protests also coincided with an ill-fated experiment
with black education in Connecticut. Prudence Crandall, the mis-
tress of a school begun for white children in 1831, told Garrison, "I
have been for some months past determined if possible during the

remaining part of my life to benefit the people of color." In 1833 she admitted a black girl to her school, and then decided she would turn the whole Canterbury school into a refuge for black girls. The reception in the Nutmeg State was quick and brutal. Manure was placed in the school's well, stones were thrown at the school and its students, merchants would not sell their wares to them, classes were disrupted by horn blowing, bell ringing, and even gunfire. The resentment culminated in a mob attack on the school. The Connecticut legislature also took action, passing a law forbidding the education of blacks from outside their state. This happened to encompass almost all of Crandall's students. Eventually, Crandall would serve jail time for continuing to teach there.

The *Liberator*'s opinion of the whole controversy was simple: "Georgia Outdone!" It was well known that throughout the South, laws consistently and expressly forbade black education, particularly in reading. By 1850, less than 7 percent of black children in slave-holding states received any kind of education. But Crandall's ordeal in Massachusetts's neighboring state was a sober reminder of how unique Boston was, in that the struggle was over conditions within a school. The overall struggle, in the North as well as the South, was about whether African American children should be allowed to learn at all. Fewer than two in six children in free states attended any sort of school a decade before the Civil War. Estimates vary widely, however, and legal scholar J. Clay Smith puts the percentage of black school-age children attending school as low as 1.7 percent. Many free black populations, such as those in New York, Cincinnati, and Philadelphia, were engaged not in integration but in lengthy struggles for *any* publicly supported schools.

Because of the black community's protest of Bascom and the Childs' controversial writings, members of the School Committee were slowly realizing that they would have to concede in some way. David Child had explicitly detailed the injustice of maintaining a large school in a tightly cramped church basement and demanded that the School Committee ask the City Council for an allocation to build a new school. In 1835 the School Committee followed his recommendation. The City Council provided $2,500 for the project, which was pooled with some money from Abiel Smith's trust. A corner lot was purchased next to the site of the African Meeting House, on the southeast corner of Belknap Street and Smith Court, for $1,935.

More than thirty years had passed since the small school had begun in Primus Hall's house; Primus had lived long enough to see the opening of the first building dedicated to black education in Boston. The school was suitably named in honor of Abiel Smith, the longtime benefactor of black education. In an 1835 ceremony to celebrate the opening of the new school, Judge William Minot assured the West End parents on that March day that the school was testimony to the "interest which the city now feels in your improvement."

The Smith School had three floors of classroom space. To facilitate heating, no dividing walls were used, so the school appeared to have three large halls. There was one teacher per floor. The primary school for the four- to seven-year-olds was located in the cellar. Above that was the writing school, where boys of ages seven through fourteen and girls seven through sixteen learned writing, arithmetic, and bookkeeping. For these age groups, half the day was spent on that floor and the other half on the top floor, which was the grammar division. There they were instructed in spelling, reading, English, grammar, and geography. Later, a small platform was built for students' recitation before the class.

We have very few recorded insights into the daily life of free blacks in Boston, particularly their educational experience. The startling exception is a rare and unusual book published in 1835 by Susan Paul, daughter of the late Reverend Thomas Paul, called the *Memoir of James Jackson; The Attentive and Obedient Scholar Who Died in Boston, October 31, 1833, Aged Six Years and Eleven Months.* Jackson had been a black boy attending school on Beacon Hill before his death. The young child made such an impression on Paul that she decided to write a short book honoring the goodness and promise of the boy. It is now recognized as the first African American biography.

It was appropriate for Susan Paul to write this piece of abolitionist literature about a child because she did so much to involve the children of Beacon Hill in the abolitionist struggle. In *James Jackson* she relates the day when she first told the class about the reality of slavery. To be sure, this small manuscript is a book about their free life amid much prejudice, as southern slavery is not mentioned until near the end of the work. James learned that there were thousands of black children who, unlike him, "were not allowed to read, who had no schools, nor any books. These persons she said were slaves."

The teacher goes on to describe whipping and the cruelty that children in bondage were subjected to. James is profoundly disturbed by this horror and goes home to pray, "O lord, pity the poor slaves, and let them be free, that they may have their liberty, and be as happy as I am." Some children in those classes were former slaves themselves, but most were children of free blacks. For them especially, Paul's story shows that teachers tried to impart to children at a young age the vast injustices of the nation. By giving her class this disturbing introduction, she was training a new generation of activists who would be part of monumental movements long after her premature death in 1841.

Before becoming a writer, Susan Paul involved the children of the community more widely through the Juvenile Choir she conducted. Using the *Liberator* for advertising, the children's choir sang sold-out shows, where they were able to raise money and heighten awareness about abolitionism. During the New England Anti-Slavery Convention of 1834, they sang a new song written by Susan Paul called "Mr. Prejudice."

*Pray, who is Mr. Prejudice,*
*We hear so much about,*
*Who wants to spoil our pleasant songs,*
*And keep the white folks out*

*They say he runs along the streets,*
*And makes a shocking noise,*
*Scolding at little colored girls,*
*And whipping colored boys. . . .*

*A colonizing agent hired,*
*We're told he has a whip,*
*With which he flogs our honest friends,*
*And drives them to the ship. . . .*

*We wish that we could catch him here,*
*We think he'd hold his tongue,*
*If he should see our smiling looks,*
*And know how well we've sung.*

*However strong the rogue may be,*
*Kind friends, if you'll unite,*
*Should he peep in, oh, never fear,*
*We'll banish him tonight.*

This is a remarkable song, showing the early age at which the children of this community were made aware not just of their status but of their responsibility to protest against it. As with Paul's book, the song deals with discrimination, segregation, and colonization in ways that children can fully understand, while simultaneously expressing these themes to adults.

Susan Paul wrote *James Jackson* to show whites that "the moral and intellectual powers of colored children are inferior to the power of others, only as their advantages are inferior. Let, then, this little book do something towards breaking down that unholy prejudice which exists against color." The power of children singing "Mr. Prejudice" did inspire action. After the white abolitionists heard them sing, they passed a resolution committing themselves to work against slavery, as well as segregation and unequal treatment in "taverns, stages, and steamboats." Schools were not mentioned in the resolution, as the movement toward integrating schools was still a few years away. However, Paul's ability to remind abolitionists of the injustices that the children of Beacon Hill faced would have a long and valuable impact.

The fact that the School Committee built the new Smith School did not stop all black protest about inferior treatment in schools.

Smith Court. The Smith School and African Meeting House are on the left. William Nell's house is on the right. *(Courtesy of the Society for the Preservation of New England Antiquities)*

The school may have been in a more pleasant building, but it was still the only school without a play yard, trees, or shrubs. The children were taught only the most basic subjects, whereas other city students learned composition, declamation, history, bookkeeping, algebra, geometry, natural history, and drawing. A letter in the *Liberator* in 1836 criticized Boston papers for devaluing the prize-winner of the annual examinations at the Smith School when they printed the names of winning students from all city schools except the Smith School. The *Liberator* did print the names of the Smith School winners, but the rest of the Boston press treated these students much as William Nell had been treated. In fact, almost ten years after Nell's painful experience, Franklin medals were still being denied to Smith School children.

William Nell and others signed the first petition for the abolition of the Smith School in 1840, little knowing that they were embarking on an epic siege. At first, the struggle and disputes were about concerns that affect all school systems, now and then: control over the hiring and firing of teachers, oversight of the curriculum and classroom discipline—small but crucial matters, and yet hardly issues that change the course of a nation's history. The original petition, as far as we know, no longer exists. Who could possibly have cared about the poor back side of Beacon Hill and an obscure little school that never attracted more than 150 students even at its peak?

Nell did not know that his dream of creating equal education for all children would also cost a former classmate her job. Nancy Woodson, who had ranked with Nell at the top of their class when both were denied Franklin medals, went on to become a favorite teacher. Less than a year after the petition of grievances, the School Committee sent a message about Nell and others' agitation by firing Woodson without explanation, replacing her with a white teacher. The black community sent numerous petitions asking for her reinstatement, to no avail. They were forcibly reminded of their powerlessness against the white school bureaucracy. Agitation against the Smith School started in earnest again in 1844.

William Lloyd Garrison described Woodson's replacement, the white schoolmaster Abner Forbes, as "eccentric in his manner of saying and doing certain things." A Williams College graduate, he had worked as a private tutor in Washington, D.C., before arriving in Massachusetts and being hired to teach at the Smith School. He was chosen in part because of his abolitionist sympathies, and indicators at first promised a productive and fruitful relationship with black parents. He worked hard, also teaching night classes for older members of the community and offering lectures at the Adelphic Union, and there was also his pleasing attendance at abolitionist functions. At the time that he was appointed to the Smith School, the *Liberator* wrote that the black students could "desire no better commendation."

Yet relations between Forbes and the black community started to sour sometime after the first protests against segregated schools began with Nell's signed petition. Representative of the School Committee's attitude was an August 1841 report on all Boston schools that concluded, "The Smith School is mentioned last, because in any enumeration of the schools according to their negative conditions, this must be placed last." It seemed the hard work of leading the school was starting to exhaust and irritate Forbes. In its quiet but oft-expressed disdain for the humble Smith School, the School Committee conceded that Forbes had to "encounter embarrassments of [a] various and complicated nature, which are unknown in other public schools."

Despite this, because he was teaching African American students, he was paid less than other teachers in Boston. This was galling, especially after the School Board acknowledged that "the labors of Mr. Forbes are necessarily more arduous than those of any other instructor in the city." Above all, he was frustrated by the growing number of students who were the children of fugitive slaves, and, further, that all black children possessed "traits of character peculiar to themselves, which are extremely difficult to bring in to proper subordination." He estimated that more than nine-tenths of the students were "extensively poor," and that each of them was liable "at any time to move from the city."

Nothing Forbes did antagonized the black community more than declaring, in a School Committee report of 1843, that he would henceforth refuse to teach "transient and vagrant children." Forbes's resolution was immediately seen as blatant disrespect for the brutal realities of these fugitive children's lives. In fact, it appears that Forbes's whole opinion and estimation of blacks had declined during his time at the school. He claimed that "the colored people manifest but little . . . interest in the education of their children." This was an especially maddening observation, considering the years of toil the Beacon Hill community had endured to initiate this school for their children and the varied educational societies and night classes for adult members of the community that they were supporting without help. However, it was not simply his view of blacks that was changing; he was soon calling abolitionists a "most peculiar sect."

Meetings of the black community in the early spring of 1844, led by John Hilton and his younger associates Nell and Morris, produced firm protests against segregated schools and the cruelty of the current teacher. Allegations of Forbes's maltreatment of children were intended to augment the general arguments against segregated schools, places parents saw as painful and harsh. They argued that this poor state of affairs only showed that "we will never have a good or flourishing school under this system." The petition signed by members of the black community pointed out, "People are apt to become what they see is expected of them. It is hard to retain self-respect, if we see ourselves set apart & avoided as a degraded race, by others." Parents lamented that however well behaved the children of black Beacon Hill were, they were nonetheless considered a "contamination to your children."

The School Committee was not about to abolish the Smith School, but their members felt obligated to investigate the black community's extremely serious accusations against Forbes. He was charged with administering excessive punishment, using inappropriate language toward children, neglecting his duties, and voicing debasing opinions of African Americans.

During six and a half days in June 1844, the School Committee presided over heated hearings. The committee heard 86 witnesses and 103 statements testifying to Forbes's cruelty and 40 witnesses whom Forbes had assembled to refute the charges, although only 7 of them were parents. As the hearings went on, parents, pupils, and even former coworkers recalled stories of boys being ferruled on the soles of their feet, and they spoke of instances when Forbes allegedly pulled students' hair and ears. Recess time at the Smith School was expected to be observed in total silence. Forbes blamed a boy named James Brown for creating noise by getting into a scuffle with another child, an accusation that the child claimed was untrue. Brown was whipped on the soles of his feet until he confessed. The boy was only eleven years old. Such whippings were particularly stinging, considering that some of these children were recent escapees of slavery.

A parent named Angeline Gardner related one of the most disturbing stories. When her child had not returned from school as expected one day, she walked up Beacon Hill to the Smith School to look for her. As she was walking through the school, she saw three children huddled together in a darkened room. At that point, she was thunderstruck to hear Forbes call her child a "vile wretch," threatening to have her taken to the House of Corrections if she disturbed his school. In fact, one girl testified that she chose to stay at the House of Reformation of Juvenile Offenders rather than go back to the Smith School.

The hearings, which were widely covered in the Boston papers, had the effect of giving the rest of Boston a window onto the isolated world of this segregated school. Hilton, Nell, and Morris were seeking not only Forbes's removal but the removal of segregation itself. However, the general population of Boston was more than skeptical about this hearing. Hilton, Morris, Nell, and other black leaders were called "assailants" and "co-plotters." One editorial writer for the *Boston Courier* accused the agitators of being "lovers of intermixture."

Such editorialists reveal how widespread the feeling was that the charges against Forbes were fabrications. Many outsiders could not accept that only a few years earlier Forbes had been praised as a leading and idealistic abolitionist and now was being vilified. One writer went on to suggest that ungrateful blacks were out "to destroy the character of the teacher," and that he was but an innocent casualty in their take-no-prisoners war on segregation. It is impossible to evaluate fairly the charges against Forbes today, but when confronted with the sheer volume and intensity of the complaints against him, it seems that a genuine resentment of Forbes's treatment of students was the driving factor in the hearing. Forbes's controversial "trial" served to invigorate action against segregation, but Forbes was not, as has been suggested, used cynically by the integrationists for their anti-segregationist purposes.

The *Boston Courier* clearly leveled a charge that Hilton, Morris, and Nell had been put up to this vilification of Forbes by white abolitionists. The *Boston Olive Branch* agreed with this assessment, regretting that they had "yielded to the injurious advice of their professed friends," these "inflammatory reformers." This would be a constant accusation throughout the years of the school struggle. The idea of a downtrodden and largely powerless community forcefully articulating their interests was novel and, to some, impossible to conceive. The conviction that African Americans were docile and unintelligent was still omnipresent. Thus dismissive opponents felt free to rationalize their stands, condemning both white and black abolitionists with the accusation that the latter were dupes, the former cynical opportunists.

The School Committee was not swayed. In a statement read by Frederick Emerson, Ralph Waldo Emerson's brother, the committee dismissed almost all of the charges against Forbes. However, considering the antipathy the black community now held for Forbes, they judged it would be impossible to send him back to the Smith School. Nonetheless, the committee emphasized that to release him would be "an act of injustice to him, and an example of injurious effect upon the schools." Therefore, Forbes would continue his career somewhere else in the Boston school system.

Although Beacon Hill parents had managed to rid themselves of Forbes, their leaders were still furious that he had not been dismissed as a teacher, and moreover, that their charges were held as untrustworthy. Soon after the Forbes hearing, the School Committee reluctantly took up the remonstrations of the black community against the Smith School. They had a valuable ally on the committee, a Unitarian minister and reformer named John Turner Sargent. Born into a rich shipping family, Sargent rejected family business pursuits to become a minister. The only other man to join Sargent was George Hillard, the law partner of another firm believer in integrated schools, young Charles Sumner. Nell called Sargent and Hillard the "faithful among the faithless."

A realization was setting in that something more radical would be needed than just petitioning an antagonistic school board. Hilton, Nell, and Morris had been planning for this. John Hilton announced that "the colored parents of this city are recommended to withdraw their children from the exclusive school, established in contravention of that equality of privilege which is the vital principle of the school system of Massachusetts." Nearly a half century earlier, the black community had struggled mightily to initiate this groundbreaking school, but new notions of equality were now strong enough that Hilton, Morris, and Nell were willing to see it shattered to wipe out segregation.

The *Liberator* quickly endorsed this new drastic step, writing, "All colored parents [are] to see to it, at whatever inconvenience or expense, that none of the children be sent to the Smith School." However, many in Boston were puzzled to see the black community abandon their community school. The *Boston Olive* wrote that to boycott the Smith School was to "deprive their children altogether of the advantages so freely tendered," and all for a cause that was certain to fail: "One thing is certain; the white population will not consent to admit the colored children into the schools."

Hilton offered to host classes in his living room on Belknap Street. Just as Boston's first school for blacks began in the living room of another Beacon Hill community leader, now fifty years later the children were back in private residences. It would be another five years before any kind of alternative school took shape. Nevertheless, Hilton, Morris, Nell, Garrison, and others endorsing the boycott had a powerful influence on the community. By the end of 1844, the boycott had cut attendance at the Smith School by 40 percent.

Over the next four years, the number of children at this school, which used to educate 100 children every day, declined to an average of 66. By 1849 the daily average was down to 53, with the boycott incorporating half of the original student base.

Forbes, who had been sent back to the Smith School until the School Committee could name a replacement, became increasingly maddened by the boycott. The integrationists who would "not send their children to the school on any consideration—however great the inconvenience[—]"mystified him. He tried to teach the students who stayed, but he found that "I was left wholly without a First class and I did not fully organize one till sometime in November, most of who[m] were taken from the third class."

The boycott held strong as 1845 dawned. Even after Ambrose Wellington was appointed new headmaster of the Smith School, attendance remained low. The School Committee continued to deny medals to deserving Smith School students and continued to punish the black community by refusing to publish in Boston newspapers their children's exam results. The boycott was clearly irritating the committee.

Hilton, Morris, and Nell decided to lead their campaign under a new name, the School Abolishing Party. It was an interesting name, implicitly linking the abolition of slavery with the abolition of segregated schools. The School Abolishing Party gave Hilton, Morris, and Nell a full regimen of responsibilities. Morris was still studying hard under Loring's tutelage, but he also found time for activism.

Nell, seven years older than Morris, found himself continually impressed by the younger man's dedication to the law and steady rise to success. A polite rivalry was developing between the two, but Morris seemed to have the upper hand. Nell was forced to ruminate on the direction his own life was taking outside his political activities, which did not provide financial help for his sisters. Feeling that his fellow activist Morris enjoyed "every prospect of success," Nell concluded, "it ill becomes me to be napping." He added, "I must confess myself at a loss what string to pull."

Nell considered following Morris's path for a time, but eventually he gave up the idea of becoming a lawyer when he realized that his Garrisonian ideals weighed too heavily on him. Garrison had declared that the Constitution was nothing less than a corrupt compromise with the slave-holding powers. Thus, as a new lawyer before the Massachusetts bar, Nell realized he could not take the oath of allegiance.

While Nell pondered these questions, the School Abolishing Party considered how to bypass an increasingly belligerent School Committee through legislative means. Wendell Phillips and Ellis Gray Loring were called upon to go back to the State House to testify, this time in an effort to end segregated schools once and for all. They proposed a bill to the Joint Standing Committee on Education that made illegal the exclusion of any child from a public, tax-supported school. The enforcement measure of the proposal was mild (though it would pay great dividends in later legal contests); the statute simply proposed that every child must receive monetary compensation for any unlawful exclusion, the amount determined and collected through legal action against the city or town. Without this provision, the *Roberts* case could never have been initiated.

Critics were immediately up in arms. Some were concerned that

Boston would be inundated with litigation from the black community. To others, it was primarily the threat of integrated schools that was unsuitable. The *Boston Olive Branch* wrote of the legislation,

> May good men and heaven defend us from such social intercourse of the two races, as it might destroy the usefulness of our excellent schools, or lead to the abomination of the unnatural amalgamation of the two races, whom God intended should ever be distinct. . . . Give the negro his liberty, but KEEP HIM IN HIS PLACE.

One legislator, half joking, told Phillips, "We in Boston know that such schools are illegal, but we mean to have them."

Phillips's proposed bill was not immediately rejected. Instead, politicians did what is done when they are forced to pass a bill they do not like; they revised the measure until it was ambiguous and equivocal and would, as Phillips remembered, "not secure our object." Instead of allowing children to sue if excluded from a school, the new bill permitted the students to sue for monetary compensation if they were denied "public school instruction." This was a subtle semantic difference, but the change meant that since black children always had public school instruction offered to them at the Smith School, such a law would probably not help black parents without a very liberal interpretation of the law by a judge.

Even to test the statute, a legal suit was needed, which meant hiring a lawyer, which cost money. Nevertheless, a claim testing the segregated schools of Boston would indeed emerge out of the black community, although not for another three years. In the meantime, the School Abolishing Party, even with the help of clever white allies, had suffered another defeat, and the boycott effort faced harder days to come.

· · ·

Parents did not lose sight of the boycott battle, and in 1846, for the third straight year, the School Committee had to address their protests of segregated schools. Further intensifying the conflict were the deteriorating conditions of the school. The School Committee knew that grammar classes were being taught without textbooks, walls were defaced, recreation rooms were nowhere to be found, and there was only a small space for a playground. Worse yet, this space was bordered by an outhouse and accessible only through "a dark damp cellar." The whole appearance of the place was "deplorable" and "unfit for the use of a school." While the 1846 petition controversies raged on, exacerbated by the School Committee's refusal to concede to black demands, the poor physical conditions the children faced were undeniable. The committee admitted, "The apparatus has been so shattered and neglected, that it cannot be used until it has been thoroughly repaired."

Frustrated that this irritating issue had not been settled by a vote in the previous two years, the Boston School Committee now decided to thoroughly deal with the issue. They lamented, "Yet another Petition is presented this year!" For the next four months, School Committee meetings turned into hearings on whether Boston could maintain these separate schools. One such evening became so contentious that debate did not subside until past eleven at night. Appearing to speak for the petitioners was Robert Morris, Loring, and Phillips. Morris had never prosecuted a case, but Loring apparently believed that the twenty-three-year-old was ready to hold his own with these established lawyers. This trust was not misplaced, as all three spoke forcefully before the incredulous committee. Some even thought that the orations were so effective that the School Committee might vote for integration that very night, but this proved not to be the case.

The integrationists were still a minority on the School Committee, but they were growing in number. There was Henry Wilson, a rising star in the Boston political scene who would later be elected to the Senate and eventually become vice president of the United States under Ulysses Grant. Wilson showed forcefulness in firmly rejecting the idea that whites would leave the Boston schools if they were integrated. White abolitionists would be further galvanized when in 1846 the Massachusetts Anti-Slavery Society at last formally endorsed their integration efforts. The abolitionist party resolved to "afford [blacks] all the possible aid in securing the full and equal enjoyment of the public schools." The fact that it was not until 1846 that they spoke out seems to dispel the argument that equal school efforts were being manipulated and guided by white abolitionists. Despite such help, integrationists were in the minority on the School Committee for the third straight year, fifty-nine to sixteen.

The School Committee became so angry about further agitation that they vetoed a motion allowing the minority opinion to be printed. As for the majority opinion, it began with legal and administrative questions but soon moved to their collective views on race, "which the All-Wise Creator has seen fit to establish." In classic scientific racist fashion, the majority looked at the physical, mental, and moral "peculiarities" of blacks that "no legislation, no social customs, can efface." As to integration, they believed this meant amalgamation, and "Amalgamation is degradation." In the opinion of the School Board of Boston, "the less the colored and white people become intermingled, the better it will be for both races."

To validate their contentious opinion, the School Committee asked City Solicitor Peleg Chandler for his opinion on the legality of separate schools. The Maine native, who in three years would be facing Morris and Charles Sumner in the *Roberts* case, was a deeply conservative man who earlier had helped engineer the defeat of a desegregation bill in the legislature. Now battling integration on the administrative front, Chandler wrote that the majority's stance was completely congruent with municipal law, which, in his opinion, gave no preference to integration. What existed was a clear precedent for the School Committee's making necessary administrative decisions, in particular, the choice to maintain a black school, if, "in their judgement, the best interests of such children will be promoted thereby."

Wendell Phillips issued a heated rebuke to this opinion and to the disingenuous idea that the miserable Smith School was beneficial to black children. It had been a busy year for Phillips, as he had become the most articulate white voice on the school question for the abolitionists. He was carrying out a public debate not only with the city's lawyer, Chandler, but also with the liberal architect of the Boston School System, Congressman Horace Mann.

Wendell Phillips was furious that the abolitionist and vaunted school reformer Mann was against integrated schools, but he did not take into account Mann's pragmatism. Mann thought admitting blacks would raise "enough public outcry against the normal school experiment to halt it." This stance incensed the idealistic and incendiary Phillips, and he forcefully derided Mann in the press.

Chandler did not pretend to be the reformer Mann presented himself as being. Rather, Chandler was a lawyer with deeply conservative instincts. Phillips declared that Chandler was "persecuting the colored children," a man "little imbued with a knowledge of our laws or the spirit of our institutions."

Phillips was greatly aided by the minority report published against the wishes of most of the School Committee. With equal vigor, the report attacked both the racism of the committee and the idea of segregated schools. The authors asked all Bostonians to imagine the limited residential choices their fellow West End citizens had as they sent their children to school. The board's racism was threatening to obscure basic educational principles. To maintain segregated schools, in the end, was "morally injurious" even to the white children of Boston.

The Minority Committee also pointed to the integrated schools of Salem, New Bedford, Nantucket, Worcester, and Lowell. This is not to say that there had been no struggle over school integration in any of these places; Nantucket blacks had just concluded a successful four-year struggle for equal rights schools. The islanders had followed the Beacon Hill blacks' example by initiating a boycott of segregated schools in 1845, and had even threatened legal action, although no case was ever heard. But continued agitation directed toward the Nantucket School Committee brought about peacefully integrated schools in 1846. Nantucket and other Massachusetts towns were visible demonstrations to Boston—despite its larger black population—that integrated schools were possible.

To support the minority view, the committee publicized an opinion in support of integrated schools written by Richard Fletcher, soon to be appointed a justice on the Massachusetts Supreme Judicial Court. Fletcher was a typical Whig until Illinois abolitionist newspaper editor and Presbyterian minister Elijah Lovejoy was brutally shot and murdered by a mob in 1837. Fletcher was thoroughly radicalized by the death of this abolitionist martyr. Judge Fletcher, writing while Salem was going through its own desegregation controversy, saw no state law that *allowed* any school board to segregate, a direct foil to Chandler's assertion that no law required the Boston School Committee to integrate. He believed that "there is no law, adjudication or principle, which would authorize a school committee to exclude any class of white children from the white schools." Since blacks in Massachusetts paid taxes and shared the same legal rights as whites, their children were "entitled to the benefit of the free schools, equally with others."

As powerful a liberal legal voice as Fletcher was, the majority opinion dismissed his views as inapplicable to Boston simply because its black population was much larger than Salem's. In fact, there seemed to be nothing that the integrationists and segregationists on the School Committee could agree on at this point. As historian George Leveresque put it, "What presumably had begun as an honest attempt by a group of men to come to grips with a controversial issue had ended in two armed camps ensconced behind their respective reports."

The larger Boston community was just as ardently divided. The *Boston Olive Branch* represented the unabashed segregationist sentiments still running strong in Boston, calling the petitioners "whining, canting Garrisonians." The newspaper urged citizens to continue to oppose these schools because "some mixed marriages might be ultimately brought about" if children were schooled together.

Yet more mainstream journalistic voices were starting to be convinced by the School Abolishing Party. The *Boston Chronotype* fervently disagreed with the School Committee, calling them "infants, —babies of the greenest sort," producing a majority report that was "absurd and disgraceful."

The year 1846 had been one of constant roadblocks for the

school struggle. However, it was not a completely unpleasant year for Morris, as his reputation in the Boston community was growing. In September he had been selected, during a large Faneuil Hall meeting chaired by former president John Quincy Adams, to serve on a committee considering what could be done to prevent the future kidnapping of fugitive slaves in Massachusetts. This issue would become increasingly important in Morris's life. Equally significant was the fact that Charles Sumner, a young white lawyer, served on the same committee with Morris. This may have been the first time Sumner and Morris worked together, although it would certainly not be the last.

Also momentous in this year was Morris's wedding, which the Lorings hosted in their home. Despite long hours of working under Ellis Loring, Morris had found time to become engaged to a young woman named Catherine Mason, employed by the prominent Savage family as a cook. When the time came for the wedding, the Lorings made sure the ceremony would be one of "elegance," something quite atypical for a black couple in 1846. Thanks to Loring, Morris now found himself under the kindly "observation" of the wedding's most prominent guest, the former congressman, Harvard president, and Boston mayor Josiah Quincy, the man for whom Boston's famous Quincy Market would be named. The popular Unitarian minister, James Freeman Clark, conducted the wedding service. Other members of Massachusetts's high society in attendance included members of the King family of Salem, for whom, less than a decade ago, the groom had been a table servant. William Lloyd Garrison was asked to speak, but he was so overwhelmed by the beauty of the service that he could not.

Garrison made up for his silence the next week in his newspaper, describing how Morris's achievements, and the service itself, had demonstrated the possibilities "of triumph of right over wrong, of virtue and merit over all opposing obstacles, of the ultimate banishment of an unnatural and vulgar prejudice." As Morris reflected on everything he had gone through to reach that day—his father's death, the years of dreary menial labor, that daunting journey to an unknown city, and long hours of studying the law—he may have felt much the same way.

Morris's life was about to transform itself, as he was only one year away from finally passing the bar and entering the legal world. But what was to become of the school struggle, which seemed unable to make substantial progress? The one silver lining in the draconian 1846 majority report was the School Committee's stark admission that its strong inclination toward segregation could be overruled by a court decision. The black citizens "can procure redress at the hands of the civil Court."

Morris certainly understood the significance of the statement, but he did not know that another young black man's sorrow, anger, and determination would serve as his necessary spark.

# PART 2

## Equality before the Law

*Our clients made us great.*

JACK GREENBERG

SIX

# The Client

If the first school-desegregation case in American history was rooted in the long walk five-year-old Sarah Roberts took to school, it was also born in another walk, one her father had been forced to take as a boy. As with Nell's bitter childhood experience regarding the Franklin medal, Benjamin Roberts's passionate opposition to segregated schools developed in his youth. Roberts was unable to reconcile the fact that he had had to attend a different school from his white peers, and when he referred to the school issue later, he would draw on "past experiences" he shared with other blacks raised in Boston. He recalled:

Travelling from the residences of our parents, there, we passed the doors of several schools, and while we witnessed the boys and the girls of our neighbors enjoying the blessings of the nearest schools to their homes, and we were not only compelled to go by them, but several others, our feelings were any thing but agreeable. The pupils of the several schools, as we passed, took particular notice of our situation; and we were looked upon, by them, as unworthy to be instructed in common with others.

Roberts would intensely remember the feelings of being "inferiors and outcasts."

Long before Benjamin Roberts and Robert Morris ever discussed bringing a court case against the city of Boston for "the welfare of the rising generation," this humiliating walk convinced Roberts that his daughter would not attend the segregated Smith School.

When Sarah turned four in April 1847, Benjamin applied to the Primary School Committee for Sarah's admission to the school closest to their house. They lived not on Beacon Hill near the Smith School, but closer to the docks in the North End, where cold winds blew in from the harbor and swirled through the narrow streets.

To get to the Smith School from their residence on Andover Street, they would first take a right onto Causeway, a left onto Prospect, then cross to Staniford, which fed into Cambridge at the foot of Beacon Hill. From there was the steep walk up Beacon Hill along Belknap Street to the school. Despite the exertion this walk demanded, the four-year-old's ticket of admission to her nearest school was declined. When her parents petitioned the district committee, they quickly rejected their plea. Roberts then took his grievance to the General School Committee, complaining that making Sarah travel this extra distance was unfair. For a third time, his efforts were rebuked.

Frustrated by his inability to penetrate an apparently immovable bureaucracy, Roberts stubbornly chose to defy the mandate of the School Board. He resolved to take Sarah to the closest white school and enroll her directly. Roberts did indeed try this at the Phillips School, but he was turned away by Principal Andrew Cotton because Sarah did not have the required ticket of admission that each child must receive from the School Committee.

Next he tried the Otis School, where, surprisingly, Sarah was accepted. It is unclear how Roberts was able to gain admission to this school, since the School Committee had been unambiguous in their prohibitions against integration, but perhaps he had found a sympathetic principal willing to ignore the stated rules. Or perhaps Roberts had just been lucky enough to find a school unaware of the rule of segregation in Boston, though this seems unlikely. Nonetheless, little Sarah was doing what no black child had done in almost a half century in Boston: learn with white pupils.

Unfortunately, this state of affairs was not to last. Although it took several months, the School Committee finally got wind of this unusual situation and would not let Sarah's defiant father disrupt their carefully preserved system of school segregation. The School Committee saw to it that the four-year-old Sarah was removed from her new school by a police officer. The emotional damage a four-year-old might suffer from being forcibly taken from her classroom by a policeman, for reasons she most likely did not understand, is difficult to imagine. It is painful to pause and feel the true human cost, the shock and the shame, of that moment. No matter how many pages are ultimately written about this case, the hard truth of it is in that day.

This traumatic event might finally have settled the issue for a man with lesser determination than Benjamin Roberts. But instead of sending Sarah on to the Smith School, he changed his course in a dramatic and fateful way. He decided to seek out the young black lawyer who had become the talk of the black community after defeating a white lawyer in court. Considering the family legacy into which Sarah Roberts was born, it should have been no surprise that each unfavorable outcome was met by a new course of action.

. . .

Sarah Roberts, though simply "black" as far as the School Committee was concerned, was also descended from English Quakers of Rhode Island, as well as Narragansett and Wampanoag Native Americans. Her grandfather, James Easton, had been born to manumitted slaves in a small hamlet near Middleborough, Massachusetts. He fought in the Revolutionary War and, like black veterans after almost every war to follow, returned to find that such sacrifice did little to improve his social standing within his community. In the words of Roberts, Easton arrived home to "ignominy and disgrace" and the denial of "all participation in the social, civil, and political welfare of the community."

In protests foreshadowing Roberts's bringing Sarah to school without a school ticket, Easton took on the white church. Bridgewater's Fourth Church of Christ had a "Negro gallery," but Easton refused to be seated there. Instead, he bought a pew for his family in the white section. At the next service, his family sat proudly in

"Colored Scholars Excluded from Schools": engraving from the *Anti-Slavery Almanac*, 1837. *(Manuscripts, Archives & Rare Books, Schomburg Center for Research in Black Culture, The New York Public Library; Astor, Lenox, and Tilden Foundations)*

their new pew until, as his son well remembered, they were "persecuted even to the dragging out of some of the family from the Orthodox Church." Easton then decided to buy a pew for his family's worship at the Baptist Church in Stoughton Corner. This congregation reacted with the same ire. The Eastons' pew was found tarred, so the next week Easton's family brought along chairs to put in the pew box. When the pew was pulled down, Easton had his family sit in the aisles, which they proceeded to do every Sunday. Sitting on that hard church floor was a young girl named Sarah, Benjamin Roberts's mother. Benjamin would pass her name on to his daughter, who, like her namesake, became witness to a struggle for equality.

Easton was an extremely intelligent and eloquent man. Decades before Robert Morris's notoriety, Easton was known as "the black lawyer" because of his remarkable ability to grasp and deal with complicated matters. Because of the conditions of the times, he never actually secured a lawyer's education or any other formal schooling. Despite this significant gap, or more likely because of it, Easton resolved that the next generation would have better chances than he had. Accordingly, sometime around 1810 he attempted to start a manual-labor school for black children. Benjamin Roberts's passion concerning education for his children may have been formed by watching his grandfather struggle for this educational initiative.

The family had a fierce belief in education's "immense value." Roberts felt pride in the "enterprising family" of which he was a part. For more than fifteen years the school taught twenty young black men in reading, writing, arithmetic, farming, blacksmithing, and shoemaking. The school was Easton's pride and joy, foreshadowing such endeavors as Booker T. Washington's Tuskegee Institute by almost a century. Unfortunately, as his son Hosea remembered,

> The enterprise ended in total failure. . . . By reason of the repeated surges of the tide of prejudice the establishment, like a ship in a boisterous hurricane at sea went beneath its waves, richly laden, well manned and well managed, and all sank to rise no more. . . . It fell, and with it fell the hearts of several of its undertakers in despair, and their bodies into their graves.

Hosea was referring to his father, who died soon after the school closed its doors. A young Benjamin watched with distress as the school fell apart and his beloved grandfather suffered the devastation that accompanied its end.

The school's demise, however, was no isolated event, but rather a reflection of the worsening fortunes of black America in the years of Benjamin's youth. His memories of growing up black in the 1820s included being "assailed and hooted at in the streets; insults and sneers followed our path, and it was, indeed a dark day for all of us in the commonwealth." Roberts may have been made to feel prejudice from a very young age, but James Easton, a man ahead of his time, had provided blueprints for overcoming discrimination.

In 1813, about twenty years before Easton's school met its end, Easton's daughter Sarah married a young man named Robert Roberts. Roberts had been born in Charleston, South Carolina, the town of Denmark Vesey and the young David Walker. He came to Boston with ambition and ingenuity. Roberts became a valued ser-

vant to Nathaniel Appleton and Christopher Gore, and upon retirement as a manservant, he worked as a stevedore. Then he did
something remarkable; he wrote a book in 1827 called *The House
Servant's Directory*. It still makes wonderful reading today, offering a
fascinating glimpse into a vanished domestic world of antebellum
America, and remains one of the earliest books written by an
African American. Robert Roberts married Sarah Easton in 1813,
and they moved to Boston, where they had twelve children. Roberts
apparently learned a great deal from his father-in-law, James, and
was also close to Hosea Easton, a published author as well.

When not at the Gore Place, Roberts lived on Belknap Street, in
the heart of black Beacon Hill. Sarah and Robert Roberts named
their first son after her father, calling him James Easton Roberts.
Their second son's name was inspired by another figure. Benjamin
Franklin represented personal independence, hard work, good
sense, and antiracist Revolutionary ideology. One imagines his parents' pleasure when, like Franklin, Benjamin Roberts would also
begin a printing career in Boston.

Benjamin had a unique childhood. He knew that there was more
beyond his poor neighborhood and his father's job waiting upon
some of the wealthiest men in America. More than anything else,
his family's legacy of activism and self-determination shaped him.
James Easton protested segregation and started a school. His son,
Benjamin's uncle, Hosea, served a black church in Hartford, Connecticut. He carried on his father's legacy of bravery as he tried to
shield his church from hateful white mobs that rioted, shot at the
church, sacked parishioners' homes, and burned down his church.
After witnessing this brutality of racism, Hosea wrote one of the
era's most devastating portraits of prejudice in America, the 1837
tract *To Heal the Scorn of Prejudice*. This meant that in a time of dismal poverty and limited opportunities for black Americans, Benjamin had the rare experience of growing up with a father and an
uncle who were both published authors.

When Benjamin came of age, he became an apprentice in the
shoemaking business. After learning the trade, he sought employment but found only rejection. Benjamin trekked all over Boston,

showing his good recommendation, but "was refused, I suppose, merely on account of that well known crime—of having dark skin." Motivated in part by his failure, Roberts decided to find a new career that better reflected his family's legacy.

Since the age of twenty, Roberts had been writing intermittently for the *Liberator*. In a piece called "Is Slave Holding Right? Judge Ye," he wrote about the horrors of the southern states, asking, "Who would think, in this nineteenth century, this fifty-ninth year of independence, of such an exhibition?" More of his evolving thoughts were revealed in an editorial called "Are Americans Africans?" During a time when the American Colonization Society proposed to deport African Americans, this grandson of an American Revolution veteran declared: "WE ARE AMERICANS!" He wondered, since their skin color apparently made people think they belonged in Africa, "Are the whites, born in America, called Europeans?" At the time, black Boston children were still attending the "African School," and in writings foreshadowing his campaign against segregated schools, he railed against a school named after Africa. Roberts thought this name reinforced the belief that blacks did not truly belong in America. If it was to be called the African School, why did they not teach "the rules and rudiment of the African language"?

This article showed Roberts's passion about the situation of northern blacks. He displayed it again in "Bad Enough at Best," where he mourned the lack of black employment in Boston because of prevailing prejudices (a topic he knew well enough). Roberts documented the scant number of blacks in various trades and reported how they were consistently met with "little or no encouragement."

Benjamin Roberts was twenty-three in 1837 and had recently suffered the deaths of both his mother, Sarah, and his uncle Hosea Easton. Writing for the *Liberator* would not be enough for Roberts. He wanted the control over his own writings that his father and Hosea Easton had, while demonstrating the fighting sprit of his grandfather James Easton. Furthermore, there were legitimate critiques of the *Liberator* that pointed to the necessity of a black paper. Garrison was known to leave out advertisements for black-organized events of which he did not approve. In the end, no matter how much emphasis Garrison gave to the community life of black Boston (and with the help of William Nell, this was considerable), without a newspaper of its own, the black community's voice was muffled, interpreted and inflected by a white abolitionist perspective. This came to bear most often on nonintegrationist blacks, whose ideas were given no voice in the *Liberator*. Though Roberts was an integrationist, he might have agreed with historian James Horton's analysis that a black newspaper would have had a stronger emphasis on "areas of employment, training, self-esteem, and racial pride."

Bearing this in mind, in April 1838 Roberts set out to establish something new. The result was his *Anti-Slavery Herald*. Because this was to be the newspaper of the black community, he wanted it printed entirely by blacks. Just as his grandfather's school had taught black young men practical trades, Roberts wanted to teach his young trainees printing and composition. This was an ambitious endeavor, especially considering the precarious position of previous black papers around the country.

While struggling with financial troubles, these papers had focused largely on freedom for the slaves. The first such paper, *Freedom's Journal*, debuted in New York in 1827. *Freedom's Journal* was coedited by the former Boston schoolteacher James Russworm, but it soon folded for lack of money. Its successor, *Rights for All,* survived for only three years. Frederick Douglass would later pour $12,000 into his paper, only to see the *Northern Star* also collapse in 1860. In general, free blacks were so poor that they did not have the extra money to support such ventures. Day-to-day survival was hard enough. Nevertheless, seventeen black papers appeared before the Civil War, though few of these existed before Roberts's 1838 attempt, and none had ever been edited by a black person in Boston.

Bearing this in mind, Roberts sought to gain an endorsement for his paper from the white community so that benefactors might support it. With Garrison understandably not eager to help, Roberts sought out Amos Phelps, a prominent white abolitionist he did not know well. A native of Farmington, Connecticut, Phelps had come to Boston and fallen under the spell of Garrisonian abolitionism. Now a minister, he had recently left his post as editor of an abolitionist paper named the *Emancipator*. Phelps endorsed Roberts's project, though he confessed, "of the character of the paper, I can say nothing." He wrote that in the short time that he had known Roberts, he believed him to be "a young man of enterprise and character." Thus, he gave his "hearty approbation" that Roberts would succeed in his establishment of an office for "colored lads" and the paper they would produce.

One month later, Phelps's story changed dramatically. Though no copies of Roberts's paper, the *Anti-Slavery Herald,* survive, historians agree it had a militant tone that greatly displeased Phelps and other white abolitionists. Wanting nothing to do with this paper, Phelps now demanded that his recommendation be returned to him. When Roberts stopped into the offices shared by the Massachusetts Anti-Slavery Society and the *Liberator* on Cornhill Street in Boston one June day, he found a note from Phelps addressed to him.

As he opened it and began to read, he was greatly surprised by Phelps's withdrawal of support. He begrudgingly returned the recommendation, but included a furious letter of his own.

In it, Roberts laid out years of frustration with paternal white abolitionists, feelings that had boiled over with their recent denouncements of his paper. His anger was made more direct because it was mixed with the pain of watching his endeavor fall apart—in much the way his grandfather's manual-labor school did a generation before.

Phelps's associations with Garrison were well known, and Roberts was convinced that "there has been and *now is,* a combined effort on the part of certain *professed* abolitionists to muzzle, exterminate and put down the efforts of certain colored individuals." Roberts believed Phelps and others were spreading rumors that he had secret intentions for his paper far different from what he had first told the abolitionists. The editor called this "Base misrepresentations! False accusations!"

Roberts wondered how whites expected the position of blacks to rise when they were not supported in their efforts. Garrison had written in 1831 about a paper in Albany, New York, founded by a black man: "To this, and every similar enterprise, we wish the most triumphant success." This sentiment seemed to be true except when the paper was started in Garrison's own city and sphere of influence.

Yet Roberts's anger was about more than just one man. As in the modern civil rights movement, the abolitionist movement featured a real, though largely covert, tension between more militant blacks and their white "allies." What is remarkable about this Roberts incident is that these tensions were generally not written of, that is, not until Frederick Douglass came into conflict with Garrison a decade later over the start of his own paper. Douglass, like Roberts, had experienced patronizing attitudes at the hands of white abolitionists for a long time. Most famously, after hearing Douglass give an eloquent and articulate speech, one antislavery agent told him, "People won't believe you ever was a slave, Frederick, if you keep on this way. Better have a little of the plantation manner of speech than not."

Ten years before an issue of Douglass's *Northern Star* went into production, the *Anti-Slavery Herald* had come and gone, leaving a financially strapped editor livid about the white abolitionist establishment. Roberts told Phelps, "I was not aware that so many hypocrites existed in the Anti Slavery society. According to what I have seen of the conduct of some, a black man would be as unsafe in their hands as in those of Southern slaveholders."

Five months after Phelps demanded that his recommendation be returned, Roberts printed a notice in the *Liberator* announcing with "deepest regret" that the *Anti-Slavery Herald* had been discontinued. Restraining his previous venom reserved for Phelps, Roberts calmly maintained that training young boys while trying to run a paper had made his way harder. Nevertheless, he resolved now to travel, making speeches that promoted the "principles" of such a paper, making "every endeavor" to see that the effort revived.

What might have been the most cutting aspect of this failure was the lack of support Roberts received from the black community. He had struggled to create a newspaper speaking for his people, but he had underestimated the depths of loyalty in Boston that existed for Garrison. Most African American readers simply felt they already had a community newspaper in the *Liberator*. However, Garrison was not reassured by Roberts's failure and became so distrustful during this time that he persuaded the Anti-Slavery office to open an intelligence office. William Nell, Garrison's most loyal ally in the black community was in charge of ensuring support for the regular abolitionist leaders. Roberts's now-aborted competition with the *Liberator* was not the only rumbling in the growing black abolitionist camps. Some African Americans began to withdraw from the Massachusetts Anti-Slavery Society, forming a new organization where their voice was clearer. The painful and divisive issue of women's rights and their full participation was also causing controversy. Many women and men believed that the female was an essential part of the abolitionist cause. With all this in mind, William Nell and John Hilton presided over a meeting at the Smith School calling Garrison, who supported women's full participation, "bold and fearless." They also declared, "We denounce every colored person who is an enemy to Garrison (if any there be) as a foe to liberty."

There was no mistaking the message this sent to Roberts. He withdrew from the leadership of the black abolitionist community of Boston for a decade. This promising young man seemed to disappear into his printing work and family life. He even left Boston for a time. He married a young woman named Adeline and moved to nearby Lynn to raise a family. The move to Lynn, which was then America's center for shoe manufacturing, suggests Roberts may have been so disillusioned by his editing experience in Boston that he returned to his first trade of shoemaking for a time. Still, he did not fully abandon printing; in 1841 he was responsible for publishing Lynn's first city directory.

Evidently, Roberts could not stay out of Boston for long. Though still reluctant to participate in abolitionist circles, he opened a printing establishment on Washington Street in late 1843. He declared himself "prepared to execute, at short notice, every variety of letter-press printing, in the neatest manner, on most reasonable terms." He found work printing books, pamphlets, and various items for Masonic groups, churches, black literary societies, and local abolitionist groups. One of his major achievements of this quiet period was printing R. B. Lewis's *Light and Truth,* a long-forgotten, though groundbreaking, four-hundred-page history of black and Native American peoples drawn from ancient and modern writings.

This was also a time of family change. In June 1842, scarlet fever claimed the life of Benjamin's twenty-month-old son, Thomas. It was not long after this death that the Robertses were blessed with a daughter, and they decided to honor Benjamin's recently deceased mother, Sarah. The first Sarah Roberts had sat in protest in a white church as a child. As an adult, this elder Sarah became known as a formidable leader and activist herself, notable in a time when Maria Stewart's experience of being shut out from the leadership elite showed the difficulty of being a female abolitionist.

· · ·

By 1847, Roberts had been quiet for some years, shying away from visible social action. In that long decade, soon after the collapse of his trade school, his grandfather James had died. Roberts's uncle Hosea was despondently living out his years following the destruction of his church. Benjamin never explicitly wrote of their fate, but he would not, in the end, let their discouragement prevent him from making one more great principle-based exertion.

Roberts decided he must embark on what he called a "practical experiment." This test was to enroll his four-year-old daughter in a white school to see if she would really be expelled on account of her color. When he discussed his plan with friends and associates, he found little enthusiasm for the effort. He was told that if black children attended white schools, "big boys among the whites would whip and frighten our little boys; and great girls would sneer and cuff at our small girls." Roberts was not deterred by these ominous forecasts; in fact, he dismissed naysayers of his plan to test segregation as "old fogies."

On the morning of April 15, 1847, he and Sarah set off for

school. When a near-disaster ensued with little Sarah's eventual removal from her classes by a Boston police officer, Roberts did not hesitate to take the next ambitious step for his "practical experiment." A lawsuit now presented itself as a realistic and logical next step.

Up to that point, black Garrisonians such as William Nell had taken such a bleak view of the Constitution and the whole structure of American law that they did not see the legal system as being anything but an unholy compromise with slaveholders, a union that had to be dissolved. Roberts, by contrast, trusted that the denial of equal school rights was in "direct opposition to the Constitution and the laws of Massachusetts, respecting the equal rights of ALL the inhabitants." This meant that the "insignificant and trifling assertions" of the despised School Committee need only be overruled by a reasonable judicial decision. Although the School Committee may have doubted the legality of desegregating the schools, they had, perhaps unwittingly, previously admitted that black citizens could "procure redress at the hands of the civil Court."

It seemed not to matter to Roberts that Robert Morris had been practicing as an attorney for only a year when he sought him out for his services. Despite his inexperience, the young black lawyer was the talk of the West End after his defeat of a white attorney only a few months earlier. The *Liberator* called Morris's triumph "memorable in the history of the colored people of this State, if not of the Union." According to J. Clay Smith, preeminent authority on the history of black lawyers in America, Morris's first victory had also been the first lawsuit brought by a black lawyer on behalf of a black client. That case, over "services rendered" for which a black man was not paid, was typical of Morris's early work, which usually involved settling estates and wills or disputes over small claims. Though these cases allowed him to make a living, he had by no means become well-to-do in his first year as a lawyer. By the end of that year he had a personal income of only $152. Despite this, the *Liberator* steadfastly attested to Morris's "aptness for business," which served him well in setting up his own practice.

The year 1847 had also been the first year of Morris's marriage, and he faced a crisis far more important than the paltry income generated by his legal practice. Soon after the wedding, his new wife, Catherine Mason, was "called by grace" in a powerful conversion to the Catholic faith. To Morris, this was totally unacceptable. He was heavily involved in the Methodist church in Boston and had grown up with a powerful bias against all things Roman Catholic. This prejudice was already strong at a time when there were comparatively few Roman Catholics in America, but his powerful distrust toward Roman Catholicism had grown dramatically by 1847, with a titanic influx of immigrants from largely Catholic European nations. The 1845 potato famine in Ireland sent thousands of impoverished and starving Irish men and women—hurt by bad crops and harsh trade policies—to America.

Many of these Irish Catholics landed in Boston, where tensions with blacks quickly grew. Irish leaders, looking at the black struggle for civil rights, asked, "In the country of the whites . . . what right has the Negro either to preference or to equality, or to admission?" Morris heard these protestations of black equal rights, and his dislike of these people's religion only grew.

He found refuge from this domestic conflict in his law office in the Brazer Building on State Street, where Benjamin Roberts arrived in early 1848. The printer brought with him the elements of a case quite different from the types of claims Morris usually handled. Roberts wanted Sarah admitted to the school closest to her house, which meant Morris would have to persuade a judge to overturn the current Boston system. This was therefore a civil rights case, and he was about to become the first in a long line of black lawyers bringing civil rights lawsuits to force change.

This would be a difficult case for any attorney, much less such an inexperienced one and one appearing in a courtroom as a disdained presence. As twentieth-century Massachusetts judge Elijah Adlow wrote, there was simply "no legal precedent, no statute, no common law tradition that required desegregation where the issue of equality was raised." NAACP lawyers had a hard enough time overturning segregation in our own era, but without the benefit of the 1868 Fourteenth Amendment giving all United States citizens equal protection from discrimination from the laws or practices of any state, Morris was hard-pressed to find any legal ground to stand upon.

In fact, all Morris really could employ for this case was the 1780 Massachusetts Declaration of Rights affirming, "All men are born free and equal." Yet Benjamin Roberts seemed unconcerned with any of these considerations, as well as with the fact that Morris had only just passed the bar on February 2, 1847. Some historians have wondered why Roberts chose the unseasoned Morris instead of a more famous, and experienced, abolitionist attorney, such as Phillips or Loring, both of whom had already spoken out on the illegality of segregated schools. Perhaps his previous experience with Phelps, Garrison, and other white "allies," people who he believed had crushed his *Anti-Slavery Herald,* gave him less faith in such seemingly sympathetic attorneys.

Many years later, Roberts took immense pride in his choice of Morris when he firmly maintained, "The cause of equal school privileges originated with us. Unaided and unbiased we commenced the struggle." He would have been hard-pressed to make such a statement had he not taken his suit to a black attorney.

Morris and Roberts decided to sue on account of the 1845 statute that offered monetary compensation for any child excluded from the city's schools. Relying on this new provision was going to be difficult because Sarah had been clearly referred to the Smith School. Yet Morris still felt that going after a liberal interpretation of that law, maintaining that segregating children was essentially denying the child school privileges, was the best way to proceed.

A suit against the city of Boston for $600 for damages on account of Sarah's exclusion was duly filed. The case was scheduled to go before the Suffolk County Court of Common Pleas on the first Tuesday of April 1848.

Since the claim was against the city, opposing Morris would be Boston city solicitor Peleg W. Chandler. This was unfortunate for Morris, since by this time Chandler was well acquainted with the issue and none too pleased to be dealing with it again, having already blocked desegregation at the legislative and administrative levels.

Now was Chandler's chance to block it in the judiciary. As an expert in municipal law, Chandler would be exceedingly difficult to argue against. Having previously worked for ten years as the *Boston Daily Advertiser*'s legal reporter, he had mixed his ability to grasp complicated legal issues with crisp, clear writing.

As a firm opponent of all things abolitionist, Chandler had, while serving in the legislature in 1845, introduced a measure calling for the immediate tabling of all petitions calling for the abolition of slavery, allowing none of them to go through committees. Though this rule did not pass, it foreshadowed the tactics of southern Democrats during the civil rights movement, refusing to let the debate go forward on certain bills.

In the year that Chandler proposed this barricade against abolitionist proposals, he also served on a five-person committee that had watered down the desegregation bill pushed by the abolitionists. This was especially troubling for Morris, and a crucial problem, as he would be arguing for a generous and wide-ranging interpretation of this precise law against its coauthor. Chandler's satisfaction with segregated schools had been further on display when he had gone toe to toe with Wendell Phillips in their competing opinions for the School Committee.

Chandler was a powerful and focused personality. As one friend remembered, "In dealing with individuals as a negotiator he was unrivaled." His large physical frame helped him in this area. The lawyer, who looked for all the world like Brigham Young's bearded twin with spectacles, was an aggressive advocate who told his clients, "Stick, Stick, Stick, is the Motto of this office."

Yet there was another, more vulnerable side to Chandler. Many viewed his post as city solicitor as a natural jumping-off point to wider fame and power, with one peer predicting that he was to be the "foremost man of our City and of our Commonwealth." Unbeknownst to his colleagues, however, he was in the beginning stages of losing his hearing. Listening well and completely to witnesses and opposing counsels was becoming more and more difficult. His brilliance and robust energy would compensate for his failing body only for so long, especially in a job like city solicitor, where he was responsible for dealing with every case the city of Boston was a party to. He was coming to the painful realization that many of his ambitions would go unfulfilled and his time in public life was fleeting. Still, his strong Swedenborgian faith helped him bear his "heavy affliction with fortitude." But Morris knew none of this, and probably shared the opinion of Wendell Phillips that Chandler was effective and fervent in "persecuting the colored children."

Morris's wife, Catherine, gave birth to their first son, Mason, two months before the first hearing of *Roberts v. the City of Boston,* and one can imagine this giving Morris a further sense of urgency. Now he was about to argue a crucial school-desegregation case, one whose result could well determine whether his own child would someday attend open schools.

The only documentation surviving from this initial hearing in the Suffolk County Court of Common Pleas is an agreed set of facts signed by both Chandler and Morris; this means that for the most part the first *Roberts* arguments are lost to history. There is no reason to believe, however, that Chandler departed far from his 1846 report for the School Committee, in which he explained not only that there was no municipal law requiring integration, but that there was nothing depriving the School Committee the full and reasonable ability to classify its students any way it wished.

Recovering the line of Morris's reasoning is more difficult, though the facts that are included in the shared statement seem to suggest certain things about Morris's contentions.

In the agreed set of facts, a brief history of the School Committee is first recounted, as a major question of the case centered on whether they had the legal eminence to enforce these distinctions. Also included was the 1845 legislation that Roberts was suing on behalf of, along with the official regulations of the primary School Committee for assigning students to schools, including their 1846 resolutions against desegregation. It seems Morris saw to it that the full text of the School Committee rule dictating *"Scholars to go to the*

*Schools nearest their Residences"* was part of this report, showing the conflict this regulation created with the idea of a single black school serving children all over the city. This was the crux of his argument: that forcing the "colored children" to attend a "colored school" was illegal.

Morris also introduced evidence about Sarah's daily walk. It was calculated that the Smith School was twenty-one hundred feet from Sarah's house near the water on Andover Street, though that measure was as the crow flies, which meant her actual walk was substantially longer. On Sarah's direct route, she passed "the ends of two streets in which there are five primary schools." The closest primary school was a mere nine hundred feet from Sarah's front door, meaning that had it not excluded her based on her race, her walk to school would have been more than cut in half.

The court records also make it clear that Roberts was a participant in the boycott of the Smith School after Sarah was forcibly removed from the Otis School. It was conceded that Sarah could have attended the Smith School "at any time and her father was so informed, but refused to do so." Instead, he had brought her back to a white school and tried to enroll her one more time about two months before the case. Perhaps, to test segregation one final time before litigation, on February 15, 1848, Sarah marched up to a white school once more and once more was rejected.

Equally interesting is what was not introduced in this first argument's stated facts. There was clearly plenty of evidence as to the inferior facilities of the Smith School relative to other white schools in the city. This had already been amply documented in various minority reports and newspaper articles over the previous decade. The peeling paint, the tiny play space—these were just a few of the problems. Children as old as sixteen had to sit at desks designed for seven-year-olds, a humiliating and physically painful experience. On the issue of books, for example, an 1848 report in the School Committee papers reveals that the Mather School had nine hundred volumes valued at $550, whereas the Mayhew School had another four hundred worth $300. And the exclusively black Smith School? Its "library" contained one volume, worth $3.

Still, Morris seemed to have made a conscious decision not to use any of this evidence in the case against segregated schools. One reason for this reticence may have been that in the following year, the School Committee was about to embark on a campaign to renovate and repair the Smith School. When NAACP lawyers were pressing for desegregation in the South a century later, one common tactic among school districts avoiding desegregation was to fix up, or "equalize," the facilities reserved for black people. Morris seems to have been anticipating this diversionary strategy by resisting what must have been a temptation to introduce a mountain of evidence showing that the black school was shoddier and worse equipped than the white ones. Renewed funding could always change that physical reality.

What could not be shifted so easily was the emergence of an over-arching moral principle, one stating that segregation made *any* school inherently inferior, regardless of the specifics of the school.

A decision was not released until October 1848. Morris and Chandler apparently had previously agreed that a judgment would be entered *pro forma*. It was the intention of Morris to appeal if there was an adverse outcome, and this would expedite the process. The lawyer Richard Fletcher, quietly sympathetic to abolitionists, was still following the issue of segregated schools ever since advising Salem's mayor in 1844 of their inherent illegality (and then offering a similar message to the Boston School Committee). As it transpired, Fletcher was only a few months away from being appointed to the Massachusetts Supreme Judicial Court. He recommended to Morris that he appeal the vital case to that court.

Though Morris clearly lost the first stage of the case, this *pro forma* arrangement meant no written decision was ever issued from the first hearing. The court determined that Morris would have to pay the cost of the suit for the city, appraised at $51.30. As though losing his first civil rights case was not bad enough, the suit would now cost Morris roughly one-third of his total personal savings. This could not have come at a worse time, with Morris now the father of an eight-month-old child and his wife expecting another child. Worst of all, he had made these sacrifices for a case that at this time was almost invisible; it was not covered in any mainstream Boston paper, including the *Liberator,* typically the publication most attuned to all matters crucial to the Boston black community. Though this is mere speculation, Garrison was perhaps understandably reluctant to cover this legal action by his former newspaper rival, Benjamin Roberts, at least until it appeared more promising. Or, more simply, the case had not yet made any impact on the conscience of Boston. For that to change at the appeals hearing, which Morris was already filing for, a more influential advocate would be needed for the plaintiff.

It was Roberts who first imagined this case, and Morris who framed its initial legal arguments, but now it would require another party to eloquently defend the right of equal schools for all. The two men at last found the right man, someone living in the neighborhood and clearly on their side. With Charles Sumner, an argument would be fashioned by this new legal team that would not be surpassed for a century or more.

Boston knew nothing of this. Instead, in the next year, everyone would be caught up in a painful civil war on Beacon Hill itself.

# SEVEN

# A Gathering Tempest

William Nell had been missing from the Boston school fight since the fall of 1847. Though Nell had worked for Garrison practically since childhood, when Frederick Douglass offered Nell the position of publisher for his new paper, the *North Star*—based in Rochester, New York—the young printer readily accepted. Though Nell appears to have given Benjamin Roberts no support at all in starting a similar enterprise in Boston, Nell saw great potential in a paper owned and edited by Douglass and his partner, the brilliant black doctor and activist Martin Delany.

It was hard to leave the only city he had ever known, but after weeks of deliberation, Nell decided that not only might "Up-State" be better for his ailing health, but that being a publisher of a paper presented the possibility of steadier finances than he had ever experienced in Boston. If he had realized that feelings over Douglass's newspaper would later develop into a dismaying feud between Douglass and Garrison, it is doubtful whether Nell would have gone. For now, such open hostility was still a few years away; his mentors, Garrison and Phillips, were both wishing Douglass well with his new endeavor in the pages of the *Liberator.*

In Rochester, the young printer lived with a liberal white family named the Posts, where he became like one of them, enjoying their oysters, cod liver with lime, johnnycake, and, when his illnesses returned, home remedies of wild cherry syrup medicines. Despite this happy life, his thoughts often drifted back to Boston and the happenings there. His loyalty to Morris remained strong. After a black New York lawyer passed the bar in January 1848, the *Pittsburgh Telegraph* erroneously reported him as the first black man to do so, and Nell leaped at the chance to correct the error, at the same time using the opportunity to praise Morris's "excellence of character and correct business habits."

Equally interesting about Nell's piece is how he extolled Massachusetts for admitting Morris and Macon Allen to the bar. This praise was a jumping-off point for an impassioned overview of the continuing struggle against the Commonwealth's segregated schools. While absent from the struggle, Nell praised Morris, the man who was at the forefront of the battle.

Benjamin Roberts's reemergence from his silent period came soon after Nell left Boston. Nell, the black community's most vocal supporter of Garrison, was never listed as an associate or ally of Roberts, and by starting a competing newspaper in Boston in 1838, Benjamin Roberts had perhaps put himself in a provocative position. Working purely from negative evidence, Nell seems to have been quite distant from Roberts, as there are no records of Roberts's attendance at any community meetings led by Nell throughout the 1840s. With Nell now hundreds of miles away from Boston, Roberts was noted as a more consistent and vital presence in the integrationists' community meetings. His leadership was needed, because they were now facing their first significant opposition within the black community.

Thomas Paul was the son of the late minister Thomas Paul, the man revered for bringing about the construction of the Belknap Street Church, among other achievements. Rev. Paul, along with Nell's father, William Guion Nell, was part of a generation that did not seek integration, instead focusing on black unity and "self-elevation" on Beacon Hill. While William Nell's activism was different from his father's, the younger Paul stayed much closer to his father's ideals as he sought change and improvement within the black community. His father had shown the possibility of change from the ground up with the expansion of his once humble church, and Paul intended to do for the beleaguered school on Belknap Street what his father had done for the African Meeting House next door.

It was also the revered memory of his illustrious father that made the son so much of a threat to the integrationists. But Paul was a man suffering from chronic poor health, and in the end, was not like his father at all with his timid and ineffectual manner. His cause was not lost, however, for he possessed a partner in his family who would prove to be an aggressive and assertive advocate, though perhaps not as wise as loyal. What Paul suffered from in shyness, his older cousin Thomas Paul Smith more than made up for in self-assurance and brashness. Smith worked as a secondhand clothes dealer but had the mind and oratorical abilities befitting someone of a high social standing. The school struggle would finally give him an opportunity to put his abilities on display. It would fall to Smith to force the issue of defending the segregated school on behalf of his more passive and withdrawn cousin.

It is noteworthy that these two men would become the defenders of segregated schools, for, unlike most free blacks in Boston, they had actually attended integrated schools. Both had initially been educated in the segregated school on Beacon Hill. When Smith finished his education there, he applied, but was denied, a high school education in Boston because of his skin color. Through connections to Wendell Phillips, he was able to gain admission to the prestigious Phillips Academy in Andover, Massachusetts, where he stayed for two semesters. Either because of this experience or in spite of it, it seemed to sour Smith on the idea of attending schools with whites. He came to firmly believe black children needed to be in their own schools, where they could be "cheered on by the unanimous shout of encouragement of all [their] fellows with no jeers or unkindness to make heavy [their] heart."

Thomas Paul had been taught at the Smith School under Abner Forbes a few years after his cousin had finished. While a boy in Boston, he apprenticed with Garrison at the *Liberator*, a job he shared with Nell. As his cousin had, he wanted something more than just the Smith School education, and after his father died when he was seventeen, he enrolled at the Noyes Academy in Canaan, New Hampshire. Noyes Academy was an abolitionist experiment in integrated education. Though it is not known what happened at Phillips to turn Smith away from integrated education, we know exactly how Paul's experience influenced him. He suffered a horrendous experience at Noyes, which went a long way toward explaining his later actions.

The New Hampshire townspeople were displeased with the racial makeup of this new school in their area. It was said of the school, "Fourteen black boys with books in their hands set the entire Granite state crazy." After various disruptions of the school, Canaan citizens finished it off once and for all by roping the school building to one hundred yoke of oxen and dragging it into a nearby swamp. As his school was being hauled away, a frightened young Paul watched from a hiding place behind haystacks. Paul went on to graduate from Dartmouth University, where he was well liked, but the experience at Noyes Academy never left him.

After Dartmouth, Paul came back to Boston. Though he had the rare claim of being a college graduate, he was floundering. An article in the *Liberator* praised his achievements in school but asked citizens to seek him out and give him advice on a direction for his career. The president of Dartmouth had recommended he go into the law, but Paul decided he would rather teach. In 1837 he tried to start an alternative black school to the Smith School, which would teach more diverse subjects, such as natural philosophy, Latin, and Greek. At the time, Forbes was still teaching at the Smith School, and by starting a new school, Paul was demonstrating a belief that segregated schools were fine, as long as they were taught by black teachers who would not treat the black children as inferiors. His school never got off the ground, and he moved on to Albany, New York, serving as principal for a school of black children. Paul later moved onto a similar school in Providence, Rhode Island, but as the 1840s wore on, he became increasingly homesick for his native Boston.

At that point Paul and his cousin Thomas Smith, who was already in Boston, decided it made perfect sense that he should become the principal of the Smith School. The problem with this idea was that the Smith School was at the center of the heated campaign against segregated schools. Therefore, before Paul could return to Boston, Smith had to do two things. He had to ensure the integrationists were unsuccessful in closing down the Smith School, and he had to convince the School Committee that it would be a good idea to release Ambrose Wellington and install Paul as the new headmaster.

Fortunately, these two undertakings seemed to reinforce each other, as the thought of Paul taking over the Smith School might make the idea of keeping it open more attractive. The fact that Smith's mission began at the same time as the commencement of the *Roberts* case guaranteed that both sides of the school debate would soon be in greater conflict.

With the Roberts case pending in the court of Common Pleas in the fall of 1848, Smith began a petition drive in the West End to have Paul put in charge of the Smith School. He told many citizens, some of whom were illiterate, that his petition would not affect the question of segregated schools but simply put Paul at the head of the school—if it continued. For men like Benjamin Roberts, this formulation of intent appeared on the petition he signed. However, the petition that eventually reached the School Committee, while still bearing their names, had a quite different preamble. Roberts, a man fighting school segregation, now had his name on a document praising the Smith School, saying it was offering blacks the "greatest advantage."

Smith's trick, not to say brazen dishonesty, was to be the first shot in what would be a war between two increasingly bitter sides. Roberts and his integrationist allies were livid about being hoodwinked over the petition. It was now clear to the integrationists what Thomas Paul's return really was about, and they resolved to fight any move that might prolong the existence of the Smith School. The savvy Smith put integrationists in the uncomfortable position of opposing a qualified black teacher simply because his appointment would make the segregated school more sustainable. Nevertheless, integrationists were willing to take this thorny position because of the higher principle of equal rights.

A "remonstration meeting" was called to protest Smith's sly petition. The volatile Roberts first stood up to revile Smith, calling him "a young ambitious bigot" interested only in his "selfish gratification." He moved onto the petition itself, which he called "a misrepresentation, a fraud, a deception." But it was when the impudent Smith arrived at his own remonstration meeting that the room erupted.

Roberts embarked on collecting the names of those who wished to have their names removed from the petition, which ended up being about a third of the original signers. A report was filed with the School Committee calling the petition a fraud. Featured in the report was a letter written by Robert Morris from his State Street law offices, explaining how he was "opposed to the appointment of Mr. Thomas Paul," and adding "the colored people are decidedly opposed to the measure proposed by Mr. Smith."

In early August, a large community meeting in the Belknap Street Meeting House proved to be a turning point in the growing fury within the community. The integrationists essentially decided that if Smith would not play fair, neither would they play by established rules. What was not made clear was that this particular meeting concerned the abolishment of the school. Smith nonetheless spoke up for the removal of the current white principal as the better course for saving the school.

Then came a surprise. The usually diffident Thomas Paul walked into the meeting and proceeded to denounce the integrationists as "incorrect and calculated." Roberts passionately expressed his belief that Paul was interfering with the abolition of the school. Roberts proposed the approval of a written statement of the meeting, one written by the business committee that he and Morris belonged to.

Smith believed that the audience, full of vocal friends and enemies of the Smith School, was left "thunderstruck" at the audacity of the committee, believing these "resolutions" had been written and planned beforehand. Smith and Paul were further angered that none of the resolutions had anything to do with particular ideas for improving the school but instead were declarations of the community's equal school rights.

Despite Smith's disapproval and the "peculiar manner" in which the resolutions were created, most passed the meeting after a "protracted and warm discussion." Smith attempted to defame Roberts by insinuating that the printer had no interest in integrated schools until he had "a case in law," referring to the case still pending—one from which Roberts might still receive $600 in damages. He also berated Morris, who had just moved to Chelsea, as thus being "not interested in the Smith School." Paul proposed that an alternative committee should write up new resolutions, but he found little support.

On invitation from Thomas Paul Smith, Roberts did put aside his anger long enough to accompany him to the Smith School in the fall of 1848, presumably for some discussion and lobbying. Joining the adversaries was the newcomer Reverend Leonard Grimes, a freeborn Virginia black who had worked alongside slave catchers until he led escaped slaves out of the South. This odd group approached the shabby Smith School when "the sky was clear and the day was glorious." If only what they found inside the school was as pleasing.

The men saw evidence of the success of the ongoing integrationist boycott, as they found only eighteen children in the school. Smith wrote that all felt "sorrow and mortification" at the tattered and dilapidated school, an institution begun with so much hope after its construction in 1835. Although Smith and Roberts shared consternation at the state of the school, they also saw different solutions. Smith could not resist sharing his irritation with Roberts, who he thought was "disregarding the interests of the people" with his quixotic movement for integrated schools. This caused Roberts to oppose "all measures for improvement of the Smith School." Of course, the main improvement Smith was seeking was a new principal. Despite their exploratory trip to the school, the two men were simply not going to see eye to eye.

A young girl stands in Smith Court, in front of the African Meeting House. *(Photograph by Halliday Historic Photograph Co.; courtesy of the Society for the Preservation of New England Antiquities)*

Smith, however, did not get his wish for his handpicked new principal in 1848, as the School Committee voted 12 to 10 to not replace Wellington with Thomas Paul. The School Committee recognized the "deep seated feeling of dissatisfaction" blacks felt with their school but thought that firing Wellington was premature. They also maintained that they felt "no sympathy" for the integrationists' sentiments, adding, "nothing can be crazier" than their ideas.

. . .

In the summer of 1849, cholera spread from the throbbing metrop-
olises of Philadelphia and New York and swept over Boston. The hot
summer months meant that the north side of Beacon Hill, with its
overcrowding and deficient drainage, was especially susceptible to
this epidemic. The distressing death rates on lower Beacon Hill
were not as dreadful as in other wards of the city where destitute
Irish immigrants lived. The dead were piled in plain burial wagons
headed for the cemetery.

In the summer of 1849, despite the pall of death hanging over
Boston, the integrationists found reason to be heartened with an
event Nell later saw as foreshadowing desegregated schools in
Boston. For the first time in Boston's history, black children were
included with the rest of the city's young people in the Fourth of
July celebrations. The man responsible for this pivotal moment was
none other than the black community's old friend, Rev. John Sargent, steadfastly on the side of integration while serving on the
School Committee. Sargent demanded that black citizens not be
"colonized" on Independence Day. Thanks to his persuasive argument, black parents proudly watched their children march with
white children in the "procession and festival in honor of the day."

It was also decided that an appeal should be written for the
mayor and City Council of Boston, in hopes that they could somehow influence the decisions of the School Committee. The idea to
appeal to the City Council paid off quickly. The aldermen decided
to appoint a special committee to study the desegregation question
and hold a hearing on the night of August 8 at City Hall. To address
the City Council was a huge responsibility, as this was "the most enlightened assembly that could have been collected in the city." Morris, Hilton, and Roberts were all to speak, but so was Thomas Paul
Smith for the opposing view.

As an old veteran, Hilton was honored with the chance to speak
first, with his "respectful manner." Morris was next to address the
gathering. A *Boston Post* writer acknowledged him to be "a man who
is much esteemed for his moral and intellectual worth." On this
night, however, it seems Morris spoke a little too long, with even his

friends admitting that he was somewhat "tedious." Morris ended his speech with an account of the integrated schools of his hometown Salem as being an example of what was possible in Boston.

Benjamin Roberts took the stage to read all the memorials, petitions, and resolutions that the integrationists had collected over the previous months. The *Post* conceded that Roberts's presentation was "well arranged, clothed in good language," and showed "much talent."

Yet according to the *Post*'s version, it was Thomas Smith who stole the evening. He was repeatedly interrupted by applause as he pleaded for the continuation of the Smith School. With "eloquence," "wit," "ingenious arguments," and "sarcasm" that could have come from "a young graduate of Harvard," he spoke from his personal experience. Smith foresaw black children being scattered throughout Boston schools bringing only "scorn," while the Smith School was a place where black children would have "their feelings defended and protected from outrage or indecency." The *Post* described this as an "outpouring of the soul." Smith even expressed a position that acknowledged the integrationists' principle that blacks deserved the same rights as whites, "legally and constitutionally," but then asserted that keeping open the Smith School was a matter of "mercy and humanity" for children choosing not to go to integrated schools, preferring a safe "asylum."

If only this line, and tone, of argument could have been sustained. Smith had powerful and important arguments to make— some of which, to this day, are still being assessed and debated. The issue of black-only schools is still a controversial topic, and he clearly moved both white and black listeners. Then the moment was tarnished by a turn to more rhetorical excess, a tactic that too often ruled both sides of this dispute. Smith finished his presentation by accusing the integrationists of selfish motives, of having "little or no interest in the education of the rising generation."

By mid-August, the new school year was fast approaching, and a new decision on the school question was due from the School Committee. Efforts were redoubled to get more petitions in. The integrationists filed a new request with 201 names, and the Smith School supporters submitted one with the names of 66 "Colored Clergymen and Parents." Even the Smith School children were brought into the petition battle as the integrationists gathered the support of 38 children, though the Smith School supporters found 42 children who wished to see the school remain open.

The integrationists claimed that their ranks represented "the cream of the colored population. We have the property and intelligence with us." Black people of the relatively prestigious professions, such as clothiers, tailors, barbers, and waiters, signed their names to petitions calling for integration at about double the rate of those who signed Smith's petition. By contrast, unskilled and unemployed people were far more likely to support Smith and Paul. Nevertheless, the integrationists were not an elite, as a quarter of their movement was made up of unskilled and unemployed workers.

Smith took to the press again, publishing an editorial railing against the integrationists. "Who says the Smith School was established for our degradation?" he cried. He believed "there is no equality" when men like Morris and Roberts are able to "demand the abolition of every institution among ourselves." This assertion must have been frustrating and perplexing to Morris and Roberts, faithful members of the black Masons and members of multiple social and literary societies for black men. For them, the issue was about equal rights, and their zealousness for the abolition of the Smith School had been born out of the denial of these equal rights in Boston. Smith saw them as far too eager to throw away "an institution formed expressly for the education, elevation, refinement and benefit of the colored youth of Boston."

Two days before the School Committee was to release their opinion based on the newest campaign, another meeting was held on the school question. The black community was now meeting every Monday night to debate integration and, for its supporters, how to mobilize to get it. At this August 27 meeting, the Independent Baptist Church was packed with an enthusiastic crowd. Though the majority of those gathered were in favor of integration, Smith showed his usual assertiveness when he stood to defend his beliefs. As Smith began his speech, he admitted he now realized that he was part of a minority view.

At that point the elderly Hilton interrupted him to score the line of the evening, saying that Smith "was mistaken in representing himself in the minority, for John C. Calhoun, Henry Clay, the American Colonization Society, and the entire pro-slavery community, were with him." Smith School supporters found themselves utterly frustrated, as they felt there was "too much party spirit to do good." In response to the treatment of Smith, when Morris rose, he too found himself trying to speak through "confusion, discord, gag and excitement." Throughout his speech hisses and applause would be heard, since for both sides the "object seemed to be to hear one side, or nobody."

William Nell was living in Boston full-time again and anxious to be back in the thick of the school battle. He rejoined the battle just in time, with the worst fears of the integrationists confirmed two days later, when on August 29, the Special Committee of the Grammar School Board issued a majority opinion reaffirming segregation. There was more than a subtle note of impatience in the writing, as the committee may have felt their repeated rebuffs to the concept of integration should have settled the issue by then. With $2,000 recently appropriated for repairs for the dilapidated Smith School, the board was particularly disinclined to entertain the notion of closing it. They accused many of the integrationist petitioners of being non-Boston residents interfering with the city's affairs, ignoring the fact that many of those people had left Boston as a form of protest precisely because of the segregated schools. Mocking the integrationists, the committee wrote that the abolition of the Smith School would mean the "Ethiopian would be washed white: Social distinctions would be all done away." There was to be no integration, for the board foresaw that Beacon Hill's "Bowdoin School, Phillips School [would] be thronged, long thronged with colored children and youth."

The only good news was that a former Massachusetts representative, Charles Theodore Russell, had written a stinging rebuke to this report. He was a minority of one, but his moral and legal reasoning spoke with significant impact. He believed any city that would subject blacks to the same taxation must allow them the same school privileges. Russell thought segregation would "not only destroy the schools, but the government which rests upon them." Russell's rebuke would be very influential in the arguments in the *Roberts* case that would be heard at the end of the year.

Thomas Smith now claimed that he was not against integrating the schools so long as the Smith School remained open. To the integrationists, this distinction was of no consequence. While Smith may have genuinely held a nuanced view of the issue, it is clear that whites exploited this conflict within the community to their advantage. One *Liberator* article spoke for many:

> But, however much we can blame the Committee, in what terms can we speak of those colored citizens who have sided with them? I know not the motives of these men, but for their course in this matter, they deserve to be held in universal contempt. Had it not been for their interference, in all probability the school would have been abolished.

Because of the disastrous majority report and the fact that the first day of school was now two weeks away, the pressure was on.

The next Monday night a mass meeting began with a prayer and quickly proceeded to emphatic denunciations of the School Committee. William Nell took to task the clergy members on the committee, asserting that their "illiberality (saving a few honorable exceptions) has been manifested in their uniform opposition to every effort for the overthrow of American slavery." With equal malice, he spit at Thomas Smith and his "evil machinations." Smith's talent was undeniable, and his speech at City Hall especially had given the School Committee additional cover to decide against them.

It was important to Nell, perhaps because of his uncertain and distant relationship with Benjamin Roberts, that it be publicly stated at this meeting that the long campaign *did not* begin with the

*Roberts* case. Nell felt some in Boston believed that were it not for the suit, "we...would not now have moved in this matter." After being gone from Boston for two years, he wanted none to forget that "we have been petitioning them for a redress of grievances, independent of any such suit." Nine prointegration resolutions were passed, though so many people spoke on the heated issue that the meeting did not adjourn till past eleven.

Yet, at last, Thomas Paul gained his long-coveted appointment at the Smith School despite warnings about his health from former employers in Providence and his poor interview skills. The School Committee overlooked these detractions because he was their best hope for ending the integrationist movement. Another reason Paul received this appointment was a letter that Smith had given to the committee from Dr. James McCune Smith, known as the best-educated black in America. Thomas Smith, with typical sleight of hand, had sent him a letter based around the query, "Do you think that under existing circumstances the colored teachers succeed better than white ones would?" Smith dishonestly represented the school struggle in Boston as being over what color the teacher might be, ignoring the whole issue of desegregation. Under this false pretense, McCune Smith, a great supporter of integration, sent back a well-thought-out explanation as to why Paul would be the better teacher for the Smith School.

It was not until months later that McCune Smith, much like the many signers of Thomas Smith's first petition the previous year, discovered with anger and mortification that he had unwittingly provided assistance against the integration movement he so strongly supported. His articles in Boston papers speaking of "the grand instincts of equality" were now too late. Paul had already been appointed by the School Committee, and as the first day of school dawned, it seemed as if the integrationists were at last firmly beaten by Thomas Smith. Something dramatic was needed to change the fortunes of the integrationists. Nell saw this as "a people's trial hour."

Days before the first day of school, much of the black community took a break from their struggles and ventured out to Worcester for the annual West India Emancipation Day. Leaders such as Morris and Nell possessed a keen sense of world events affecting their local struggles, and this special day was popular for recognizing a crucial anniversary of freedom. Emancipation in countries so close to the American South could not help but signal hope for change. People gathered each year to rejoice at "the deliverance of eight hundred thousand" while "aiming at the great and glorious object, the liberation of three million of our fellow countrymen."

On the morning of the celebration, so many Bostonians gathered at the train depot that they filled fourteen cars. The integrated railroad travel that existed now was a hopeful reminder of the power of their activism.

This was an important day for Robert Morris, as the twenty-six-year-old was asked to speak alongside four of the most famous reformers and thinkers in America. He shared the stage on that hot August day with Garrison, Phillips, Theodore Parker, and Ralph Waldo Emerson. Morris's new co-counsel in the *Roberts* case, Charles Sumner, was also asked to speak, but he declined because "engagements detain me at home." Garrison, Phillips, Parker, and Morris were all fiery men who more than pleased the audience with rousing speeches, but the deepest impression of the day was left by the more serene, contemplative Emerson. Emerson had not planned to speak because of illness, but he decided, because of the importance of the occasion, to speak anyway.

Emerson looked out over the vast crowd, this movement of committed reformers who were now so clearly fulfilling his own ideals for the progress of humanity. They were fighting against a slave-holding South that he saw as nothing less than barbarous. "They are still in the animal state," he said. Yet this was not to be an embittered speech. Still hoarse, Emerson gazed beyond the crowd, far off into the crystal sky. He told the crowd to congratulate themselves for their activism, which showed them to be "under the control of higher laws than any human will." As for the fate of this movement toward equality, Emerson assured them, "Revolutions, as we say, never move backward."

# EIGHT

# No Neutrals

The debate over integration versus self-imposed segregation in the name of community strength has played itself out in various ways throughout our national history. There has never been unanimity on this troubling question among African Americans. W. E. B. DuBois and Marcus Garvey, the NAACP and the Black Panthers, Martin Luther King and Malcolm X—they all disagreed with each other forcefully. And yet, as passionate as holders of competing principles have often been, and continue to be, one is hard-pressed to find an incident where this debate led directly to violence within the black community.

One such moment, however, came on September 17, 1849.

Robert Morris and his integrationist allies were gathered at a meeting in the Belknap Street Church. Then, unexpectedly, they were "assailed by a volley of stones and other missiles." What distinguishes this violence from the near death of Garrison at the hands of a white mob in 1835, and other dangerously violent moments in the abolitionist saga, is that it was started by fellow black citizens. The stone throwers were free black Bostonians. The fact that Beacon Hill residents were rioting over the question of closing the Smith School shows how visceral, and volatile, the issue of integration had become by late 1849. Between Morris's loss in the case before the Court of Common Pleas the year before and the appeals hearing in the Massachusetts Supreme Judicial Court scheduled for

Engraving of the Abiel Smith School for black students in 1849, the year of the *Roberts* case. *(Courtesy of the Boston Athenaeum)*

December, a struggle between integrationists and segregationists over the school question engaged and inflamed the black community. The passion over the issue reached a dangerous zenith on that September day.

The direct catalyst for the violence on the evening of September 17 was a protest the integrationists had engaged in that morning. It is not clear whether Nell, Hilton, Morris, Roberts, or any other leader gave explicit orders, but as children, teachers, and parents arrived at the Smith School for the first day of school, they found integrationists forcibly blocking the entrance to the school. The integrationists, having already pulled their children out of the school in the boycott, evidently now envisioned a new drastic step: keeping *all* children out of the segregated institution.

In fact, the boycott had been so successful that only twenty-three children had even registered for the school, but to Nell, these remaining children were being "seduced into the Smith School." The integrationists did not resort to physical violence, but every other possible means was used to keep the children from entering the school. Eventually, the Boston police arrived, and the integrationists scattered into the complex warren of small Beacon Hill streets and alleys. Unlike the late 1950s scene in Little Rock, the police then escorted children *into* a segregated black school to avoid the threat of militant integrationists.

That evening, a meeting was held at the Belknap Street Church. Perhaps as a result of the morning's drama, this was an especially large meeting of integrationists. In the packed space, both Morris and Nell rose to exhort them. During this flurry of orators and proposed resolutions, some began to notice with unease that other members of the community, known to be Smith School supporters, were starting to gather near the doors. They stood, silently observing from the back of the room but not speaking, unlike in so many previous contentious meetings. Then, on cue from some of the leaders, the dissenters began disturbing the meeting with hisses and "other demonstrations." Morris and others tried their best to implore the audience to ignore the disruptions and to focus on the business at hand. The Smith School supporters then exited the building, and leaders inside the meeting hall again asked for order.

This order lasted until the shattering of the first window. Pandemonium overtook the room as glass hit the church floor. Terrified people scurried to find safety in the increasing melee. The Smith School supporters standing at the back of the room had, upon leaving the church, regathered on Belknap Street and begun hurling cobblestones through the same vestry windows through which Nell had watched William Lloyd Garrison create his Anti-Slavery Society.

Integrationists huddled down, many already with severe bruises from the projectiles being hurled into the room. The screams and commotion coming from the church woke much of Beacon Hill, and a large crowd of witnesses quickly assembled to watch the rioters surrounding the integrationists, who were still inside the church, most still throwing "missiles of all sorts."

When the police arrived, making it the second time they visited this Beacon Hill cul-de-sac in one day, they set out to settle disputes within this community that they may have only dimly understood. As was the case in the morning, however, the police were effective. The black segregationists soon scattered, with none arrested.

The integrationists then emerged from the church, stunned by what had just taken place. Nell saw some of his comrades trying to make light of the situation by picking up the stones that had been thrown, making sure they were "preserved as trophies of the prowess of those who resort to such methods of appeal." It was ironic that the men who resorted to violence to save one black community institution had now vandalized another. The incident might not have happened had the integrationists not raised the ante with their protest in the morning, but now Smith School supporters had taken their battle to a new level. As the first week of school wore on, children found police patrolling the area around the school to make sure there would be no further incidents. Though many integrationists saw themselves as the victims of an unjustified attack, they immediately strove to take the initiative and to better organize the boycott of the Smith School.

Though the boycott was five years old, it had never been run with very sound organization. The first priority was to improve the "independence" schools. The primary obstacle in the success of these schools was that they were also all-black, which meant parents, for the sake of future integration, were being asked to trade in one segregated school for another.

On Monday, September 24, integrationists boldly returned to the site where only a week before they had been attacked. Nell, covering the meeting for the *Liberator*, could hardly believe that after the previous week's debacle the church was again crowded. It was as if the experience of undergoing the attack had given the movement a new urgency, causing their numbers to increase. The twelve-person committee went over the measures of organization for the first grammar class of the Independent School. Time was spent as-suring parents about the value of education at this makeshift school. A large part of the meeting was spent soliciting donations to pay teachers at these boycott schools. Decades earlier, much of the money for the first black school in Boston had come from the com-munity itself, and now their leaders were asking for precious money they had been saving for their proverbial rainy day—for "the pres-ent is indeed a dark and rainy day."

For the boycott to work, the integrationists had to decisively win public opinion in the black community once and for all. The sizable audience was told

> that in our battle for freedom, the influence of all colored men and women is indispensable. In their fire-side and tea-table conversation, their free and easy talk during business hours, down town or up town, in the street, store, kitchen or parlor, or wherever they are, should be, as an all-engrossing topic, equal school rights, and them-selves their language should be—"We want no neutrals among us."

Considering all the issues facing the community—slavery, colo-nialization, poverty—for school rights to be pushed as the "all-engrossing topic" speaks to the depth of commitment to this cause. And yet, their "no neutrals" policy was a heavy burden for many in the community. Certain successful black shopkeepers found them-selves unable to support the boycott for fear of losing their white clientele, as well as some black neighbors on the other side. Al-though much of this campaign had been planned in churches, black ministers sustained a deep ambivalence about this militancy, some fearing that if schools were integrated, they would lose black members of their church to white churches.

Despite these unconvinced elements of the community, just the continuation of the boycott had to be considered a great success for the integrationists in 1849. Thomas Smith had seemingly won the day, according to the School Committee's report and their appoint-ment of his cousin to the head-mastership of the school, and yet, did any of that really matter if no one was attending the school? In fact, it was after the appointment of Paul, which was done to break the back of the boycott, that the integrationists were able to create the lowest attendance numbers in the history of the Smith School. Thus, they met their biggest threat with their most effective organizing.

The boycott was an exceptional concept because, despite any declarations by the School Committee or Thomas Smith about the virtues of segregated education, it was now rendering the city's conception of education ineffective and a fiscal mess. Because the School Committee had in the past preferred to spend more on white children, they were now faced with the increasingly unpalatable necessity of maintaining a school for a handful of black children, which was economically unfeasible. Before the height of the boycott in 1849, the School Committee spent $29 for every white child in the Boston schools. Now, because of the need to maintain the Smith School, they had to spend $76 on the few black children still enrolled in the Boston schools. Thus, the integrationists were cannily forcing a prejudiced School Committee into the prickly position of spending more than twice as much on each black child as they were spending on a white child. This state of affairs could not continue, for the School Committee would soon have to make a decision about how large a price they would have to pay for the luxury of segregation.

When the boycott started in the wake of the Abner Forbes controversy in 1844, the Smith School regularly had more than one hundred children in attendance every day. By 1849 that number had been effectively cut in half. After Paul's arrival and the reenergizing of the independence school movement, the attendance had again been cut in half, so in the spring of 1850 Paul was left with an average of twenty-five children per day.

With the *Roberts* trial approaching and the school agitation becoming more visible, members of the Boston community who detested the very idea of integration began to make their opposition more vocal. The *Boston Post* editorialized, "Law or no law, our citizens of the West End will not suffer the infusion of forty to fifty colored boys and girls among their own children." The article suggested that if this desegregation became a reality, these students would again encounter the kind of harassment that made them demand separate schools in the eighteenth century. Otherwise, the *Post* writer claimed, whites would leave the Boston schools. This was an early version of the threats of white flight that would mark much of the desegregation debate in the late twentieth century.

Thomas Smith was also back in the fray with a long article in the *Liberator*. After reiterating his position on the continuation of the Smith School, he went after Robert Morris for what he saw as personal attacks. Smith also questioned Morris's motives as a lawyer, claiming the young man "scorns the country, gets men in scrapes and gets them out...and for what? Who does not know? For that very gold, which he affects to believe dazzles every body's eyes but his own." Morris's and Smith's distaste for each other had clearly passed beyond differing ideologies and into very personal animosity.

The integrationists continued their Monday night meetings; Nell described these meetings as times not just for lengthy speeches but "free and easy reunions" among friends within the community. Instead of just listening to their orators, people could be found in the meeting hall discussing their various experiences in protesting the schools, comparing notes, and proposing different plans of actions. It was also an opportunity for the women of the community to be actively engaged in political action. Angeline Gardner, who by day worked as a washerwoman, served on a committee of boycotting mothers that prepared refreshments for the hectic meetings, solicited money for the temporary schools, and distributed the money that was brought into the movement. To Nell, it was the women of the Beacon Hill community who kept "the flame alive in the dark hours of the struggle when some men despaired of victory."

At a particular meeting in late October, community members expressed how they had brought this once obscure issue to be talked about in the schools, families, papers, journals, and "highways and byways of the city." Also discussed was the upcoming *Roberts* case and the glimmering hope that this court battle could ring the death knell for segregated schools in Massachusetts. Robert Morris also gave a "spirit-stirring speech," describing horrors still happening at the Smith School and telling the story of a black boy unfairly dragged into Police Court by his teacher. Morris, nearly a month before his moment in court with the *Roberts* case, implored all in attendance, "Let us war upon the whole scheme of wickedness, and let the measures for our success become the great thought of our lives."

A November meeting on the same topic received even more attention from national figures. An exceptionally large crowd filed into the African Meeting House upon the announcement that the heralded Frederick Douglass would be speaking on the Boston school fight. Unfortunately, Douglass never appeared, but his absence was compensated for by fiery speeches from Charles Remond, Wendell Phillips, and William Lloyd Garrison. For Phillips and Garrison, this was the first anti–Smith School meeting they attended. They both played commanding roles in the marriage and railway struggles, and Phillips had written much on the school question in the earlier years of the fight; but the year 1849 had brought Nell's, Morris's, Hilton's, and the rest of the black integrationists' opportunity to lead.

With the *Roberts* case only weeks away, the two now appeared at the November meeting. Phillips congratulated the boycotting parents "on the union they had exhibited in their struggle." He offered a historical overview, placing their determination for education in the context of the long labors in the North for quality common schools. As for Thomas Smith's part in disrupting this process, Phillips proclaimed that he had committed "treason" against his community. Garrison and the black abolitionist Remond of Salem made similar affirmations of the school struggle, with Remond predicting that "a brilliant victory would soon crowd their exertions." Garrison foresaw a similar outcome, trying to reenergize the quest by reminding the adoring crowd they were fighting not just for themselves but also for white children.

Even the integrationists' vigorous opponent Thomas Paul conceded that the integrationists had been very successful. They had gotten more than three hundred members of the community during the previous nine months to put aside their day-to-day struggle for survival to engage in at least fifteen meetings demanding integration. In fact, while his supporter Thomas Smith could claim victory in the School Committee's maintaining the Smith School, he could hardly claim victory over public opinion in the black community. His followers now comprised only about 10 percent of the community.

The majority of the School Committee, in their rejection of integration in 1849, had made reference to the upcoming *Roberts* case in the Massachusetts Supreme Court, writing, "To Caesar they appealed and to Caesar they should go."

# NINE

# A Brahmin of Black Beacon Hill

Despite their differences, Abraham Lincoln held Charles Sumner in affectionate exasperation, though the senator constantly harangued him on the plight of black Americans. One day in 1862, during one of the worst stretches of the Civil War for his administration, Sumner reproved Lincoln's actions in appointing a provisional governor in North Carolina who had recently closed a school for black children. Standing in the War Department office, Lincoln asked in weary frustration, "Do you take me for a School Committee man?"

Sumner coolly replied, "Not at all. I take you for the President of the United States; and I have come with a case of wrong, in attending to which your predecessor, George Washington, if alive, might add to his renown."

But in 1849, when Robert Morris appeared in Sumner's offices at 4 Court Street, Sumner was far from influencing American presidents. Instead, he seemed mired in a profession for which he had little affection. He certainly loved the idea of the law, but it was the everyday drudgery of law practice that he disliked. Sumner would rather be in his own world reading Shakespeare, Dante, or Homer, conversing in French about art, considering great political questions, and writing lectures and letters to English friends. Yet, when he was asked to argue for the *Roberts* case on appeal, it was for him a reminder of the best the law had to offer. He was so eager that he took the case without payment.

Charles Sumner in 1846, a young lawyer three years away from the *Roberts* case. *(Crayon portrait by Eastman Johnson; courtesy of National Park Service, Longfellow National Historic Site)*

If Benjamin Roberts had any hesitancy in letting the well-known Sumner work on his case, he never said so. Perhaps this was because Sumner represented a different kind of white man to many. Frederick Douglass, a man who clashed with white reformers such as Garrison, said of Sumner, "None have uttered the feelings of the black man so well." Both Roberts and Morris would share this high opinion of him and carry a fierce devotion for Sumner for the rest of their lives.

.  .  .

Sumner grew up in the heart of the black community on Beacon Hill. His father was the liberal-minded sheriff of Suffolk County, who struggled to feed his nine children. As a child, he watched his father's friendly relations with and customary bow to people of all races, and he was raised with an awareness of the plight of free blacks that many, including passionate abolitionists, did not have. His father believed, "The best thing the abolitionists can do for the people of color is to make their freedom a blessing to them in the states where they are free." It was said of him that "he would be entirely willing to sit on the bench with a negro judge." Charles would absorb these ideas, as well as his father's aversion to segregated schools.

He began attending the Boston Latin School at age ten and won the Franklin medal. While there, the gawky, awkward boy learned about discrimination based on one's background. The school was made up of the sons of the Boston aristocracy, of which Sumner, the sheriff's son, was not a part. As a boy, Wendell Phillips would not even speak to Sumner because he was from the "wrong" side of Beacon Hill. Sumner pushed on with his studies, however, because he was raised with the ideals of equal education; as his father wrote, this was "the poor man's birth right." Nevertheless, these experiences would help shape Sumner's sensitivities toward those on the north side of Beacon Hill. Comfortable with black people, he had often addressed the Adelphic Union and was a near fixture at J.J. Smith's barbershop, where he would engage with members of the black community in heated debates on issues of the day. Sumner, often seen by others as stiff and aloof, still understood that a barbershop was the best place to gauge and learn of public opinion.

Sumner perplexed people all his life. His strong sense of principle often blinded him to common, everyday interactions. When Julia Ward Howe once asked him if he had ever seen Edwin Booth act, he replied, "Why, no madam—I, long since, ceased to take any interest in *individuals*." She laughed and replied, "You have made great progress, Sir—God has not yet gone so far."

It was true that he was too literal by half. Holmes wrote, "If I told Sumner the moon was made of green cheese, he would immediately say 'No, it isn't,' and proceed to line up a long list of weighty arguments." His sense of humor, thus, was limited, if nonexistent. "Poor Sumner can't take a joke, of any kind. He is as literal as a Scotch guide-board," wrote Richard Henry Dana in his journal.

Phillips said he was like a cat "without smellers," lost in social situations. When asked if he had ever used a joke in any of his speeches, he answered honestly, "No, I never did." (It is a marvel he and Lincoln got along as well as they did.)

Sumner matriculated at Harvard at age fifteen. Phillips remembered returning from various social events with groups of high-spirited students in the wee hours of the morning only to see a solitary candle burning in the window of Sumner's room, where he had been up all night studying. This preparation would pay off in his success in college, and then law school. According to Sumner, a lawyer should be a moralist, scientist, philosopher, and scholar. Above all else, he saw the law as giving him the best opportunity to help humanity.

When he was twenty-three, he took a trip to Washington, D.C., and for the first time witnessed slavery. He saw people so brutalized that they were "nothing more than moving masses of flesh. I have now an idea of the blight upon that part of the country in which they live." Back home in Boston, his growing abolitionist zeal was strengthened by reading the *Liberator,* though he read it selectively and without falling in thrall to its zealous editor. Sumner, like Frederick Douglass, Ellis Gray Loring, and many other abolitionists, came to disagree with Garrison's disunionist ideas, based on the editor's notion of the Constitution as being nothing more than a slaveholder's document. Sumner chided Garrisonian Wendell Phillips for defaming the Constitution while still living under its protections. He found no nation was without some history of oppression, so he believed his best path as an abolitionist was not to renounce government but to "exercise any influence among my fellow-men, by speech, by the pen, by my vote," to create a more just society and have proslavery passages in the Constitution expunged.

The idea of constitutional color blindness had been brewing in the young counselor for a long time. He could not understand the logic of denying the rights of citizenship to a certain race. If blacks were excluded, "Is the Indian race also excluded? Is the Mongolian excluded?" The fallacy he found was "How can you 'curtail of their fair proportions,' & limit words, which of themselves express no limitations, derived from color or race?" If this was so, America would have to say to the rest of the world, "Come," and then add, "but all who come must be of the purest white, or you cannot have offspring entitled to privileges & immunities of citizenship."

On his grand tour of Europe in 1838, while visiting a university law school in Paris, Sumner noticed the calm presence there of students of African descent. These young men were "well received by their fellow students," and "their color seemed to be no objection to them." In Sumner's homeland, there were no black lawyers yet and few integrated educational institutions. He confessed that "it seemed very strange." Reflecting on the sight of these blacks and whites learning together, and the sad contrast with what he had seen when growing up, Sumner rejected any ideas of racial inferiority, writing in his travel journal, "It must be, then, that the distance between free blacks & the whites among us is derived from education, & does not exist in the nature of things." Drawing on these European memories, Sumner would tell Americans, "It is well known that the prejudice . . . is peculiar to our country." These prejudices were "akin to the stern and selfish spirit that holds a fellow-man in slavery."

This realization shows the emerging feelings that would drive him to do so much on behalf of both black education and black lawyers in the hard years to come. Sumner saw education as the most crucial function of society: "The true grandeur of humanity is in moral elevation, sustained, enlightened and decorated by the intellect of man." Many people believe such noble things, and few endure the criticism and abuse that go along with actually working to uncover this grandeur.

Not only was Sumner an imposing orator of "bass sonority," tiring of the law, but he was, in the mid-1840s, undergoing a dispiriting time. He found his life lonely and depressing. He had run for and lost a position on the School Committee in an effort to aid his friend Samuel Gridley Howe and, further, lost a considerable amount of money to an effort to help Mann's educational reforms. Harvard Law School was resistant to his being named to replace his old mentor, Professor Joseph Story. Perhaps worst of all, he had been selected to present the important and honored July Fourth oration for the city of Boston, and it turned into a near disaster.

In the Tremont Temple, before a vast crowd, the young man, resplendent in blue coat and white pants, looked like a Greek god —tall, handsome, with thick, long chestnut hair carefully combed over his brow. His confident and dignified presence promised a triumphal speech, but then, on this martial holiday, he proceeded to praise the cause of universal peace. In the dinner at Faneuil Hall, some twelve speakers rose to roast the audacity of the orator.

Coming to Sumner's rescue was none other than Peleg Chandler, who later recalled that he decided to "throw the whole thing into broad farce." To protect his friend, Chandler first gently criticized the speech and then asked what more or better one could expect from "an old bachelor. How could a man who never knew anything of domestic broils feel competent to speak of war?" After some laughter, he quickly raised his glass: "To the orator of the day!"

Yet all was not gloom. Sumner, believing that "morals is the soul of all politics," was buoyed with an overwhelming sense that the world was about to change. Religious Millerites in Boston were boldly predicting that the world was about to end, but the transformation Sumner sensed was an altogether different kind of cultural shift. All across Europe, people were rising up in open liberal rebellion against the old order, and the spirit of revolution was in the air. There was a growing faith, in Europe and in America, that human goodness could at last prevail.

When the *Roberts* case came to Sumner, he was ready. He was fired up with a deep hope that in resisting the Mexican War of James Polk and speaking out against the perceived rise of the "Slave Power" in Congress, things were changing. The American "Newness" he believed in was actually a worldwide current. In 1848 Sumner felt himself part of a larger political transformation. He had been a member of the "Conscience" Whigs, who disagreed with the "Cotton" Whigs, the faction of the party more comfortable with slavery. Yet the Whig coalition could not long survive the divisive impact of slavery. In 1848 Horace Mann, the future senator Henry Wilson, the future governor John A. Andrew, and Sumner gathered in Sumner's Court Street law offices for long discussions on what to do about this encroachment of the "slaveocracy." They believed the South's growing power in Washington, D.C. (as well as in the business offices of Boston's State Street), was twisting and corrupting "free" states. Sumner's later nomination to the Senate was born from these anguished discussions. The Free Soil party stood for free labor, free speech, and free people, and this would be, until the rise of the Republican party, his new political platform. As the *Roberts* case approached, the possibility of Sumner's entrance into politics loomed, coloring all his thoughts and hopes, though he would have been aghast if anyone had labeled him ambitious. The prospect of elective office seemed to him extremely unlikely, and he suspected it would come, if it ever did, at too high a price for his honor.

As Sumner gravitated toward a life in abolitionist politics, he realized that the old Beacon Hill world he had grown up in now found his liberal views abhorrent, too radical. Once, driving down Beacon Hill with Dana, he bitterly swept his hand toward the neighborhood, and particularly the home of George Ticknor—who had exiled him from his parlor due to his views—and said, "There was a time when I was welcome at almost every house within two miles of us, but now hardly any are open to me." Even George Hillard, his old law partner at 4 Court Street, complained that all Sumner talked of was "slavery and the Mexican war," as he utterly neglected his law practice.

The summer of 1849 brought the tragedy of the death at sea of Sumner's brother Horace. His ship sank nearly in view of the Jersey coast, and his attempt to float to shore on a plank from the ship was to no avail. Margaret Fuller also died, with her new husband and child, in the same tragedy. However, it was another death that truly threatened to overshadow the *Roberts* case, even in the minds of its attorneys. *Roberts* had the misfortune of coinciding directly with one of the most infamous crime cases in American history.

The very courtroom (with the same judges presiding) where Sarah was to have her day in court was also being used in the sensational trial of a Harvard professor who had brutally murdered an associate. The nation was transfixed by this crime.

No one believed at first that John Webster was capable of such a crime. As a professor at Harvard, he was the picture of meekness.

Yet Webster had a large secret debt to the miserly Beacon Hill resident George Parkman. More a tight landlord than an academic now, Dr. Parkman wanted the money Webster owed him. He stalked the timid Webster at parties and frightened him by showing up at the back of his lecture hall.

On November 23, 1849, Webster's visceral resentment of Parkman detonated. Parkman had walked down from his home on Beacon Hill, along Cambridge Street, and into the Harvard Medical College for an appointment with Webster. At some point during their angry exchange, Webster bludgeoned Parkman to death in his laboratory. Days later, Robert Gould Shaw was posting notices all around Beacon Hill concerning the missing Parkman. On Saturday, December 1, at the unveiling of the statue of Aristides in Louisburg Square, the gathered crowd talked only of the missing man.

It would not be long before the police visited Webster's laboratory, the place Parkman had been last seen, only to find bones in the furnace and other assorted body parts scattered and hidden around the room. Thrilled crowds gathered around the Medical School, and it was quickly established that the grisly remains were indeed Parkman's. The *Boston Herald* declared, "At no time within the recollection of any citizen of Boston has there been so great, so general an excitement."

Charles Sumner and the prominent attorney Rufus Choate corresponded about possibly taking on the case of defending Webster, but both decided that the sensational publicity would not be worth it. Sumner had a private conversation with Charles Francis Adams about possibly serving on the legal team after receiving a personal letter from Webster from the Leverett jail. They decided it was not a good idea; after all, it would be hard to make a case that this was an innocent man, when portions of Parkman had been found in Webster's furnace and private vaults.

At the conclusion of the trial in March, and after the instructions to the jury were given, Sumner and Richard Henry Dana retired to the old Bell in Hand tavern to wait for the verdict. After an hour and a half, they heard the jury returning and rushed back to the courthouse to hear a resounding "Guilty."

The spectacle of the case seemed all consuming. During the

days of the Parkman trial, sixty thousand people were, at one time
or another, ushered in and out of the courtroom as authorities
tried to let as many curious spectators as possible see the quiet mur-
derer. It is estimated that almost half of the population of Boston
saw at least a few moments of the trial. The great heavy doors of the
courthouse had to be replaced. Reporters from all parts of America
and Europe covered the drama. The judge that Webster faced was
the same one who would preside over the *Roberts* case within that
month: Lemuel Shaw.

. . .

A lawyer who appeared before Judge Shaw on many occasions was
once watching an artist sculpt a lion and jested, "Why that's the best
likeness of Chief Justice Shaw that I have ever seen." Severe as he
was, his was unavoidably the face of Massachusetts law. Strong and
gruff, austere and quick, with a sharp rebuke for the lawyers who
appeared before his bench, Shaw was a living legend long before his
thirty years as chief justice ended in 1860.

The respect, not to say near veneration, by which he was held was
of a piece with his imposing physical frame. The judge was short but
had a powerful aspect. His head was topped with a mane of chestnut hair that he was in the habit of tousling into shagginess upon
arrival at his office. His face was wide, massive, and somber, with a
wide mouth and a great nose. He was ugly, but magnificently, im-
pressively so. When he spoke, it was with a deep, low intonation, except when his speech turned into a savage growl at the hapless
lawyers before him. He spoke slowly and with so many pauses that
at times a lawyer would start to speak only to have the judge inter-
rupt to start up again. He was said to think and consider slowly, and
though he was able to grasp the course of a motion in an instant,
he declined to rush to conclusions. He moved slowly, in the judge's
chair as well as when taking his well-trodden lumbering path from
his home to Court Street and back each day.

Shaw lived in one of the finest Georgian houses on Mount Vernon Street. It had a refined interior filled with mahogany furniture.
Outside his house, a quick left off Mount Vernon Street would place
him on Belknap Street, where the Smith School stood just down the

street. Not only was Shaw familiar with school issues, having served on the School Committee, but he was only a few hundred feet from the black community of Beacon Hill and their controversial school.

His great, mountainous presence came from more than just his physical presence. Shaw was sixty-nine years old, and for the last nineteen of those he had sat as the chief justice of the Massachusetts Supreme Judicial Court. He was well on his way to the 2,150th opinion he would write, and of these, he wrote in the minority only three times, an astonishing record. This is a testament to his influence on Massachusetts's law, filling more than twenty legal volumes and making him easily the most influential state judge in American history.

His life was a long and epic one in America's legal evolution. Shaw was born on Cape Cod in Barnstable, Massachusetts, during the American Revolution and died on the eve of the Civil War. He witnessed a nation that changed from a rural colony to a great urban, industrial one. As a child he lived in a country clinging to the Atlantic Seaboard, but by the time of the *Roberts* case in 1849, citizens from all over the country were flocking to California in search of gold, some three thousand miles from Boston. His natural intelligence allowed him to attend Harvard and work as a teacher— unhappily—after graduating. This was probably a significant fact for him in considering the *Roberts* case, as Shaw had not just taught in the Boston schools but served more than three terms on the Boston School Committee, the very group the integrationists had come to loathe. The Judge was not likely to share their view.

Eventually the law called Shaw away from education. He established a successful practice and over a matter of years became a fixture in Boston politics and law. When he was forty-nine, the chief justice of the Massachusetts Supreme Court passed away and Daniel Webster asked Shaw to take over. Shaw was resistant to the idea of a judge's life and the low salary, and he smoked cigar after cigar while Webster pleaded with him to take the reins of Massachusetts law. "He smoked and smoked, and, as I entreated and begged and expostulated, the smoke would come thicker and faster," wrote Webster, who estimated that a thousand cigars were needed "while settling the point." It turned out he was a natural judge, far more comfortable and proficient than he had been as a practicing lawyer.

Shaw was a conservative man who viewed the Constitution as a solemn pact. This irritated abolitionists appealing to higher laws, in which Shaw demonstrated little interest. There was a great gulf between those whose legal instincts were to appeal to this "Natural law"—overarching higher principles that nullified smaller, precise precedents. For them, the Declaration of Independence was the real and final authority when deciding slavery cases, with its noble evocation that all men are created equal and that this was "self-evident." Others went to the Constitution itself and claimed no such higher law principles. Webster, Shaw's friend and the only person who it could be said was an influence on the judge, never referred to or relied on the natural law proclamation of the Declaration of Independence.

When it came to slavery, if it was an evil, Shaw reluctantly felt it was "a necessary one, too deeply interwoven in the texture of society to be wholly or speedily eradicated." Yet, Sumner and Morris could also see that he had made very progressive decisions during his time on the bench. In *Commonwealth v. Hunt,* Shaw had ruled that a labor union, structured on the basis of maintaining a closed shop, was not a criminal conspiracy. Perhaps his most famous liberal decision came when Morris's mentor Ellis Gray Loring had persuaded him to rule against returning a girl to slavery in the *Med* case in 1836. Indeed, when he was a young man, in a speech to the Humane Society in 1811, he labeled the slave traffic as "one continued series of tremendous crimes."

Although Shaw sided with the abolitionists in the *Med* case, in 1842 he let a captured slave name George Latimer be returned to bondage in the South. The white abolitionists and the black community worked feverishly against this outcome, holding meetings and protests. When it was found that Shaw had allowed Latimer to be removed from freedom in Boston, Garrison said Shaw was to "act the part of Pilate on the crucifixion of the Son of God." Sumner had also spoken publicly for Latimer, but his opposing lawyer in the *Roberts* case took up a public defense for Shaw. Peleg Chandler wrote in his legal journal that Sumner, Garrison, and others were filled with "false morality, born from the sophistry of fanaticism."

This debate over a judge's power to appeal to higher moral reasoning, despite a lack of justification in the law, would continue to play itself out with the same cast of characters as in the *Roberts* case. For his part, Chandler affirmed Shaw's judicial restraint, writing, "A judge has nothing to do with the moral character of the laws which a society chooses to make ... the judiciary is the mere organ of society."

Morris and Sumner had to worry about not only Judge Shaw but opposing counsel Peleg Chandler, who had defeated Morris in the first hearing of the case. Sumner knew Chandler well, as their law offices were in the same building, though their friendship was a testy one. It was understood that they had very different viewpoints of the world, but at times their ideologies put a strain on their personal relationship. Chandler lamented in 1845, "For you and I to differ in opinion is nothing new or strange; but for either of us to indulge for a moment the feeling that the other has been unjust, is, I believe new and strange." He believed Sumner's recent distaste for him meant "you acted under an erroneous influence." However, Chandler had gotten under Sumner's skin by not giving an article Sumner wrote for Chandler's journal a prominent position. For this and other unsaid tensions, Chandler admitted, "I begin to feel the truth of your assertion, that I have often abused you!" The conflict at hand on December 4 was segregated schools, but these aspects of their relationship must have lingered in their minds.

Despite their squabbles, Chandler maintained great respect for Sumner and would take opposing him in court very seriously. Chandler spent much time working against abolitionist ends, but once, after reading a Sumner oration, he confided, "I find myself converted to many points of your faith." Chandler confessed, "No one can read your views without being irresistibly carried away by the soundness, the elevation and the journey of the course you point out."

It would remain to be seen whether Judge Shaw would be so carried away.

# TEN

# The Argument

The day the *Roberts* case began was cold, and bitterly so—an early-December blast in advance of winter. The ground was already covered with snow, as on the previous day the first storm of the season had swept in. The *Boston Post* described "wind blowing very fresh and veering about to all points of the compass." The storm was heavy, but the city was relieved that there had been no damage to the harbor. For those in the black community, many of whose jobs were intertwined with the labor of the harbor, the freeze that extended along the waterfront meant that there would be no more work for the rest of the season. This also meant that more blacks would attend the trial.

It was extraordinarily difficult for any story to make much headway against the growing public obsession with the murder of George Parkman. The morning papers featured yet more details of the Parkman case, with the *Boston Herald* revealing that "the thorax and the thigh [had been] found in the tea chest" and showing large illustrations of Parkman's teeth and bones. The *Daily Atlas* reported that Professor Webster was arguing that portions of Parkman's body had been put in his laboratory by someone endeavoring to collect a reward.

Walking together up the marble steps and through the great doors into the courthouse on the morning of December 4, Sumner and Morris no doubt made a distinctive duo. The old courthouse faced Court Street behind the Old City Hall, and its high colonnade of Doric pillars and lofty pediment made it seem less a legal site than a Greek temple. Sumner was described by a contemporary as a "great, tall creature" with a "delicious youthful enthusiasm." With a slender build, Sumner's height gave him a dignified and imposing presence, whereas the much shorter Morris gained his power from his engaging and pleasing personality. A friend wrote of Morris, "He had sunshine in his heart."

Historians believe Morris and Sumner were the first interracial team to ever cosign (much less argue together) a legal brief, and many at the time thought their easy and respectful partnership was itself sufficient argument against segregation. Sumner, as the more experienced and socially connected lawyer, could easily have made this appearance alone. There is no evidence that such an idea ever crossed his mind; their partnership that day was no doubt a legal argument in itself, meant to symbolize subtle and powerful undercurrents present in the meaning of the case.

Sumner and Morris were two very different lawyers, though quite complimentary to each other. Sumner was older, more seasoned, and though unhappy with the daily grind of the legal trade, at the very height of his profession in terms of intellectual prowess, historical knowledge, and familiarity with the current philosophical discussions in Europe as well as in America. In stark contrast, Morris had passed the bar only seven months before asking Sumner to "assist" him with the case. Morris still felt regret about not possessing a liberal arts education, such as the one Sumner had received at Harvard, though he resolved, "It is no use for us to stop now and worry over the slights and privations we have had to encounter, but we must avail ourselves of every opportunity to gain knowledge and improve." This contrast in their background helps to explain why Sumner was more interested in the principles and philosophies behind the law, which Morris did not concern himself with when giving advice to his many clients. Morris was a better street lawyer than Sumner. Not only was Morris practical and focused, but he had already demonstrated long, gritty, and patient determination. Morris was not the invisible partner some historians have supposed.

A potent symbol he no doubt was, but he was present as a lawyer first.

The two men were also dissimilar in their approaches to people in and out of court. Though Sumner was known to fascinate ladies with his conversation, making him one of the "social lions of the city," he did not have the humor Morris so effortlessly demonstrated. Morris was known to make even the sternest judges laugh in court and josh juries into favorable decisions.

The courtroom was a large rectangular room with high ceilings, featuring a high table for the four sitting judges, a jury box, a witness box, a clerk's desk, counselors' tables, and a roaring fireplace to keep the participants warm during a season such as this. There was a prisoner's dock with high iron railings. Blacks "thronged" the courtroom that day, all with a shared conviction that the legal team would have a decisive victory in the battle they had been fighting for years. There was the hard thump of the bailiff's staff, bringing everyone to their feet. "Hear ye! Hear ye! All those having anything to do before the Honorable, the Justices of the Supreme Judicial Court, gather round, give your attention, and you shall be heard. God save the Commonwealth of Massachusetts. Be seated!"

The road to victory, however, would have to pass through the gruff, austere judge who sat in front of Sumner and Morris. Twenty-six-year-old Robert Morris rose to speak to begin the proceedings; it is difficult to imagine the pressure of standing before a man such as Lemuel Shaw. What the integrationist legal team would have seen was intimidating and imposing. Historian Simon Schama describes Shaw as "a great warty toad at the center of the bench—immovable, unblinking, broad nostrils occasionally flaring at the suggestion of some propriety, embodying in his bulk the very weight of justice."

Shaw was so dominating in his commanding judicial authority that it would have been easy to forget that other judges sat with him on the Massachusetts Supreme Judicial Court. Yet three other men that morning looked down on Sumner and Morris from their high judges' perch, all seated soberly on either side of their chief.

Lemuel Shaw, chief justice of the Massachusetts Supreme Judicial Court. *(Daguerreotype by Southworth & Hawes; courtesy of the Society for the Preservation of New England Antiquities)*

Normally five judges served on the Supreme Judicial Court, but Richard Fletcher, having already given extrajudicial advice to both the mayor of Salem and the Boston School Committee on the legality of integrated schools, recused himself from hearing the case. This withdrawal was a great impediment to the integrationists, as Fletcher, only in his second year on the court, would have been an articulate voice in chambers for their cause and a much needed vote in the end.

Fletcher's abolitionist sympathies were not shared by the other judges, who were closer in classic Whig sentiment to Justice Shaw. Squat Charles Dewey, who had been serving on the court since 1837, was known as a pugnacious Whig. Theron Metcalf listened to his cases with the attentiveness of a former court reporter but without the imagination of his superiors. Last, there was the court octogenarian, the somber and courtly Samuel Wilde, a veteran of the ill-fated Hartford Convention, who had been on the bench for thirty-four years.

Robert Morris rose to speak first for his young plaintiff. A contemporary said Morris "tried cases on facts, and left the refinements and technicalities of law to others who had mastered them." In this case, those "refinements" would be for Sumner to lay out with rhetorical splendor later in the day, with Morris first setting forth the facts of the case. This arrangement made sense, as his working the case made him fully conversant with the details. He had done the digging work for eighteen months. Morris began by presenting the agreed set of facts that he and Chandler had signed off on after the first hearing of the case.

Peleg Chandler, seated not five feet away, was silent at the opposing table. There was nothing yet to object to, nothing he had not previously agreed to. One wonders what he found more interesting that day: the odd and unsettling sight of a black man in this setting or being forced to face Sumner in a case that he and his friend could hardly have disagreed about more. Their lives were diverging now, and the painful ache of the growing and widespread abolitionist sensibility was forcing them beyond simply opposing sides in a seemingly minor case. Chandler could not have realized it, but from that day forward, their experiences were diverging forever, his to a more quiet local practice, Sumner's to national renown.

Morris then proceeded to summarize Sarah's repeated attempts to obtain a ticket of admission to the school nearest her house, where there had been ample room for her. He explained how her father, Benjamin, had brought her to the school, where she was

The courthouse in Boston, where the *Roberts* case was heard, when newly built in 1836; viewed from Court Street. (American Magazine *iii, no. 3 [December 1836]; from the authors' collection*)

"ejected therefrom by order of the said committee." With this necessary foundation provided, Morris now sat down, turning the case over to his friend. With the audience in the room being overwhelmingly black, one can only imagine the pride felt by those watching and hoping, investing their expectations in Morris.

Sumner now rose and dramatically placed his long, handwritten argument in front of him, ready to take a more philosophical look at the issue of segregation. Indeed, his words constitute one of most wide-ranging and powerful statements about the state of America ever written. Legal scholars have argued over smaller aspects of the argument, but few have doubted its lasting impact or the argument's uncannily shrewd anticipation of nearly all future arguments against racism in our national life.

Sumner, as a writer or political speaker, was never particularly known for his originality, but henceforth he would be renowned (and often reviled by numerous enemies) for his stately eloquence,

his ability to marshal both contemporary ideas and arcane historical resources. In this case, he was building on the arguments made
by black citizens in the form of petitions and *Liberator* articles over
the previous decade. This is not a trivial matter, for as Sumner's
words have become more and more famous, the fact that they were
so rooted in the creativity of members of the West End community
becomes more significant. The problem with Sumner's sustained
cascade of high rhetoric, often delivered in numbing and exhaus-
tive detail, was simple: could he make this argument compelling?

He most certainly did in the *Roberts* case. In that moment his talents came together to fashion a statement that, quite unlike the vast
bulk of his speeches, is truly timeless. He knew this case was important to a group of people he admired and had come to love, and he
certainly sensed the potential importance of the decision to his city
and state. Yet not being a national figure at this time, it seems he allowed himself to write in a direct and persuasive style, elegant and
noble without surrendering to the ponderous and self-regarding
excesses he later became prone to. It was as if he wanted the free
blacks crowding the courtroom to fully engage with his ideas and
feel uplifted. He masterfully built on ideas and concepts that had
been fermenting in the black and white abolitionist communities
for the last decade, bringing them together in ways that had never
been done before, and have hardly been bettered since.

As Sumner readied himself to begin speaking, he inwardly felt
his mind "weakened" by thoughts drifting to the Parkman case, the
horrific "details of the murder." No doubt this odd distancing sensation derived from the fact that he was standing in the same courtroom space that had served the Parkman case. He forced himself to
forget those ghastly thoughts and concentrated on the task at hand.
In front of a packed courtroom of black supporters and brooding
judges (one contemporary said Shaw looked like "the statues of
Gog and Magog in the Guildhall in London"), Sumner opened with
a simple question: "Can any discrimination of color or race, be
made, under the Constitution and Laws of Massachusetts, among
the children entitled to the benefit of our common schools?"

Judge Shaw, pen in hand, was already scratching away. In the

Boston Social Law library today, fifty-two great heavy volumes of his notes still exist, and one can read his twelve pages of notes taken down as the lawyers spoke that day. His later printed decision would be based largely on these swift and comprehensive notes.

Shifting the burden of the question from the integrationists to the segregationists, Sumner wanted to immediately take the high ground. Sumner wanted the judges to consider not whether the School Board had the power under Massachusetts laws to integrate its schools, but whether they had the power to *exclude* certain groups from certain schools, and then to send them to others "at distances from their homes less convenient than those open to white children."

Turning away from legal questions, Sumner began talking about Sarah, reminding his listeners that this was, after all, a case about a girl's future. He compared the great, wealthy city of Boston with this five-year-old child, this girl "of degraded color, of humble parents, still within the period of natural infancy." Yet this child was raised in the spirit of a family who had been fighting against segregation for generations, and as so many civil rights figures in the years to come, she was "strong from her very weakness."

It is not recorded if Sarah was in the courtroom that day, but it is likely that she was sitting with her family, as Sumner then emphasized: "This little child asks at your hands her *personal rights*" and by doing so, asks for the rights of black children across the state. In word-play reminiscent of the expression that slavery was that "peculiar institution," Sumner asserted that segregated schools were the North's "peculiar institution." He pointed to how the controversy had been fought in the School Committee and even the press for years, and this was now the opportunity to "cause it to subside for ever."

Sumner was forthright in acknowledging that while he would discuss the legalities of segregated schools, "I cannot forget that the principles of morals and of natural justice lie at the foundation of all jurisdiction." On one hand, this was a dangerous path to go down in front of Justice Shaw, who in the *Latimer* slave case had shown his disinterest in "natural justice" in favor of obedience to current laws. On the other hand, Sumner faced the same dilemma that Morris had faced in the first hearing of the case. Without the future Fourteenth Amendment to draw on, there was little constitutional ground to stand on. This meant that Sumner would be forced to make as much a moral and philosophical presentation as a legal argument, but this was his natural bent, and he eagerly pursued it.

His first point was his most important and soundest in terms of law, reminding the judges that they were all bound to one concept, which was "according to the spirit of American institutions, and especially of the Constitution of Massachusetts, *all men, without distinction of color or race, are equal before the law.*" He intentionally used the word "spirit" here because he was giving a very progressive reading of "American institutions," many of which still sanctioned racial slavery. But unlike radicals such as William Lloyd Garrison, Sumner looked at the Constitution in the most favorable light possible. Whether or not the Constitution was supposed to guarantee equality was not a settled issue in 1849. John Calhoun, one of the nation's most powerful senators, was arguing that equality was a profound misreading of the Constitution. So to support his bold assertion that all persons were equal before the law, Sumner first had to trace evolving ideas of equality. In the autumn, his New York friend John Jay had sent the lawyer a packet of books, which he exhaustively mined for information needed for this argument on the complicated concept of equality.

Linking the principles of democratic government to Christianity itself, Sumner explained that any idea of legal equality was rooted in "the sublime doctrine of the Brotherhood of mankind, enfolding the Equality of men." He followed these ideas through the ancient philosophers and the slow penetration of equal rights into the policies of the state. Despite the civil wars fought over the monarchy in England, it was left to a poet, John Milton, to write, "With fair Equality, fraternal state," because equality as such was never codified or clarified in the institutions of England or its "unwritten Constitution."

To find more concrete declarations of equality, Sumner turned instead to the French Revolution and the ideas of men in the era of social philosopher Jean-Jacques Rousseau. In his 1755 encyclopedia, Diderot wrote an article on natural equality, which he believed to be "the principle and the foundation of liberty." Sumner observed that at the time this was written the king was founding a school for nobles, which was "in defiance of the principle of equality—but in entire harmony with the conduct of the School Committee in Boston." But the king lost his head in the revolution, and in 1791 a constitution was written that affirmed: "Men are born and continue free *and equal in their rights.*" This was the end of superiority, nobility, feudal rule, and distinctions of birth. The French Revolution went through changes in leaders and regimes, but the idea stayed the same in a new constitution two years later, which pronounced: "All men are equal by nature, *and before the law.*"

A counterrevolution of conservatism doomed these ideas in France, but Sumner now revived them for America. His excursion into French philosophy and history was not an idle historical exercise (though his listeners were no doubt shifting a bit in their seats), because it provided him with a crucial, and historic, assertion that would make this day notable. He seized the opportunity to translate the phrase *"égalité devant la loi"* (equality before the law) into English for the first time. Once said, it could not be unsaid. Sumner took a French theory and began the process of making it into an American legal instrument.

The first utterance of these four words is a pinnacle in American law, a moment for which Sumner has justifiably received much acclaim. However, Robert Morris may have had more do to with the phrase's incorporation than previously thought. Seven years earlier, Ellis Gray Loring, his mentor, with whom he was working very closely at the time, was testifying before a Massachusetts legislative committee on the illegality of segregation in transportation, when he uttered a similar idiom, "Equal before the law," which was almost the same as Sumner's "equality before the law." This suggests Morris may have seen the applicability of his mentor's 1842 axiom for the *Roberts* case. It was then up to Sumner to translate from the French a new way to express this vital and universal concept.

The main constitutional foundation Sumner had was the Massachusetts constitution's assertion "All men are born free and equal."
He argued that Massachusetts was thus a state founded on the con-
demnation of every form of inequality. Sumner understood that
there would always be differences in the natural endowments of
every person, in intelligence or mental capacity. However, these natural differences have no effect on "civil and political equality" because all must have—and he repeated that phrase again—"equality
before the law." Indeed, those four words were "the Great Charter
of every person who draws his vital breath upon this soil . . . whoever
may be his parents." All distinctions must disappear before the Constitution. Hitting on his rhetorical rhythm now, Sumner contended,
"He is not poor, or weak, or humble, or black—nor Caucasian, nor
Jew, nor Indian, nor Ethiopian—nor French, nor German, nor English, nor Irish; he is a MAN—the equal of all his fellow-men." Radical words for 1849.

Having made an impressive impact with this homily on equality's
true place in American law, Sumner moved on to speak more
specifically about whether there was any legislative justification for
segregated schools. The answer to this was simple. "The legislature
of Massachusetts, in entire harmony with the Constitution, has
made no discrimination of color or race, in the establishment of
Public Schools."

He proclaimed that the legislature was too kind, "too mindful of
the Bill of Rights," to make such distinctions based on birth. Sumner went over the laws concerning schools in the state. There was
nothing in the books that suggested segregation was the law of the
state, and even when special needs were mentioned, *all* children
were to benefit.

Having done the best he could to show the basis for equality in
the state constitution, the legislative branch, and the judicial tradition of the state, Sumner began a more moral appeal rooted in the
daily life experience of the black community. Segregated schools
were "a source of practical inconvenience," something whites never
had to experience, so how could this possibly be equality? He suggested the old adage was right, and if it was true that education was

brought to every man's door, then a black father "is obliged to go for it—to travel for it—often a great distance."

He went over Sarah's long walk to the Smith School, emphasizing this was not even close to the most egregious example of children having to travel immense distances. Nonetheless, if little Sarah had to walk only an unnecessary twelve hundred feet, where was her "equality before the law"? To Sumner, "This simple fact is sufficient to determine this case." To some, these twelve hundred feet might seem trivial, but to others a "paltry tax on tea" might have been just as inconsequential. However, "the insignificance of a fact cannot obscure the grandeur of the principle at stake." It was over that tea, and its inconvenience, that in that very city, the people of Boston "went to war for a principle." For black families all around Boston, Sarah's, and countless other children's, inconvenience revealed a much deeper principle—this equality before the law that Sumner was struggling to clarify.

This brought Sumner to his next history lesson, about the nature of what he labeled as caste. Today, the word *racism* has taken a marked ascendancy in social discourse, but it is instructive to go back to an earlier formulation that the West End citizens would have been very familiar with and that Sumner used so effectively. It was hard to deny that the idea of caste accounted for the separation of races, especially after Sumner read from the School Committee's majority report of 1846: "The distinction is on which the Almighty has seen fit to establish, and it is founded deep in the physical, mental, and moral natures of the two races." He nearly sputtered, "Words more apt than these to describe the heathenish relation of Caste, could not be chosen." He traced the emergence of the word *caste* and showed how it had always been intertwined with racial ideas. He compared what the School Committee was mandating to something resembling the separation of the Brahmins and Sudras in the dense caste system of India, though he added, "The offence is greater with us, because, unlike the Hindoos, we acknowledge that men are born equal." Sumner then quoted sixteen Christian leaders from around the world explaining that caste ran contrary to the message of Jesus. During these long passages, it is abundantly clear that Sumner had departed once and for all from a legal argument and was exploring something more universal.

Having asserted caste to be a reprehensible human institution, Sumner angrily asked what exactly in Massachusetts law gave any School Committee the power not just to make administrative decisions but to "brand a whole race with the stigma of inferiority and degradation, constituting them into a *caste*."

Here was a taste of the fire Sumner would scorch the Senate with over the next two decades as he cried, "They cannot in any way violate that fundamental right of all citizens, Equality before the law. To suppose that they can do this, would place the Committee above the Constitution." The School Committee could indeed deal with qualifications such as "age, sex and moral and intellectual fitness." But race was simply not such a qualification because it "is not to the skin that we can look for the criterion of fitness for our Public Schools." Sumner did not deny that these educational bureaucrats had legal discretion over some matters, but they did not have license that could supersede "the Constitution and laws."

As if he could see inside the great engines of Shaw's mind as it was forging a justification for segregated schools, Sumner now tried to preempt an idea that the School Committee could "furnish them an equivalent." Later Sumner may have wished he had not opened this legal Pandora's box, as he now argued against the idea of "separate but equal." Perhaps his instincts told him that Shaw would seize on some logic in this vein and that he should dispel it. Sumner asked how anyone could call the Smith School a true equivalent when one class of citizens was forced to meet by themselves. The school differed in "spirit and character" from one bringing all children together under the banner of equality. To Sumner, "It is a mockery to call it an equivalent." Even if the Smith School were "well endowed," it would not secure blacks equality, and they were not bound to accept it.

True equality could be found only in full acceptance to *common* schools. Comparing this to the treatment of Jews in their European ghettos, "this compulsory segregation from the mass of citizens is of itself an *inequality* which we condemn with our whole souls."

This opened the doors for the School Committee to initiate "one school for Unitarians, another for Presbyterians, another for Baptists, and another for Methodists. They may establish a separate school for the rich." Introducing the first touch of humor in the argument, Sumner pondered the absurd, suggesting the School Committee could "exclude the children of mechanics from the Public Schools."

With this disarming sally, Sumner brought the question back to slavery. "The same words which are potent to destroy slavery, must be equally potent against any institution founded on inequality or *caste*." A much younger Justice Shaw had dealt a great blow to slavery in Massachusetts in the *Med* case, and Sumner was now challenging him to see the same logic applied in this case.

Sumner then delved into the most radically forward thinking of his case. In 1953 Thurgood Marshall used Dr. Kenneth Clark's famous doll tests to help prove that segregated schools gave black children a sense of inferiority, and Supreme Court chief Earl Warren made special mention of these psychological tests in his written judgment. A century earlier, Sumner made exactly the same observations but without reference to scientific tests or social science studies. Yet he challenged everyone in the courtroom to be honest with themselves on the prime question, "Who can say, that this does not injure the blacks?"

With words anticipating the *Brown* decision, Sumner asserted that segregation gave all blacks a "peculiar brand," a clear and lasting "stigma" that "deprives them of these healthful animating influences.... It widens their separation from the rest of the community, and postpones that great day of reconciliation which is sure to come."

In a very early version of the logic that affirmative action defenders in the public university system would employ, Sumner made the radical leap that without the diversity that many groups bring to a school, "the whole system of public schools suffers also." He even went so far as to declare (italics are ours): *"The whites themselves are injured by the separation. Who can doubt this?"*

Then, in the passage that affected his contemporaries the most, the lawyer revealed a vision of what common schools in America could do:

> The school is the little world in which the child is trained for the larger world of life. It must, therefore, cherish and develop the virtues and the sympathies which are employed in the larger world. And since, according to our institutions, all classes meet, without distinction of color, in the performance of civil duties, so should they all meet, without distinction of color, in the school, beginning there those relations of equality which our Constitution and laws promise to all.

At his most prophetic, he forbiddingly warned the whole nation, "A degraded or neglected class, if left to themselves, will become more degraded and neglected." Segregation had to be ended, or a dark future for all was in store.

It was abundantly clear to Sumner that "prejudice is the child of ignorance. It is sure to prevail where people do not know each other." Anyone, or any institution, setting up barriers to this process "directly interferes with the laws of God."

Sumner realized he had been talking for a long time, even in an age when listeners were more patient and indeed anxious to be treated to fine, and extended, oratory. In fact, he had been speaking for about two hours, but he was not quite done. With Morris seated next to him, he spoke of his own experience of seeing young black law students in Paris. He reminded his spectators of how Massachusetts had ended slavery, repealed the marriage prohibition, and ceased segregated transportation, and now it was time to end the "last of [slavery's] footprints."

Taking his seat next to Morris after his argument, Sumner said that America had changed. In the words of legal scholar Andrew Kull, this legal team had set forth an argument "so comprehensive that the arguments of the next hundred years would not add significantly to the themes he developed." This was the first great charter drawn up for the entitlement of blacks to equal education. Yet the

Peleg Chandler, Morris and Sumner's opposing counsel in the *Roberts* case. *(Willard Photograph Collection; courtesy of the Social Law Library,
Boston)*

argument pointed to more than that. "Equality before the law" was
now a promise of those corresponding principles for all citizens.

This was quite an act to follow, especially because opposing counsel Peleg Chandler was a logician, not an orator on a par with Sumner. Sumner had asked the question, "Can any discrimination of
color or race, be made, under the Constitution and Laws of Massachusetts, among the children entitled to the benefit of our common schools?" The question Chandler began with showed their
differences in approach. The city solicitor had no interest in trying
to re-create, or even answer, the visceral social and moral argu-

ments Sumner had evoked but wanted instead to stick to the simple issue of whether Sarah Roberts was entitled to compensation of $600 from the city. So he asked, "Has the plaintiff been in fact excluded from public school instruction?" And if so, "has she been unlawfully excluded?" Chandler believed the city charter did give the School Committee these powers, but before he was able to elaborate much further, time had run out for the day, in part because of Sumner's lengthy argument. Chandler would continue the next day.

As Morris, Sumner, and the confident crowd left the court, Sumner found himself believing he could have done a much better job. Somewhat like Abraham Lincoln's dissatisfaction with his Emancipation Proclamation, Sumner was left uneasy, writing a few days later when sending the argument to his brother, "I could make it much better." As the true impact of the argument began sinking in, however, Sumner's view of it would change dramatically.

When court readjourned the next day, Chandler continued his unadorned argument. He did his best to begin sympathetically, demonstrating the respect he had for Sumner by admitting "many of the propositions of the counsel for the plaintiff." But Chandler, and probably Shaw too, resented Sumner's sanctimonious moral appeals, maintaining that the case should be argued "as one of pure law." Thus, the simple answer to his question of whether Sarah Roberts had been denied public school instruction was *no*. He emphasized that a distance of twelve hundred feet was actually reasonably close to her residence. Chandler declared that the five-year-old child had "no reason to complain" and cited instances in which a white child might not go to the school nearest her residence. To him, instruction at the Smith School was "as good as any other school['s] in the city." Ignoring the stigma of segregation that Sumner had espoused, the conservative Chandler thought the idea of blacks repudiating the Smith School made as much sense as "a white child [who] refuse[d] to go to her appropriate school, because it was white."

The crux of Chandler's legal argument lay in his affirmation of the administrative powers of the School Committee, all of which were granted under the city charter. Backing off from some of the more contentious statements about Sarah and her walk, he declined to offer his opinion on the expedience of separate schools. What Chandler wanted to make clear was the School Committee's *"legal right"* to create these schools if they saw fit, and then be "responsible to their own consciousness, and to the public." And yet, he could not avoid the validity of the schools completely, as he spoke again on how "this separation was no more unjust to blacks than the whites." Referring to Thomas Smith's campaign, Chandler said that little had changed since blacks had requested the school fifty years earlier, and he maintained that "the colored population were still in favor of the school." Of course, thanks to the very visible activism of the integrationist population, this was a difficult claim to support. In the flow of his argument, however, Chandler believed that he could confidently speak on behalf of the black community. He had more to add.

Chandler, in using the "separate but equal" logic that he hoped Justice Shaw would seize on in his final judgment, maintained that there was not a "wish or desire to deprive the colored race of any rights, legal or moral." And attempting to seem particularly sympathetic, Chandler claimed that "there was no desire to add to the prejudice and wrong already suffered by the colored population." He singled out the boycotting integrationists as "those who neglect these means," which help elevate their people. Finding their crusade quixotic and destructive, he chastised those who would "withdraw their children from the schools, and cherish a feeling of discontent and unhappiness." He crystallized the perception of so many Bostonians that this whole struggle was not only misguided and foolish but, more, that their discontented activist leaders were profoundly ungrateful, as they already had so many advantages not shared by other members of their race. Nell commented on this reasoning when he wrote,

> The position of the colored citizens of Boston is in many features a peculiar one; for while with truth it can be said that they enjoy cer-

tain facilities denied to their brethren in nearly all other sister cities, yet the extremes of equality and proscription meeting in their case, as indicated by the pro-slavery School Committee Board.

Chandler clearly did not see it that way. He sat down after having given a capable, though hardly inspired, defense of the status quo. All that remained was for the fathers of the city to speak.

# ELEVEN

# A Doctrine Is Born

Unlike the first hearing of the *Roberts* case, the appeal received much attention. On December 10 the *Daily Evening Traveler* devoted seven columns to it, almost the entire front page, printing Sumner's argument in its entirety. The editor commented on the unusual length of the piece for a newspaper but hoped that it would not stop readers from studying it. Most mainstream journalists of Boston had traditionally been hostile to the integrationists' demands, but now this paper called the argument "clear and convincing," "learned and sound—embracing a very comprehensive view of the whole matter."

Less surprising, the *Liberator* enthused over Morris and Sumner's handling of the case. Garrison called Sumner's argument "luminous and profound." In a particularly prophetic moment, Garrison acknowledged this was not just a matter of "temporary local interest," but "will be long matter of debate in this and other States, and the comprehensive view of Mr. Sumner will long be a treasure-house for other laborers to draw from." He had no idea how right he would be. As for the outcome of the case, Garrison had been so taken aback by the resonance of Sumner's argument, he forecast, "There can be no doubt, it seems to us, that it will be in favor of the plaintiff, and therefore against an odious complexion caste." The *Liberator,* over the course of multiple issues, also printed Sumner's argument in total.

Sumner's friends were equally pleased with his efforts. John Gorham Palfrey, a Unitarian minister and congressman, read the argument with "the highest satisfaction" and immediately predicted it would rank as one of Sumner's best-remembered acts. Estimating the opinion of the black community, Nell informed Sumner, "[Black Bostonians] repose confidence in you and are constantly praying for a successful *result* of your labors."

The argument made an impression on a future chief justice of the United States Supreme Court, Salmon P. Chase from Ohio, who enthusiastically suggested that the argument be published so as to accomplish a wider circulation of the message. None other than Benjamin Roberts came forward to carry out this idea, showing his pride in the argument Sumner had just written on behalf of his daughter. Only ten days after Sumner delivered his oration, Roberts had it in pamphlet form and for sale at the Anti-Slavery offices, and it became widely distributed. No correspondence exists, but this unusual publication clearly displays Sumner's willingness to use Roberts's printing shop as a symbolic effort, a coda to the argument itself.

One person who was not pleased with the efforts of the integrationists in court was Thomas Smith. He wrote a letter to the *Liberator* affirming his resolute belief that blacks could not count on anyone else to meet their educational needs, and thus, "We believe colored schools to be institutions, when properly conducted, of great advantage to the colored people." He did not run from the word *equality* but felt the existence of these schools was not a violation of it.

Nell believed that Smith was up to more than just editorial writing and was working clandestinely against a favorable decision. Nell fired off an angry letter to Sumner detailing "Our *industrious* enemy . . . an opponent to human progress." Though anxiously awaiting an "*immediate* and *favorable* Decision," Nell took comfort in his estimation that Smith's following was down to only fourteen members of the black community. Whatever the decision, "[Smith] has *lost* all claim to the good will of His *Brethren*."

A school meeting was held five days after the trial. A large crowd assembled, believing they would be learning the result of the case. They would have to wait another four months for that, so instead, the discussion began describing the trial that had excited so many.

Sumner's "eloquent argument" was spoken of with great approval; Sumner had already received much acclaim for his role in the suit, and that night the black community did not forget Morris and his "conduct of the entire case." Moving on, the discussion shifted to what might be their next step "should the Supreme Court return an adverse decision." Nell, perhaps with a premonition rooted in what was known about Shaw's feelings, reminded the audience that the great strategic general Napoleon always had a "next." It was decided that "should the *Bench* fail to award us justice, an appeal can and will be made to the *people* themselves." This was to be done by collecting a massive petition, utilizing citizens from "Cape Cod to Berkshire," to be presented to their legislators in the hope that they would establish a special law opening the schools to "every son and daughter of the Old Bay State." It was emphasized that if they should lose, it would be referred to as a *"temporary"* defeat.

The most contentious part of the evening came when a newcomer to Boston stood up with a substantial accusation. Lewis Hayden, who had just escaped from Kentucky, had already established a used-clothing store on Cambridge Street, and he brazenly embarked on a diatribe against black ministers' lack of involvement in the school struggle. Nell called his speech a "deserved reprimand," as Hayden named those who "retarded rather than accelerated our glorious movement." Many ministers had not supported the school boycott, and Hayden wondered whether their churches should be met with a similar boycott. Hayden distrusted all ministers after his family was separated at the auction block at the hands of a minister who sold a young Hayden for a pair of carriage horses. Hayden saw the black ministers of Boston as hardly more trustworthy. To him, these moderate ministers were "unworthy [of] the countenance of intelligent freemen."

He carried with him stories of bondage far from the Bay State. Hayden was born into a slave family in Lexington, Kentucky, in

1811. From a young age, he shared his mother's fierce hatred of slavery. This instinct was confirmed when the French general Lafayette, parading through downtown Lexington, saluted the ten-year-old-boy. Hayden remembered, "Lafayette was the most famous man I had ever heard of, and you can imagine how I felt, a slave-boy to be favored with his recognition."

Hayden served a clock peddler and learned to read from newspapers and his Bible. In 1842 he married Esther Harvey, and though they served separate masters, they found ways to be together. They had two children, but only one survived. Henry Clay, one of the most popular politicians of the era, purchased Esther and Lewis Hayden's child. Historians consider Clay a moderate on the slavery issue, but Hayden would have disagreed; soon after acquiring Hayden's wife and child, he decided to sell them. Hayden pleaded with the statesman, who coldly responded that he "had bought them and had sold them." The last sight Hayden had of his wife and child was of their being dragged away by slave traders.

Hayden married again and worked, on a lease from his owner, as a waiter in a Lexington hotel. During this period, he met a white Oberlin student named Calvin Fairbanks, who had already brought forty-one slaves north. When Fairbanks asked why he wanted to be free, Hayden responded, "Because I am a man." After a perilous route north, Hayden ended up in Canada. Once there, he wrote a letter to his former master. He explained that he was absent from his service because he had decided "to try my freedom and how it will seam [sic] to be my own master and manage my own matters and crack my own whip."

Indeed, upon seeing the clothing store Hayden maintained in Boston, one white man remarked, "Let those who are skeptical of what a slave can do, when he has no longer a master to oversee him, call at friend Hayden's store."

. . .

All the confident predictions of victory in the *Roberts* case that were heard at integrationist meetings, or proudly predicted in the *Liberator*, came crashing down in March 1850.

The court's unanimous decision, written by Shaw, was at last issued. The devastating judgment began with one sentence that ended all hopes for Sarah Roberts to attend an integrated Boston school come fall of 1850: "The general school committee of the city of Boston have power, under the constitution and laws of this commonwealth, to make provisions for the instruction of colored children in separate schools established exclusively for them, and to prohibit their attendance upon the other schools."

It was written in a grand style that would partly account for the weighty impact of the decision in the decades to come. Shaw recapitulated the facts of the case that mattered most to him, noting "the fifth of a mile or seventy rods," the difference between the Smith School and the nearest white school to the Roberts residence. The verdict was laid out with all the austere and masterly method of Justice Shaw, and details such as this gave it authority.

To Shaw, "this is a question of power, or of the legal authority of the committee entrusted by the city with this department of public instruction." He reasoned that if the School Committee did possess that legal authority, the decision over whether to have separate schools (or not) resided with them, not Judge Shaw.

Though Shaw would use different reasoning later in the decision, at that point he was writing in support of administrative judgment. Sumner had anticipated this logic when he acknowledged the School Committee had many powers, but to allow them to discriminate would be to "place the Committee above the Constitution." Shaw did not see it this way. The problem with his argument was that to decide the case on account of the School Committee's constitutional powers, he would also have to show that these powers could overrule the individual legal rights of citizens or, as Sumner put it, their intrinsic "equality before the law." To accomplish all this Shaw would need a legal sleight of hand.

What Shaw did was to accept "equality before the law," and then seize on its ambiguity to create a seemingly more benevolent and legally justifiable defense of segregated schools: separate but equal.

Shaw described Charles Sumner in his decision as "the learned and eloquent advocate of the plaintiff." He extolled Sumner's "equality before the law" as a grand phrase, one that "ought to appear in a declaration of rights," because it "pervades and animates the whole spirit of our constitution of free government." This was hollow praise. Shaw effectively discarded the guarantees of equality in the Massachusetts constitution.

So while Shaw praised the "equality before the law" axiom, he found he could not agree with Sumner's full application of it. This would mean that, for example, "men and women are legally clothed with the same civil and political powers." Shaw found it too simple to declare equality for all because "what those rights are, to which individuals, in the infinite variety of circumstances by which they are surrounded in society, are entitled, must depend on laws adapted to their respective relations and conditions."

While there is no denying that there are nuances in the law, constitutional scholar Leonard Levy has compared this paragraph to a famous satirical pronouncement in George Orwell's *Animal Farm:*

*ALL ANIMALS ARE EQUAL*
*BUT SOME ANIMALS ARE MORE EQUAL THAN OTHERS*

Though Shaw claimed blacks were full citizens of the Commonwealth, based on his reading of "equality before the law," this did not mean that there could not be separate schools for them. Especially when he saw no legislation forbidding such a practice.

Returning to his logic of administrative judgment, Shaw observed that there were schools for exceptional pupils, such as the Boston Latin School, schools for one sex, and, most obviously, age divisions that the School Committee established. Shaw felt that this power of classification could reasonably include race and was therefore not incompatible with legal equality.

Yet what of the prejudice inherent in this system?

Shaw wrote, in a sentence that survived as his chief legacy: "This prejudice, if it exists, is not created by law, and probably cannot be changed by law." In this oft-quoted passage, Shaw rejects the responsibility of the courts to ensure "equality before the law." One hundred and six years later, the Supreme Court would declare that the law could indeed change, or at least challenge, any inequality caused by prejudice.

Shaw also rebuked Sumner's argument in favor of integration because of its social good. Ignoring the success of integrated schools all over Massachusetts, he expressed a far less optimistic view of integration: "Whether this distinction and prejudice, existing in the opinion and feelings of the community, would not be as effectually fostered by compelling colored and white children, to associate together in the same schools, may well be doubted."

In conclusion, Shaw chose to ignore the humiliation of Sarah's walk, indeed expressing puzzlement as to why the plaintiffs would sue over a small difference in literal distance. Sarah's walk "to school from her father's house, is not such, in our opinion, as to render the regulation in question unreasonable, still less illegal."

Shaw crafted a progenitor for all such legal arguments to follow, one that sought to validate and defend legal segregation. It was one of the most influential decisions of the entire antebellum period and so much more. Given the racial attitudes of the time, Shaw could have probably dismissed the suit without much concern for the "equality" of the black community, but he had not done that. By accepting Sumner's premise of legal equality, Shaw was able to answer in advance future challenges posed to states and judges that wanted to impose segregation after the creation of the Fourteenth Amendment and its guarantees of "equal protection of the laws." His rationale acknowledged equal protection while denying any constitutional requirement to preclude separating the races. "Separate but equal" would become one of the most successful and useful legal concepts ever fashioned. Whether or not he intended to, Shaw had produced an idea that would long outlive him.

The philosophical Sumner had always disliked the written opinions of Shaw, finding them devoid of life or learning while still managing to be far too verbose (which for Sumner was saying something). This decision gave Sumner a new resentment of the formidable judge, a man who maintained liberal sentiments that somehow never appeared in his stately verdicts.

Sending back the books he had used to write his argument to his friend John Jay, Sumner somberly remarked that he used them, "as you have probably seen—unsuccessfully." Smarting from the loss, Sumner maintained, "I am sure, however, that the court in their opinion, have not answered my argt [argument]." Then, in either a moment of more positive thinking or just an affirmation of his bruised ego, he predicted that in ten years the rest of the law profession would concur with his argument, and not Shaw's.

Most of Boston was pleased with the decision, but there were dissenters other than the *Liberator*. The *New Englander* had seen the determination of the black community over the previous decade and felt that "our school system will suffer from an agitation on this subject which cannot be stopped while the separate schools are maintained." The writer felt that Shaw had ignored the legal and moral rights of blacks, as well as what was practical and expedient for the school system. The article closed by urging the black taxpayers to keep up their agitation until, using elements of Morris's and Sumner's arguments, this "stigma" was removed.

On April 22 dejected integrationists convened at the Belknap Street Church. Old John Hilton, the wily rights veteran who had thought his struggle fulfilled, wearily presided over the meeting. The saddened crowd gathered not only to consider the court's decision but to reenergize the community by planning "measures for further action." Nell read Shaw's decision to the group, for all those who had not yet heard the details.

In a resolution whose tone was stern and still dogged, the assemblage characterized their reaction as one of "surprise and regret." Respectfully disagreeing with Shaw's interpretation of the state's 1780 constitution, the integrationists vowed to now shift their efforts to pressure the legislature until they could *"establish justice."* They recorded "We pledge to each other our unceasing efforts, till the struggle results in victory."

A cordial thanks was offered to Sumner and Morris, though only Morris was in attendance to accept it. The duo was called "faithful, generous and devoted." It was lamented that thanks were all the community could afford to offer the lawyers, but that "renders their championship of our cause the more marked and honorable—

their reward having been found, as we believe, in the pleasure of the task."

A similar proclamation was made in commemoration of Benjamin Roberts's fidelity to his "honorable stand" on behalf of his daughter and "the school rights of the colored people of Boston." He was assured that "in the history of our struggles, and, we hope, our successes, his name will not be forgotten." A committee was even appointed to plan a "complimentary meeting or festival as a tribute to Benjamin F. Roberts for his sacrifices and efforts." There is no record of such an occasion coming to fruition.

People also showed appreciation for Nell's labors in putting together gallant events, such as the recent Juvenile Exhibition, which raised money for the temporary schools. And the group soundly recognized those parents who had taken the initiative to put their children in these schools or sought means to have their children educated outside of the Smith School. The leaders told them that they must continue to "bide their time" until the dual school system was at last ended.

Many were disappointed with the outcome of the case, but none as keenly as Benjamin Roberts. He was shocked and incensed that judges could be this "blind and deaf to the legal rights of the Massachusetts colored citizen." It was a "great injustice against the colored people perpetrated by those agents in the public service," and a "result of which was different from the expectations of us all." Now the *Roberts* case fell in line with the history of James Easton's school, Hosea Easton's church, and the failure of Benjamin Roberts's own aborted newspaper as another well-intentioned, glorious venture that somehow ended in defeat. But he would not give up.

Roberts decided to take on a mission of traveling to towns all around Massachusetts to obtain signatures for a massive petition to be presented to the legislature in favor of allowing all children to attend the schools closest to their home, regardless of their color. He wrote an announcement of this plan in the *Liberator,* explaining, "As it will require means to prosecute this effort, the friends of equal rights are requested to govern themselves accordingly." Roberts's proposal to travel in the state on this mission would be a surprising and typically resilient solution to his problems.

All of America was talking about the sensation caused by escaped slave Henry "Box" Brown and his novel and daring method of reaching freedom. Benjamin Roberts resolved to attach himself to the phenomenon. Brown had quite a story to tell. In one of the most ingenious plots of the slavery era, the 5'8" and 200-pound Brown was sealed inside a baize-lined container held shut by five hickory loops and marked THIS SIDE UP WITH CARE, and then mailed from Richmond to an abolitionist in Philadelphia. When the package arrived and the anxious abolitionist opened it at his house, Brown coolly stood up, asking, "How do you do, gentlemen?" and with that said, he promptly fainted.

Predictably, Brown was an immediate celebrity in and outside of antislavery circles. Now he was ready for a grand tour, and Benjamin Roberts received the honor of coordinating it and speaking alongside Brown. Coming off his role in a well-publicized legal case, Roberts could only increase his fame by traveling with Brown. Unfortunately, Brown was also notoriously difficult to deal with, so it proved not to be an easy task. It was decided that Brown would tell his own story, and Roberts would present a lecture entitled "The Condition of the Colored People in the United States." Behind the two men would be unscrolled a grand panorama painted in the style of the Hudson River School called *The Mirror of Slavery*. Featuring more than fifty pictures, the panorama showed the African family through the destruction of the Old World and, ultimately, men and women at the auction block and being punished. The two men also used famous paintings of the American landscape, such as Washington's *Tomb at Mount Vernon*, with powerful and shocking portrayals of the bondage permeating and corrupting these places.

Roberts had the pleasure of having the tour open in Boston on a spring evening in April 1850, in Washington Hall on Bromfield Street. Adults paid twenty-five cents and children were admitted at half price. After the performance, the duo set out for the rest of Massachusetts, where they were met with rave reviews and thronging crowds. But Roberts had not forgotten about the school issue, and he spent time collecting signatures and working on a report on segregated schools.

Roberts presented this report to an assembly at the Belknap Street Church on August 5, 1850. He utilized Sumner's message of "equal before the law," expanding on his progressive argument about the devastating effects of segregation. He saw these separate schools as the reason young black and white children who played sports together would not know each other in adulthood. For the black children, separate schools gave them an "ill-feeling" and there was nothing "to induce the pupil, if promising, to exert himself." He shared what he had seen while traveling in the Bay State: places where "the most brilliant scholars are colored," in fully integrated schools. Showing off the petitions he had collected, he then read, to the great pleasure of the audience, the names of the famous people who had signed them. Roberts declared "EQUAL SCHOOL RIGHTS"; "Nothing more, we ask—nothing less, are we prepared quietly to receive."

As encouraging as Roberts's continued work was, the integrationists had lost much of their momentum with their defeat in the *Roberts* case. Numbers were beginning to creep up again at the Smith School. The boycott could not hold forever. Part of the reason was the scattering of the boycott leadership, both in terms of vocation and location. In June, Morris, with Loring and Sumner proudly watching, was admitted to practice as a counselor and attorney of the Circuit and District Courts of the United States. Thus, Morris was now completely occupied with his burgeoning law practice; Nell was headed back to Rochester (not to work with Douglass this time, but to rest in an effort to restore his ailing health); Roberts was all over New England speaking; and the old sage Hilton effectively entered into an earned retirement from the school fight.

Yet the main reason the integrationists could not keep up their furious pace of school agitation was not the loss of the case but the rise of an issue that exploded in Boston, effectively diverting their attention and threatening to permanently disrupt their lives. It turned out that even a free black was really, always, just a slave.

# PART 3

# Let Us Be Bold

*EQUAL SCHOOL RIGHTS...*
*Nothing more, we ask — nothing less,*
*are we prepared quietly to receive.*

BENJAMIN F. ROBERTS

# TWELVE

# Vigilance

February 15, 1851, three years to the day that Benjamin Roberts had tried to enroll Sarah in the school closest to her house, began with a rainy, brooding morning.

When Shadrach Minkins reported to work at Taft's Cornhill Coffee House, he had no reason to believe that this would be unlike any other day. His place of employment was located on Cornhill Street, near the *Liberator*'s and Benjamin Roberts's printing establishment, and only one block from the courthouse. This restaurant-hotel provided Minkins with steady employment since he had arrived in Boston ten months earlier, after escaping slavery in the shipping center of Norfolk, Virginia.

What Minkins did not know as he arrived for work was that three days earlier, an ugly and hardened slave catcher named John Caphart—upon whom Harriet Beecher Stowe would later base the foul slave dealer Haley in *Uncle Tom's Cabin*—had quietly arrived in Boston from Virginia. He carried with him legal papers from Minkins's smarting owner, and more, a warrant for Minkins's arrest from a local judge.

The law enforcement agents who were assigned to assist Caphart knew that Minkins would have to be taken discreetly, so they sat down in the restaurant and ordered a cup of coffee, not knowing that the very man serving them was the man they intended to capture. When Minkins followed one of the men out of the room to give him his change, he was identified, seized, and taken away without resistance. Through a back exit they went and into the courthouse.

Word of Minkins's arrest spread like wildfire all over Beacon Hill. The mayor had already been called for reinforcements at the courthouse, because protesting masses were expected shortly. Within an hour, about 150 people crammed into the courtroom. An onlooker remembered that the mainly black crowd seemed "as if they were about to spring over the rail and tear the prisoner away." There were also a number of abolitionist lawyers who had caught wind of what was occurring and had rushed to the courthouse to help prevent the fugitive's return to slavery. But Minkins only wanted to speak to a lawyer who shared his skin color.

That was Robert Morris, and the next few hours would reveal something new about the usually calm and poised lawyer. Morris was about to do something utterly dramatic.

. . .

In 1850 the Union hung in the balance. In the same month that Shadrach Minkins had escaped from slavery, a new bill was debated in Washington that would have an immeasurable impact on his future. Three statesmen who had defined the previous era, Daniel Webster of Massachusetts, Henry Clay of Kentucky, and John Calhoun of South Carolina, were now all close to the end of their illustrious careers, and a compromise was needed to ensure that sectional tensions rooted in slavery and the differing economies would not cause the Union to die along with the three. While on his deathbed, John Quincy Adams told Charles Sumner, "I should like to teach this Mr. Daniel Webster that there is something more valuable than the Union—it is justice."

But Webster would never learn such a lesson; his unflinching commitment to preserving the Union allowed him to advocate a southern measure such as the Fugitive Slave Law, one of the five elements making up the Compromise of 1850. To Emerson, "The word *liberty* in the mouth of Mr. Webster sounds like the word *love* in the mouth of a courtesan." For the *Liberator,* the Fugitive Slave

Law was "to be resisted, disobeyed, and trampled under foot, at all hazards."

A decree as extreme as the Fugitive Slave Law could have passed only as part of a comprehensive compromise package, and in this case, a package that was celebrated as the only thing that could stave off secession and possibly civil war. President Millard Fillmore found it a repugnant aspect of the larger compromise, but signed off on it anyway without any cabinet debate. The existing fugitive laws had been vague and dependent on each state's level of support for slavery. Under this new act, captured blacks would not be allowed trials before their return to the South. Habeas corpus, the celebrated protection against illegal confinement, was a nonexistent concept for blacks. Any black person, no matter how long his or her family had been free, could be taken into bondage without any kind of judicial hearing. The return of anyone to slavery was now an administrative, not a judicial, process. Furthermore, the federal government was an active partner with the slaveholder in tracking down the missing laborers. There were harsh fines and jail sentences for not only aiding a fugitive but for not helping to capture him.

The Fugitive Slave Law had a strange and powerful impact: it forced whites who were unconcerned with slavery to suddenly become involved in the maintenance of it. Historian Leon Litwack writes, "Whites might differ on extending political and social rights to Negros, but many of them shared a common revulsion at the sight of slave-hunters searching for human prey in northern neighborhoods."

The effect of the law on northern free blacks was immediate and drastic, creating an unimaginable sense of anxiety for all. Concerns for civil rights were almost a moot point in Boston now, as the most pressing issue was living each day without getting caught and sent back to a ghastly system. The alarm was keenest for those who had recently escaped and would have slave catchers looking for them. It was estimated that about one in every four fugitive slaves in America passed through Boston at some point on his or her journey, and many, like Shadrach Minkins, stayed on. When they arrived in

Boston, they might stay at various Underground Railroad stations in the city, including Rev. Leonard Grimes's church, Peter Howard's Cambridge Street Barbershop, and Lewis Hayden's house on Southac (now Phillips) Street. When Harriet Beecher Stowe visited Hayden's residence, she found thirteen fugitives staying on the premises. Hayden had a tunnel in the back of the house that allowed for clandestine entrances and quick exits. It extended for more than several hundred yards, though where on Beacon Hill the fugitive would exit is now unknown.

In addition to shelter, Hayden would provide clothes from his store for the fugitives. Morris was available for legal help, and John Sweat Rock, Boston's first black doctor, attended to injuries and ailments a fugitive might have developed. The women of the community were particularly important, as they supplied food, shelter, and medical help.

The Reverend Theodore Parker speculated that in October 1850 there were between four and six thousand fugitives in the city. That number may have been high, but about one in five black people in Boston was thought to be an escaped slave. Therefore, the effect of the Fugitive Slave Law was devastating on the black community. Within sixty hours of its passage, 40 former slaves had already left Boston. That number would soon climb past 200. Robert Morris's African Methodist Church alone quickly lost 85 members of its congregation, individuals who hastily departed for Canada. The law also caused a mass exodus of black sailors from Boston. The district known as New Guinea, where black sailors lived, had 683 inhabitants in 1840. Five years after the Fugitive Slave Law's passage, only 50 people were living there.

Nell, Hayden, and Morris wasted no time in mobilizing Beacon Hill against the Fugitive Slave Law. Quoting Patrick Henry, they declared that America would have to give them *"Liberty or death."* Morris was named the head of a special committee that would prepare a report on how the community should handle this crisis. Five days later, a crowded meeting at the African Meeting House heard his committee's recommendations, as read by Nell. Evoking liberation images from the Bible and the American Revolution, they now called upon a higher law to justify the actions that would soon be taken. Pressure had to be applied on the commissioners not to recover fugitives; clergymen had to preach on the immorality of the law; and the whole community was encouraged to shelter and defend all fugitives. Joshua B. Smith, a caterer, brandished a long knife and told all in attendance to purchase Colt revolvers.

It was not just the black community that organized. An interracial group named the Vigilance Committee was formed in October 1850 in one of the largest meetings the hallowed Faneuil Hall had ever seen. To understand the depths of resentment that the Fugitive Slave Law stirred, consider the remarkable nature of a group, formed publicly, composed of some of the most famous citizens of Boston for the express purpose of breaking the law. The Vigilance Committee may never have been as effective as the loose network of the black community in helping fugitives, yet the fact that now there was a large and organized group joining in what blacks had been doing for decades showed that something fundamental had shifted in the urgency of the abolitionist cause in Boston. The group, which went from eighty to two hundred members in one year, boarded and lodged fugitives, gave them small sums of money, educated them on their legal rights, and helped them find jobs in Boston. Robert Morris used his ability to raise money in the black community as part of the eight-member Finance Committee. But it was Nell who may have been the most important day-to-day operative, as he administered and coordinated relief for the Vigilance Committee.

Garrison had once boasted that no slave would ever be taken from Boston. But Garrison's claim had made its way south, and it became a matter of pride there to return a slave taken from the "cradle of liberty." Slave catchers were obsessed with taking a fugitive from the place that was the embodiment of all things abolitionist. The very success of the Fugitive Slave Law seemed to ride on whether it could be carried out in Boston.

Frederick Douglass declared that "the only way to make the Fugitive Slave Law a dead letter is to make half a dozen or more dead kidnappers." Benjamin Roberts printed one thousand broadsides cautioning blacks against even speaking to police officers and plastered them all over Boston. So the stakes were even higher than the human life of the fugitive. The law meant that abolitionists attempting to save a fugitive would also be putting their lives in peril.

All of this weighed on Robert Morris, and he was determined to keep Shadrach Minkins free. Minkins was the first runaway arrested under the new law, though the Crafts had been close. Ellen and William Craft were already famous nationally for their previous escape from slavery. Ellen, who was particularly light-skinned, dressed up as a white man traveling north for "medical treatment." To cover her soft cheeks, she wore a scarf around her mouth for her toothache. Because she was illiterate, she claimed along the way that she was too arthritic to write. Instead, her devoted "slave," William, handled all matters. The darker-skinned William answered all questions, bought the tickets, and made an elaborate show of taking care of "Massa." Their plan worked to perfection.

They were soon touring with their fascinating escape story, but their notoriety made them vulnerable for recapture, and so they settled in Boston. William established a furniture business in Cambridge, and Ellen worked as a seamstress. Their tranquility, however, was short-lived. In October 1850, three southerners arrived from Georgia planning to make the shrewd Crafts the first slaves taken back under the new law. However, the slave catchers were not careful enough to keep their mission a secret. Their own home paper published their plans before they even left for Boston, so they entered a Boston that was already on its guard. Handbills, hastily printed by Benjamin Roberts, were posted throughout the city with descriptions of the slave catchers.

The fugitive hunters were constantly harassed, arrested for petty crimes (thanks to the wrangling of abolitionist lawyers), and nearly killed by a black mob. Lower Beacon Hill turned into a fortress; the *Pennsylvania Freeman* reported: "Many of the houses in Belknap and Cambridge streets are provided with ammunition.... Swords and dirks, &c, are plenty, and bayonets 'right up.'" Ellen was first hidden at Loring's house, and then with Unitarian minister Theodore Parker, and William left his shop to hide at Lewis Hayden's house.

Lewis Hayden, escaped slave and fearless community leader. *(US 5278.36.25 volume 4, Siebert scrapbooks. By permission of the Houghton Library, Harvard University)*

The week reached its climax when the slave catchers came to Hayden's house only to find a group of armed black men in front of it. The doors were double locked, the windows were barred, and two kegs of gunpowder lay on the front porch. As the slave catchers watched in disbelief, Hayden lit a torch and held it close to the kegs, removing any doubts that he was prepared to blow up not only himself but anyone else in the vicinity before William Craft would be taken back to slavery. Hayden's defiance was as much as the slave catchers needed to see. They were not ready for the violence required to capture William. That night Rev. Theodore Parker informed the southern slave catchers that they would not survive the next day in Boston, and with that, they were on their way back to Georgia.

Boston had won its first battle over fugitive slaves. A friend wrote Sumner, who had watched the whole ordeal, "You have whipped Webster." Senator Daniel Webster was furious; the carefully held peace he had fashioned was being jeopardized in his home state. The Crafts' ordeal only solidified Bostonians' resolve and confidence in their ability to defend their fugitives. These were the powerful forces poor Shadrach Minkins had the wretched fortune to enter when he was arrested on February 15, 1851.

. . .

At the courthouse that day Morris was one of six abolitionist lawyers who were desperately trying any legal maneuver to buy Minkins some time. Morris's friend Loring also joined him, but his former cocounselor Charles Sumner resisted involvement because of a pending Senate nomination. Richard Henry Dana, a brilliant abolitionist lawyer, also appeared willing to help. Loring approached Minkins, but the overwhelmed and terrified fugitive wanted to talk only to the black lawyer. Morris and Minkins spoke for a few minutes, as Morris was able to obtain his permission to file for a writ of habeas corpus.

Commissioner George Curtis, sitting in the judge's seat, wanted to hurry the process along, though the lawyers, having just gathered fifteen minutes earlier, begged for more time. Under the Fugitive Slave Law, Minkins merely had to be identified and was entitled to neither the protection of habeas corpus nor a trial. There was no telling how little time Minkins had, for there were examples of hearings lasting only five minutes before a fugitive was sent south. The fact that Commissioner George Curtis, on whom Minkins's fate depended, had recently organized a pro–Fugitive Slave Law rally also made the possibility of victory bleak. Yet the commissioner showed some equanimity when, upon hearing the abolitionist's case that Minkins could not be taken away until they had studied the Virginian's documents, it was decided that the court would recuse itself for three days. Constables cleared the courtroom.

One black man, before being removed from the courtroom, told Minkins, "Don't be afraid, we will stand by you," to which Minkins, sensing something dramatic was about to happen, responded, "If I die, I die like a man." Morris and the lawyers were allowed to stay inside and continue to plan Minkins's defense.

Dana left to seek out Judge Shaw with the habeas corpus request Morris had prepared. The usually cantankerous Shaw was in a particularly foul mood that day, thinking Dana and his abolitionist friends were trying to obstruct the wise compromise his friend Webster had worked so hard to achieve. Back at the Court House, Morris escorted his mentor Loring out of the chaotic scene, and then stopped in front of the building to address the two hundred people crowded there, all desperate for information about the slave's fate. After a few hurried words, he returned to the strategy session inside. Morris was told by Deputy Marshall to knock when he wanted to be let back in so that they could keep anyone else from entering.

Over the next fifteen minutes, Morris, trying to hide his face under a black hat, slipped in and out of the heavily guarded Court House twice more, as he and members of the community outside made quick preparations for what was about to occur. A boy standing within a few feet of the doorway heard Morris and another black man whispering. The man asked Morris how many white men were standing between the crowd and the prisoner. The answer being only eight or nine, Morris informed him that he thought they had "a good chance." It would soon become clear to the boy what they had a good chance of doing. The tension was palpable, as a handful of anxious guards stood between the vast, fuming crowd and a courtroom containing Minkins.

The time was right.

Just as it looked as though Morris would discretely once again slip back into the Court House, he violently threw open the great doors. In the shocked pause, Hayden and twenty armed black men stormed in. Guards struggled to keep their grip on the door Morris had flung open, but it was too late. Seeing the madness descending on him, Minkins got up to run, but the two guards closest to him frantically warned him that he would be shot if he left the courtroom. These guards had only a few moments before the intruders were upon them, and they were thrown aside with the same force that the men protecting the Court House door had been greeted with. One newspaper wrote it was "impossible to describe the fury of the mob."

Minkins was grabbed, put on the shoulders of four men, and carried out of the courtroom and down the stairs into the street. Everything happened so quickly that no shots were fired, and the constables were so shocked that no one even chased after the seemingly unstoppable band.

One witness saw Morris waving his hat like a gallant general and yelling, "Go ahead, men." The company passed Court Street and turned onto Cambridge, leading to the foot of black Beacon Hill. It took them only a matter of minutes to be within the geographic confines of the black community, and once there, the nerve-racking liberation of a federal prisoner seemed to turn into a festive parade, with blacks cheering and waving handkerchiefs. Morris stayed next to Minkins, keeping his arm around the frightened fugitive. One black woman stopped the party long enough to touch Minkins's head and, convinced that they had truly saved him, cried out, "God bless you." A friend of Minkins's saw him being carried away. Later, when asked if he said anything to him, he joked, "He appeared to be in a great hurry, and it is against my principles to stop a man when he is in a hurry!"

Indeed time was of the essence, as police would be swarming the Hill any minute. The cab driver whom Hayden had arranged saw the great throng surrounding him and refused to move. Livid at his cowardice, Morris and Hayden got out of the cab, needing a new plan. They then led Minkins away from the crowd and took him to hide in the attic of an elderly black widow living a few doors down from Hayden on Southac Street. Minkins would be ushered out of Boston that night and begin a journey to freedom in Canada.

With Minkins safe, all Hayden and Morris had to worry about was their own self-preservation. They were now in an incredibly vulnerable legal position, since there were hundreds of witnesses to the federal crime they had just carried out. They resolved not to flee but instead to return to work as if nothing had happened.

. . .

Over the course of the preceding ten years, members of the Boston black community had engaged in many direct actions, blocking the entrance to the segregated school or refusing to leave the white section of trains—but nothing received the attention that Shadrach Minkins's "release" did. Suddenly, the actions of this small community became the most talked about story in the nation. In fact, news of the rescue soon reached the desk of the president. An incensed Millard Fillmore held a special cabinet session and quickly issued a proclamation calling for the vigorous prosecution of the rescuers, as well as civil and military assistance in recapturing Minkins. Kentucky senator Henry Clay declared in front of a packed Senate chamber:

> By whom was the mob impelled onward? By our own race? No, sir, but by negros [sic]; by African descendants; by people who possess no part, as I contend, in our political system; and the question which arises is, whether we shall have law, and whether the majesty of Government shall be maintained or not; whether we shall have a Government of white men or black men in the cities of this country.

Little did Senator Clay know that this mob in far-off Boston was being led by none other than Lewis Hayden, a man who might never have sought to escape from slavery had Clay not so callously sold off his wife and daughter.

Papers across the country carried the remarkable Minkins escape as their lead story for more than a week. The *New York Herald* called the actions led by Morris and Hayden "the greatest outrage that ever occurred in the United States." In the South, the *Savannah Republican* called Boston "a black speck in the map, disgraced."

Equally unhappy were many Boston papers. While abolitionists were delighted by the mob's success, the *Boston Courier* called the blacks "an army of desperadoes" and added, "The question is no longer confined to the executing of the fugitive slave law. The point to be determined now is whether any law shall prevail in Boston."

Animosity toward Boston blacks had never been higher, as the article suggested that blacks, because of recent sympathy from prominent whites, thought they no longer had to obey the law. The headline of the *Boston Daily Times* was "Black Empire of Massachusetts." The *Daily Commonwealth* called Morris's and Hayden's friends the "best organized mobs in the history of the state." Considering the Boston Tea Party, this was an unwitting compliment. The spirit of those revolutionary actions was infusing the spirit of this new resistance. Crispus Attucks had died only a few hundred feet from the courthouse scene of the Minkins insurrection.

Morris returned to work after helping to save Minkins, but he could not long avoid the consequences of his actions. Two weeks after the affair, he was one of ten Bostonians arrested for their part in the escape. A small crowd formed around Morris as he was apprehended, though no riot broke out. A sum of two thousand dollars was needed to bail the imprisoned Morris out, and none other than a former mayor of Boston provided the funds. The powerful Josiah Quincy had known Morris for some time, liking him enough to attend his wedding, and now came through with support for Morris in this high-profile case.

In an incident replete with ironies, also arrested was Morris's adversary in the school struggle, Thomas Paul Smith. Nothing more perfectly demonstrated the way the urgency of the fugitive struggles had swept away concerns for all previous issues. Morris and Smith, bitter enemies only a month earlier, were united in this a life-and-death struggle.

Before Morris's case could be taken up, Thomas Sims, another fugitive, was arrested. Sims was a particularly young-looking twenty-three-year-old bricklayer and a former Savannah slave. On April 4, Sims was arrested under the false pretenses of theft, but knowing the real reason he was being detained, Sims put up a dogged fight, wounding one officer with a knife before being brought into custody. Once subdued and apprehended, Sims was taken to the courthouse. No one could now claim that Boston could not learn from the past. As Bostonians watched with awe, their courthouse was chained and roped while up to five hundred police officers stood waiting for a repeat of the Minkins rescue.

Only certain safe individuals were allowed in the courthouse, though they too had to pass under the chains. This resulted in one comical moment, as Theodore Parker wrote to Charles Sumner of his recent nemesis: "Think of old stiff-necked Lemuel visibly going under the chain! That was a spectacle!" Massachusetts's law prevented the use of jails in slave cases, so a makeshift prison cell was made for Sims in a federal jury room on the third floor of the courthouse. While he waited for nine days in this room overlooking Boston, a collection of abolitionist lawyers brought a writ of habeas corpus on account of the unconstitutionality of the Fugitive Slave Law before Chief Justice Shaw.

Fifteen years earlier, Loring had been able to convince Shaw that slavery could not extend to Massachusetts, and thus the young slave girl Med was free. But political winds had changed, and Shaw was a devoted Whig who saw the Fugitive Slave Law as the only way to hold the fragile nation, and an equally fragile political party, together. Shaw's declaration long ago that "bond slavery cannot exist because it is contrary to natural right and repugnant to numerous provisions of the Constitution and laws" was now a distant memory. Shaw, in the same casual manner with which he accepted the role of prejudice in segregated schools, now ruled that slavery had existed long before the Constitution. Thus the peculiar institution of slavery could only be "regulated to a limited extent... in this spirit it behooves all persons bound to obey the laws of the United States, to consider and regard them."

Whereas the *Roberts* case was an enormous defeat for the abolitionist cause, this Shaw decision would actually send a man back into bondage.

Though Sims was seemingly out of the reach of the black community, plans were still being hatched. Hayden and an interracial duo of ministers, the Reverends Leonard Grimes and Thomas Wentworth Higginson, developed a plan whereby stacks of mattresses would be stored in law offices, possibly Morris's, close to the courthouse. At a designated time, Sims would then jump out of the third-floor window and be carried away to freedom! When Rev. Grimes was allowed to visit the imprisoned fugitive, the desperate young man agreed to the plan, but it was not to be. In the twilight of the chosen day, Hayden and Higginson arrived in front of the courthouse to witness diligent workers applying iron bars to Sims's lone window.

At 4:30 a.m. on April 11, Sims was taken out of his makeshift jail cell with tears running down his face. A mighty force of armed men led him on a short trek down to Boston Harbor, where a boat waited to take him back to slave life. On his march to the ship bound for Savannah, Sims passed over the very spot where Crispus Attucks had bled for freedom eighty-one years earlier. Black and white abolitionists despondently watched Sims leaving.

No longer could it be said that Boston had not lost a fugitive.

. . .

By November, attention had shifted to those who had assisted Minkins. Morris and Hayden now faced the legal consequences of their actions. In August, Morris spoke at the annual British West India Emancipation Day, where two years earlier he had stood alongside Emerson on a pristine summer day with hopes of success in the *Roberts* case and no notion of the Fugitive Slave calamities to come. That year's observance was dark and rainy, and Morris spoke on the Minkins case and what it would mean for the future of slavery in America.

Unfortunately, Morris never left a personal record of his internal state in these months of awaiting trial, but it is not hard to imagine the turmoil he must have felt while facing federal treason and conspiracy charges. If that was not bad enough, he knew that the president of the United States and Massachusetts's most illustrious senator were applying pressure to see him convicted. Morris had worked tirelessly to become a lawyer, and by his mid-twenties he had already overcome staggering obstacles of poverty and discrimination to be recognized by prominent white Bostonians. Now he faced charges that would not simply disbar him but take away his freedom. All this he did for a stranger.

If it could be proven that the attack on the courtroom had been premeditated, then Morris could be found guilty of the capital crime of treason, which was possibly punishable by death. Indeed, Morris had spent long hours at Hayden's Cambridge Street store with leaders such as Parker, Phillips, Remond, and Grimes, where much strategizing to protect fugitives had taken place. However, everything happened so quickly with the Minkins rescue that this type of planning would have been unlikely.

Morris had the honor of being defended in court by a United States senator, New Hampshire's John Hale. Hale, nearing the end of his first term, had all but given up hope for reelection because of his increasingly outspoken abolitionism. Now, the senator decided to concentrate his efforts on affecting local events that were more suited to his moral sensibility. Politically he called himself "a doomed man." For someone with little to lose politically, defending a black man and other "conspirators" against charges the government brought seemed a perfectly sensible thing to do.

At a glance, one might have confused the pudgy and stocky Hale with Illinois senator Stephen Douglass, though they could not have been more ideologically separate. Hale possessed a gentlemanly manner that only thinly veiled rougher, more country sensibilities. Fortunately for Morris, years of combating proslavery men in the Senate made Hale a lawyer very much like Morris, employing forthright, commonsensical appeals laced with humor.

As for whether Morris would receive much sympathy from the presiding judge, Morris needed only to ask Loring about Judge Benjamin Curtis. Fifteen years earlier, it had been Curtis who opposed Loring in the *Med* case, arguing for the return of the young girl to slavery. His willingness to preserve the conservative status quo, coupled with his natural ambition and considerable intellect, helped Curtis attain a powerful judgeship. Most ominously for Morris, Curtis was part of Daniel Webster's loyal inner circle of friends, and Webster saw the actions of men like Morris as "treason! Treason! TREASON! And nothing else."

The biggest news in the days before Morris's legal reckoning was that thanks to Webster's influence, Curtis had been appointed an associate judge to the United States Supreme Court. Unfortunately, before he had to leave for Washington, he would still have time to preside over Morris's trial, where a conviction would be an indispensable thank you to Webster.

Yet Morris also had reasons to feel some encouragement. In June, Hayden had been acquitted despite the fact that numerous witnesses had clearly identified him as aiding Minkins, including the very driver Hayden had attempted to bribe into transporting the fugitive out of Boston. Richard Dana and Senator Hale were effective in presenting contrary evidence, and then seizing on the jury's evident discomfort with the Fugitive Slave Law. They intended to use these same strategies in Morris's trial.

Senator Webster, eyeing one final run for president, was more desperate than ever to see his home state of Massachusetts show its intolerance for vigilante abolitionists. He wrote to President Fillmore assuring him that despite the Bay State's inability to convict Hayden and black clothing merchant James Scott, he would not be deterred from pressing on with others who had been charged in connection with the rescue.

In some ways, Morris and his legal team had already won an important victory before ever stepping in front of a jury. The grand jury determined that under the existing evidence, Morris should face only misdemeanor charges, as opposed to the life-threatening treason charges that Webster had wanted and Morris had so feared. However, six months in prison, away from his young family, and a fine of up to $1,000 were still more than enough to give Morris great anxiety as he headed into the trial.

The trial began on November 4, 1851. The district attorney's key witnesses were a pair of adolescents claiming to have seen Morris with Minkins during the rush to Beacon Hill. Newell Harding of Cambridge Street recognized Morris because of his status as a well-known lawyer. Harding had been following the crowd on that February morning, and he remembered seeing Morris with his arm "laid across Minkins's hip, as I have seen friends walk together," as they moved from Southac Street to West Cedar Street.

Fifteen-year-old John Mack knew Morris's face because he had recently seen him trying a case. He claimed to have been standing in the courtroom when Morris had made his three trips in and out, and Mack heard him speak to another man as to their chances of being able to free Minkins. This was the prosecution's primary evidence: that the rescue was a premeditated affair, thus a treasonous crime. Once the rescue had been carried out, the intrigued boy followed the crowd down Cambridge Street, seeing Morris accompanying Minkins most of the way. By the time he reached Garden Street, Mack pushed through the throngs surrounding Minkins to be within about eight feet of the fleeing fugitive, but by that point Morris had disappeared. After the boys' testimonies, along with three men who claimed to have seen Morris in the cab with Minkins, the district attorney was satisfied.

Dana opened his defense of Morris on Thursday, November 6, passionately making a case for acquittal based on the Fugitive Slave Law's unconstitutionality. To the Massachusetts jurors, he lamented "the great increase in the power of slavery, and the effect of the laws to support it." But hedging his bet on the appeal of these political sentiments, he also boldly claimed, "We shall show, not only that Robert Morris had no lot or part in this rescue, but that no such plan ever existed." Dana went as far as to assert that the president of the United States was pushing for Morris's prosecution.

Dana told the court that Morris had been walking home from the courtroom when the unruly procession of Minkins's liberators passed by him. After that, Morris was doing nothing more than working in his law offices in the Brazer Building on State Street and talking to passersby about the day's wild occurrences. Finally, Dana asked, Why would anyone, especially a man who spent his whole life advising black people about respect for the law, flaunt it so publicly?

The defense called numerous witnesses to testify about Morris's law-abiding character, the most prominent of these being former Boston mayor Josiah Quincy. The respected city elder described his decade-long friendship, one that had begun when he observed Morris studying under Loring. Mayor Quincy described how throughout that time he found Morris to be "peaceable and good." Then the defense turned to none other than Loring, the perfect witness because of his own background in persuading juries. Loring proudly told how he had known Morris "intimately for thirteen years," and that the young lawyer's reputation was "excellent in every respect."

An especially peculiar sight came with the next character witness, a somewhat shocking and totally unexpected appearance by Chief Justice Lemuel Shaw. A better witness for a Boston jury could not be found, for everyone remembered the *Roberts* case. Shaw proceeded to testify that Morris had not accompanied Dana to his office when Dana had unsuccessfully sought the writ of habeas corpus. Moreover, Shaw had no memory of seeing Morris in the crowd carrying Minkins away and placing him in the cab. This was confirmed by six other witnesses called by the defense, including one man claiming to have shared an umbrella with Morris during the melee.

Concluding Morris's defense, Hale masterfully showed contradictions in the testimony of the government's witnesses. Then Hale poured on the fulsome oratory, knowing that people's mounting distaste for the Fugitive Slave Law was Morris's great hope. Hale wondered aloud how Morris could be guilty of freeing a slave if slavery was in fact an unnatural state. If the Fugitive Slave Law was totally contrary to the Constitution and humanity's moral sense, how could anyone be convicted for circumventing it? Turning away from the court and staring right at the jury, Hale proclaimed,

You have got to *swear* he was a SLAVE! that a man whom God made
and whom Christ redeemed was a SLAVE, a *thing,* and not a MAN!
And you have got to find that there was a conspiracy, because parties
here intimated to officers of this Court that there was a God in
Heaven who would judge them for their works.

When Hale finished, a thunderous burst of applause broke
through the courtroom, an unusual reaction to a criminal defense
lawyer's closing statements. Hale effectively cut through the increasingly absurd nature of the whole proceeding with his startling
assertion that there was no way Morris could be guilty of a crime
that was not really a crime.

As Sumner had done months earlier, Hale effectively turned a
courtroom into an abolitionist meeting house. Morris was so grateful to Senator Hale that he led a drive to purchase an eight-volume
history of England for the senator, since "the advocates for the colored race in this country can look for few earthly honors." Hale
would pass these gifts on to his children as proof that their father
"had some share of the respect and regard of the oppressed."

District Attorney George Lunt's closing argument was in marked
contrast to Hale's poignant oration, as a newspaper described his
efforts as "very plain." He recounted the numerous witnesses who
had seen Morris with Shadrach Minkins and maintained that
whether the escaped man had been a slave or not was irrelevant.
And to jury members who might be apprehensive about the consequences of separating Morris from his wife and children, who
seemed to have been in the courtroom while their husband and father awaited his fate, Lunt coldly stated, "Robert Morris should
have looked at them and *he* should have thought of his wife and
children, before he engaged in the commission of this crime." In
marked contrast to the ovation Hale received, when Lunt finished,
"a profound silence prevailed."

The two sides waited through Sunday and Monday, when state
elections where being held, for court to resume on Tuesday. By the
time court recommenced, Judge Curtis realized something would

have to be done to counter Hale's passionate closing statements, in which he had effectively said that if the jury found the Fugitive Slave Law unconstitutional, they must acquit. Curtis, breaking with usual judicial precedence in a manner abolitionists called judicial tyranny and antidemocratic behavior, avowed that this conclusion was not so. In his charge, he told the jury they were to consider not the legality of the hated law but only "the facts as found." Curtis also made clear the ease of finding guilt in this case. The question was not just whether Morris had planned, or even helped in, the rescue but "if he was present and did nothing to prevent it, this would render him guilty." This was a powerful directive, tantamount to instruction to the jury to find Morris guilty as charged. This was what the jury was left to ponder when they began deliberating at two-thirty in the afternoon.

Would Morris's apparent guilt, under Judge Curtis's charge, outweigh the depths of resentment felt against the Fugitive Slave Law, so eloquently voiced by Hale?

By nine-thirty the next morning, Morris found out the answer was no. Morris, like Minkins in his new life in Montreal, was a free man.

# THIRTEEN

# New Alliances, New Divisions

The results of the Minkins trials had been as much a triumph for the abolitionist cause as the rescue itself had been.

After Morris was acquitted, the *Commonwealth* wrote that the lack of convictions must have been "mortifying" for the district attorney and was proof that the government had made a "fatal mistake." Many were still convinced of Morris's role in the affair; the *Boston Bee* assumed his guilt in an article about the case, in which the "not guilty" verdict was supposed to have been the result of fine lawyering. Morris, now freed of all charges, would not accept these suppositions, writing to their editor, "I think I have now a right to stand clear in the judgement of this community, and cannot but think it ungenerous in the conductors of an influential paper still to hold up to public odium a young man whose good name and honest toil are the only reliance of himself and his family."

Despite Morris's efforts to preserve his reputation as a man of law in Boston, few in Boston would soon forget the remarkable events of that February morning. Hayden, Morris, and dozens of unnamed members of the community openly defied the wishes of a president and the government—all in the name of a higher law.

The Minkins controversy epitomized Morris and Hayden's growing partnership as radical leaders of the community. Morris used his connections with white society to gain access to the courtroom and to white abolitionist allies, at which point Hayden, with his deep ties to the humblest persons of Boston, was able to influence that courtroom in powerful direct action.

The recent ordeal did not derail Morris's growing reputation as a lawyer, which was no longer notable solely because he was black but because of his skill and, more, sustained nerve. Experience gave him the invaluable ability to think on his feet. A fellow lawyer was amazed at how his "self-possession seemed perfect. He never seemed confused or taken by surprise." His indictment on treason charges did not significantly hurt his career. Morris became the second African American to hold a judicial post when Governor Briggs appointed him to be a magistrate to Essex County. In his private practice, he followed after Loring, balancing activist pursuits with railroad law. He was responsible for the books of one of the wealthiest railroad companies in the state. This seems fitting considering his protests over segregation during the transportation battles of the 1840s.

This was an era of change in Morris's life. Commenting on the school boycott in 1852, Nell wrote, "Boston is fast losing many of her intelligent, worthy, aspiring citizens, who are becoming taxpayers in adjoining localities, for the sole advantage of equal school rights." Cambridge, Charlestown, Roxbury, Salem, and New Bedford were all recipients of some of Boston's largest black taxpayers who wished to extract their investment from Boston real estate. Following this trend, Morris decided his taxes would no longer support segregated schools for his son, Robert Jr. (Mason had not survived infancy). He relocated to Chelsea, which was close enough to continue his professional life in Boston but far enough away to ensure that Robert Jr. would attend free public schools with students from all backgrounds.

Along with the Morrises' change in residence came a resolution of the spiritual gulf that existed in the young couple's marriage. Morris had been passionately opposed to his wife's unusual conversion to Roman Catholicism. Painful antagonisms between blacks and Irish were too strong for Morris to understand why Catherine could accept their religion and thereby reject his Methodism. His love of Catherine, however, eased his hostility toward something that was so much a part of her. Aside from the religious conflict between them, theirs was a tender and devoted marriage. One friend was impressed with how, in his wife, Morris always "found a ready sympathizer and an earnest helper in all his undertakings."

It was a gradual process, but long-standing biases melted and unfriendly feelings began to wane. With his young family and by himself, Morris prayed until an answer came to him. This conversion of a leader of the black community to the religion of a group locked in a destructive relationship with them could not have been taken lightly.

The black population of Boston numbered only around 2,000 during the 1850s, whereas the Irish population had climbed to 53,000. Thus, many blacks felt they were in a city and in a labor market becoming increasingly dominated by a group that openly despised them. Morris's personal charisma and intelligence were substantial enough to keep favor in his community in the long run. Twice every Sunday he attended Mass, he never missed monthly confession, and he began teaching classes, as he had at his old Methodist church.

While teaching these Sunday school classes Morris took a particular liking to an impressive eleven-year-old boy who was already teaching classes himself. The boy's name was Patrick Collins, and his family had arrived from Ireland with thousands of others in 1848. While Boston was overflowing with Irish, the town of Chelsea, where the boy's family had moved, was not. At the school he was sent to, he was one of ten Irish children in a class of one hundred. As a result, he remembered being "sneered at, jeered at, hissed at, beaten and hunted like wild animals." The journey home from school every day was spent fighting for his life. In 1854 a Scottish immigrant nicknamed Angel Gabriel led a crusade against the Irish in Morris's Chelsea, where Catholic churches and houses were destroyed. Despite the fact that young Collins's house had been fortified, the mob found him and broke his arm in the melee.

The relationship Morris and Collins developed defied the conventional paradigm of Irish-black relations and deserves consideration as an antidote to traditional historical accounts of ethnic relations in antebellum Boston. Morris sympathized with the boy, because he surely understood oppression. Just as Loring had taken a boy from the ranks of the poor and the despised and trained him for a better life, Morris proceeded to do the same for Collins. Collins had been selling fish and oysters for money, but Morris offered him a new job as office boy for him, a position in which Collins served until 1857.

Collins loved his new work and the cheerful employer who took a chance on him. Just as Loring's view of the potential in Morris had been accurate, so was Morris's appraisal of Collins. In 1901, after years of success as a lawyer, Morris's office boy became mayor of Boston. Today an imposing statue of the great mayor can be seen on Commonwealth Avenue in Boston.

Morris's relationship with Collins was indicative of the remarkable rapport he had with many Boston Irish. When he first entered the law, most of his clients were black, but eventually Irish people made up about three-quarters of his practice. He was once known as the "black lawyer," but now he was just as often called the "Irish lawyer." Despite their reliance on Morris, some prejudices died hard. The thick-skinned Morris recounted how anytime an Irishman would get in trouble, their friends would say, "Straight up to nigger Morris." In truth, Morris continued to deal with a variety of cases, including his first capital case, when he represented a young black woman for the murder of her child.

. . .

While Morris was building these bridges to the Irish community, ties within the abolitionist community were under greater strain than ever before. At the heart of this conflict—one that threatened to derail any further progress on the school struggle or any collectively mobilized activism—was a clash between Garrison and Frederick Douglass.

In the midst of this increasingly malicious and disturbing feud, Nell and Morris found themselves on opposite sides. Douglass had for some time been dissatisfied with Garrison's immoderate ideas about the Constitution as nothing more than a slaveholder's document. Garrison's slogan was "No union with slaveholders," but Douglass thought a more constructive saying would be "No union with slave-holding." Douglass thought that Garrison unnecessarily conceded the country's founding texts to the enemy and would, by dissolving the Union, leave slaves totally defenseless. To Douglass, Garrison was surrendering the abolitionists' greatest potential weapon, which was the liberal declarations of freedom found in the Constitution's preamble, which not only governed the rest of the document but could make the status of slavery impossible to sustain.

These divergent views on the nation led Douglass to accept participation in party politics, something Garrison urged freed blacks not to do, viewing involvement in the political framework of the country as an affirmation of the current corrupted system. But Douglass had lived as a slave, and this created a pragmatism born out of a fierce urgency, something Garrison could never share.

Egos were also on the line. Garrison still resented Douglass's need to start his own paper in 1848, not just because of the competition for subscriptions among black subscribers but also for the contest for the domination of the abolitionist movement. Particularly mystifying to Garrison, who had long taken to heart the acceptance he had received from many blacks, was Douglass's declaration that his paper would do "work which it would be wholly impossible for our white friends to do for us." That is, "the man who has SUFFERED THE WRONG is the man to DEMAND REDRESS," otherwise expressed as "Who would be free, themselves must strike the blow."

Forgetting the example of Benjamin Roberts's *Anti-Slavery Herald*, Douglass maintained that "for the first time in the western continent, there is a press under the entire control and direction of colored persons." And blacks around the country responded to Douglass's success. One evening in Philadelphia, where both Douglass and Garrison spoke, Douglass was introduced as "the staunch advocate of Liberty in which time could never erase the memory of so great a champion," and Garrison was merely cited as "first to cry hold to the tyrants of the south."

Many were now responding to Douglass's message of political participation, and Garrison realized he was losing his hold on the people who had loved and supported him for so many years. It was this tension that probably caused Nell, always loyal to Garrison, to discontinue working on Douglass's paper and return to Boston. Then all-out warfare between the two camps erupted in 1853.

A meeting was organized in Boston for Frederick Douglass to speak on August 2, 1853, at the Twelfth Baptist Church. Morris, a friend and admirer of Douglass, was chairman of the meeting. This may have been Garrison/Nell territory, but Morris quickly showed where his allegiances were. With a fiery rhetorical cadence, he introduced the black editor as "*the* advocate of freedom."

Douglass spoke for an hour on the conditions of their people across the country, interrupted only by a brief discussion with Morris when Morris took exception to Douglass's endorsement of the idea of a national manual-labor school for black boys. Morris chided Douglass for the support of any segregated school, using the example of the Smith School, a "foul blot upon the city of Boston." Douglass took his point but still believed, in light of circumstances around the nation, that a manual-labor school was a promising idea.

But this was a small debate between two allies, totally unlike what transpired when Nell rose to speak. The evening took a turn for the dramatic when Nell announced he had come to speak out against Douglass. Douglass's former assistant editor now said that he was "unkind, ungenerous, and ungrateful to his old and tired friends, particularly to Mr. Garrison."

Douglass, a man who had once beaten his slave driver within an inch of his life, did not take personal attacks lightly. He demanded that Nell produce the articles to prove such things. Nell sheepishly backed off, explaining he did not have such writings with him, as he had not been anticipating this debate. That said, this dispute was picked up again a night later at the Belknap Street Church. Nell now supplied numerous articles from Douglass's paper that he claimed proved Douglass's unkind spirit, and they began contesting over each one, especially as to their respective evaluations of Garrison.

Morris had had enough. Still smarting from Nell's speech of the previous night, he interrupted, unloading pent-up grievances. Nell and Morris had come up together in the leadership class of the Boston community and had been public leaders together of the school-rights struggle for almost a decade. Morris, like Douglass, was frustrated by Garrison's reluctance to encourage blacks to play a part in the political system that was so crucial for their full citizenship. Morris's father, York, had rallied black voters in Salem during Roberts's childhood, and Morris was not one to lightly discard this legacy. Furthermore, Loring had earlier left the ranks of Garrisonians over his realization that disunion was not the answer.

As early as 1848, Morris had written of his support for the small antislavery Liberty party in the *Liberator* because of the need for "political efforts and political machinery to accomplish objects needed for the public welfare." Yet the Liberty party did not show the potential for inroads into the political mainstream that the Free Soil party did by 1853. Thus, Morris and Hayden came out in support of the Free Soil movement. In fact, much of the black community did, as shown in the election of 1850 in which the Boston Free-Soilers ran strongest in Ward 6, the area comprising black Beacon Hill. Morris's frustration that Nell would not make these same pragmatic gestures helped account for the wrath he directed to his old comrade on that night.

According to Douglass's later account of the evening, it had been Nell who started the fight between them because he had "two accounts to settle at once, and a most pitiful work he made of it." It seems Nell put his friendship with Morris on the line because he felt the lawyer had been thoroughly disloyal to Garrison by engaging in these political activities. Whoever started with whom first, Nell felt Morris was soon making an "ungenerous and ungentlemanly attack" on him. Much to Nell's chagrin, it seemed most Boston blacks decided to side with Douglass and Morris. Nell was still loved and respected, but he could not realistically stand up to the towering figure of Frederick Douglass, a man who, although no longer living in Massachusetts, was now the foremost spokesman for free blacks nationally.

Things got uglier. In his paper, Douglass wrote of Nell and his allies as "my bitterest enemies, and the *practical* enemies of the colored people." He called Nell a "Contemptible tool," a "pitiful tool" being used and unappreciated by Garrison. Garrison responded with a vicious reply to Douglass. Garrison, in the lowest moment of his career, made insinuations in the *Liberator* of an affair between Douglass and an Englishwoman working on his newspaper. Douglass then proclaimed that Garrison secretly believed in black inferiority. Eventually, tempers would cool, but damage had been done to relationships within the movement.

As for Nell and Morris, no letters between them exist after this juncture. The obliteration of their decade-long partnership could not have come at a worse time. Boston's black children were still attending the decrepit Smith School, and Boston was poised for the trauma of another fugitive slave case. The issue, however, that Morris now expended most of his energy on in 1853 would have been especially well suited for their old affiliation. Morris was fighting for the right of blacks to serve in the militia, and it was Nell's grasp of history that started this movement.

The struggle for blacks to enter the Union army was, like the school boycott movement, a decades-long struggle, with many of the same leaders bound in shared action and agitation. It was Morris and Nell who first led, each in his distinctive way, the movement for Massachusetts blacks to be among the first African Americans to serve in the Civil War. Morris began his effort in 1853, indebted to Nell's remarkable history of black militant patriotism. His book, *Service of Colored Americans, in Wars of 1776 & 1812*, was a groundbreaking history that inspired pride rooted in the bravery of soldiers in previous generations. This bold affirmation of his people's stake in our common history received positive reviews in mainstream papers all over the nation, many of which were shocked that a black man had the ability to compose such a history.

Morris decided to battle against a section of the militia law permitting only "white male citizens" to serve. The effort began in 1852 with twelve petitions to the state legislature and the mayor's office for the inclusion of blacks in the militia. They were enough to get Morris an audience before the state's Committee on the Militia. The speech he would give would become a great charter for the movement of black military participation in Massachusetts, culminating in less than a decade with the creation of the famed Fifty-fourth black regiment in the Civil War.

On March 3, 1853, Morris entered the great golden-domed State House on Beacon Hill, its long corridors lined with imposing depictions of Massachusetts's military history. Before a collection of state senators and representatives, Morris began his testimony by tracing the history of emerging civil rights over the previous thirty years, especially highlighting the long struggle against Boston's segregated schools. Before the influential lawmakers, Morris could not resist briefly expanding on that subject, reminding them, "The colored children are compelled, against the wishes of the whole colored population, to attend a separate and exclusive school. I trust the proper authority will soon repair this act of injustice, and banish from our midst this last relic of unchristian caste."

Concentrated legislative advocacy for desegregated schools was still two years away, and Morris was there for another purpose. He acknowledged the opposition to true black citizenship. Morris cleverly used the words of Webster's friend, the conservative Judge Shaw, to make his point. The arguments of Morris and Sumner in the *Roberts* case had not persuaded Shaw to demand integrated schools, but the judge had indeed conceded that blacks were "entitled by law, in this Commonwealth, to equal rights, constitutional and political, civil and social." This acknowledgment by Shaw made it difficult for anyone to argue that blacks had no place in the state militia.

Morris's research went back to the law books of the old Massachusetts Bay Colony, which required all free black males over sixteen to serve in the militia. It was not until 1792 that they were excluded, based on a national militia law. Morris drew on Nell's historical research, giving the legislators a comprehensive history of the loyal service blacks had provided to the state and the country in times of war. Morris emphasized, "In times of peril and great danger, the colored people have always been called upon."

Showing his pragmatism, Morris offered to lead an independent company so that blacks might serve not alongside "sensitive and nervous" white soldiers. Morris suggested this regiment would be called the Massasoit Guards, named after a Native American chief who had been an ally to the Bay State. All would be invited to join their ranks. Such a charter had recently been extended for a group of Irishmen, and Morris saw no reason why blacks should not be extended the same opportunity. He entreated them to remember "we are laboring to raise ourselves in the estimation of our fellow-citizens" because "we hunger and thirst for prosperity and advancement."

Morris gave a brilliant speech, but it was to no avail. Black activist William Watkins, accompanying Morris to the State House, thought there never had been a chance for approval, and he ended up calling the whole incident "a humbug—a legislative farce."

Nell was hurt and frustrated that Morris wanted none of his help. He thought they should be united in such a righteous cause, but he was helpless now that Morris and Hayden "lent their influence against me." Still angry about the Douglass-Garrison debate, Morris continued to make what Nell perceived as "extraneous and ungentlemanly" attacks on him. Morris wanted to fight the militia battle not with his old ally Nell but with the help of some other associates from the school battle.

One of those people would be Benjamin Roberts. Soon after the *Roberts* case, Roberts had traveled with Henry "Box" Brown all over New England. Brown had nearly been recaptured and sent back to slavery during a stay in Providence, Rhode Island. After this scare, Brown decided it would be safer to tour only in England. Roberts did not accompany him, perhaps because of Brown's increasingly erratic behavior. Brown had turned into a drinker and gambler, and Roberts appealed to Robert Morris for legal recourse against Brown. Eventually Brown disappeared into obscurity in England.

Back in Boston, Roberts worked for the Vigilance Committee by printing warnings that appeared all over the city. But he was anxious to give newspaper publishing another try. In 1853 he premiered a new effort, the *Self-Elevator*. Roberts published the semimonthly on Washington Street, where subscriptions could be purchased for one dollar. His first paper had focused on abolitionism, but now Roberts was more interested in what was happening in the life of northern free blacks. He would "agitate the cause of general improvement among the colored people, especially in regard to mechanical employments and scientific pursuits." The first issue of the *Self-Elevator* was devoted to the militia struggle. The *Self-Elevator* may have been as short-lived as the *Anti-Slavery Herald* (though the circumstances of its demise are not as well documented), but Roberts used its brief life to aid in the fight for military representation.

Morris also received major help from another character in the *Roberts* case. Charles Sumner, whose life had changed dramatically since arguing on behalf of Sarah Roberts, took up the military issue as well. When Sumner had accepted the *Roberts* case, he was a dissatisfied Boston lawyer, but now, four years on, he was a nationally known United States senator. When elected in 1851, flags floated all over the city and "entirely across Washington Street." Crowds assembled to discuss the fortunes of their native son, especially on State Street, where Morris worked.

The era of Daniel Webster's appeasement of the South was over. When Webster died in 1852, the *Liberator* proclaimed, "The magnificent failure of his life is over." Sumner was now in Washington advocating abolitionist ends with unflinching vigor and moral zeal (passions that often infuriated and perhaps unwisely antagonized his fellow senators). One of his first articles of business was to begin demanding the repeal of the Fugitive Slave Law, which had so ravaged Sumner's home city.

Sumner had not forgotten Morris after their days in court together during the winter of 1849. On June 27, 1850, Sumner and Ellis Gray Loring had accompanied Morris to the office of the clerk of the Circuit Court of the United States. Their purpose that day was to see Morris admitted to practice in the Circuit and District Courts of the United States. In the next decade Sumner used the fact that Morris was now a counselor in the federal courts as an antidote to suggestions that blacks were not entitled to the rights and privileges of citizenship. This historic occasion was a tribute not just to the success of Morris in his young legal career but to enduring alliances crossing over racial lines.

In 1853 Sumner threw his weight behind the militia issue. He was selected to be part of a convention that would examine possible revisions to the Massachusetts constitution. He used this opportunity to attack the use of the word *white* in the section on the militia. With the same fire that he used to champion "equality before the law" on behalf of black schoolchildren, Sumner now demanded to know on "what grounds do gentlemen make any discrimination in the case of the power over the national militia."

Once again Morris had begun the momentum for a cause, and Sumner assisted with his celebrated eloquence. As in the *Roberts* case, Sumner's words could not bring down the object of their objections, as the convention deferred to the belief that an integrated militia would violate the national Constitution.

With the militia effort rebuked in 1853, the following year would be a time when renewed energies finally returned to the school struggle. Attention had been diverted, not only by the defeat in the *Roberts* case, but because of the Fugitive Slave Law cases that rocked Boston. To be sure, 1854 would see a major slave case and national events with ramifications affecting all black Americans. But this time these factors would not be enough to stop the final onslaught on Boston's segregated education, a siege a decade and a half in the making.

FOURTEEN

# So Close to Passing

When Edward Pindall sat down next to his white classmates on the first day of school in 1853, he harbored a secret.

Even Nell, a friend of Edward Pindall's father, was never sure if William Pindall was white or just so light-skinned he was able to "pass." Edward's mother's lineage was Native American, black, and white, and she too had noticeably light skin. Thus, it was not surprising that at first glance it was hard to tell that their son Edward had anything but European blood.

The Pindalls lived within the confines of the black community but did not want their son going through a segregated education in the ramshackle Smith School. So William Pindall presented Edward to Andrew Cushing, chairman of the Committee of Primary School District No. 9, for admission to the white school closest to their house. Pindall made no references to the boy's African ancestry, and the unsuspecting bureaucrat raised no questions about it.

So Edward began attending school with his white counterparts, the first black child to do so since Sarah Roberts had in 1847. After two weeks at his new school, his experience, sadly, started to resemble Sarah's. Like Benjamin Roberts's daughter, Edward would see only two weeks of integrated schooling before whispers about his true identity became louder and louder, culminating in a note from Cushing. Cushing had done some research on the Pindall family, finding that he had been duped into allowing Edward to attend a white school. The School Committee member informed William Pindall that Edward would no longer be welcome at the white school, but that he could enroll in the Smith School.

Pindall resolutely ignored the School Committee's instruction and sent Edward back to his white school the next morning, in the hope Edward would be accepted there. This was a false hope, as the former teacher, Miss Turner, turned him away. Pindall's response to the removal of his son was much the same as Benjamin Roberts's had been. He sought out Robert Morris.

Morris took the case, and they decided to sue the city of Boston for $500 on account of Edward's unlawful exclusion from a public school. Morris now had his opportunity to redeem his defeat in the *Roberts* case. The *Pindall* case would be Morris's second chance at obliterating segregated schools, and this time he would handle the case without the assistance of a famous cocounselor.

There was, however, a problem in the nature of the case. Nell, now reluctant to give Morris credit for anything, pointed out the limitations of the lawsuit when he observed that even a favorable outcome "affects the one individual, or perhaps, the few others who can pass the examination of a skin-scanning committee; but it is of no advantage in establishing the principle that all children, of whatever complexion, are equals before the law."

This was true, but Nell overlooked two aspects of the case that Morris understood. First, the case was meant to display the absurdity of racial distinctions in school. Edward Pindall had been unable to sit with white students because he was somewhere between one-sixth and one-eighth black, though evidence of this was hardly visible. What reasonable citizen of Boston could possibly think this was logical? The "one drop of blood" concept seemed far more suited to the "barbaric south" than the supposedly liberal Massachusetts. It is important to recall the multiracial lineage of the Roberts family, for whom race seemed a mere social construct, as they were quite aware of their Indian, English, and African bloodlines. If Morris could convince a jury of the irrationality of separating out someone as pale as Pindall, and then get him admitted to a white school, this crack in the wall of segregated schools could be the beginning of the end for the whole system. Furthermore, with Shaw's "separate but equal" doctrine in place, any other direct challenge to the current system was legally impossible.

Regardless of the outcome of the *Pindall* case, the most direct effect would be to refocus Boston's attention on the almost forgotten issue of segregated schools. At the time of the *Roberts* case, the integrationists' boycott of the Smith School had reduced its average attendance from more than 100 to as low as 25. Four years later, that number had steadily crept back up. The temporary protest had ended because of the drain on time and money, and many parents, like Robert Morris, moved their children out of Boston or found private schools within the city. But those less fervent about the cause let their children begin attending the Smith School again. The average number of 25 students in 1850 went up to 37 in 1851, 44 in 1852, 51 in 1853, and 54 in 1854. This was still half the number of students who had been there before the integrationist boycott, but the trend toward a growing number of students returning to the Smith School shows how passion on the issue of segregated schools was waning considerably before Morris brought the *Pindall* case to court in 1854.

Inaction on the school issue after the *Roberts* case had not gone unnoticed. In 1852 the writer of a letter to the editor of the *Liberator* expressed "impatience" with "waiting . . . to see some movement of the colored citizens of Boston, in relation to the Smith School." It was not that Nell and Morris discounted the issue, but there were so many distractions. Yet, moments such as when Nell stopped at a Cambridgeport school exhibition in the spring of 1853 and watched children of different colors seated next to each other, "without the least apparent sign that such a spectacle was otherwise than ordinary," reinvigorated him to continue the fight for the realization of a scene like that in Boston. So Nell plowed along with his newfound employment as a copyist and accountant, waiting for something to jolt new interest in the school matter. That stimulus would be Edward Pindall.

Morris initiated legal action on behalf of Pindall, but while waiting for their day in court, a rear-guard attack on segregated schools began. A complaint about Pindall's removal was filed with the Boston City Council, and after they examined the matter, a remarkable report by the Committee on Public Instruction, composed of the mayor, two aldermen, the president, and four other members of the council, was issued on April 3, 1854. The City Council had no authority to manage the schools, but they could advise the stubborn School Committee, and they chose to do so on this issue. Some on the committee met the young boy and were "astonished, that any objection should be expressed at the admission of the boy to any of our public schools." They maintained that "few would suspect, without a close examination, that he had African blood in his veins." Thus, they objected to his exclusion from public schools.

The report did not stop with Pindall. This opened the whole question of the validity of separating students based on race. The committee reminded readers that Boston was the only municipality in Massachusetts still segregating its schools, though there were no specific rules or regulations guiding the practice. Those attending integrated schools, the committee believed, would grow up "without that unchristian prejudice against color." They entreated the School Committee to at least give this openness a "fair trial." Shaw had given them the power to change the system if they chose to, and the City Council thought integration would be a success. Echoing Charles Sumner, the committee urged *"equal rights and equal privileges."*

The report was a bombshell. This was the first time school integration had been endorsed by an official Boston committee. Suddenly, the Pindall matter set in motion a total rethinking of the possibility of integrated schools. The City Council at first endorsed the committee's recommendation to integrate Boston's schools, although after a close vote, they tempered their position by asking the School Committee to reexamine the issue. Nevertheless, this was unprecedented progress on the issue, and after the long limbo, intense attention was finally back on segregation.

Unfortunately, less than two months after the report, that attention was momentarily wrenched back to the plight of fugitive slaves, with the most infamous recapture in Boston now under way. Per-

haps the most notorious fugitive story of all, Anthony Burns's capture and humiliating public loading on a ship in Boston Harbor
bound for Virginia, changed all attitudes. After an ill-fated abolitionist rescue attempt to free Burns failed, Boston finally had had
enough. Now the courts were unable to prosecute the abolitionists
who had tried to rescue Burns. Even old-line "Lords of the Loom
and the Lash" conservatives were swayed by the sickening sub-
servience to the slave states. Businessman Amos Lawrence said it
best: "We went to bed one night, old fashioned conservative, compromise Union Whigs, and we waked up stark mad Abolishionists."
Again the nation was shocked at the audacity of Boston.

Illinois senator Stephen Douglass sent sectional tension over slavery to a new level when he introduced the Kansas-Nebraska Act.
This legislation ended any peace brought by previous compro-
mises, by allowing the people of these new states to decide whether
or not they would allow slavery. Thus, warring factions in these new
territories lined up to battle over this question, and the result was,
if not the real beginning of the Civil War, at least a vivid preview of
the violence to come. Bostonians sent weapons to their allies on the
frontier. Extremism and inflamed passion on all sides had never
been higher.

Despite these winds of tumult, the integrationists tried to stay focused on their goals. The City Council, even with their encouraging
report, had been unable to persuade the recalcitrant School Committee to desegregate the schools, so Morris had no choice but to
push on with the Pindall lawsuit. So in late October, Morris and Edward Pindall walked into the Court of Common Pleas. They faced
what amounted to a debate on the boy's skin color in the hope that
this might be the path to equal education.

The opposing lawyer was a vastly different man from Peleg Chandler, whom Morris had faced in the *Roberts* case. No longer city solicitor, Chandler was busy revising the city charter, planning for the
development of the Back Bay, as well as the creation of a vast space
to be called the Boston Garden. George Hillard, former law partner
of none other than Charles Sumner, had replaced him. Hillard had
been one year ahead of Sumner at Harvard Law School, and they

set up a congenial practice together at 4 Court Street, in the heart of Boston. His relationship with Sumner, the white individual most identified with the process of integrating schools (plus the fact that Hillard himself had introduced a prointegration motion while a member of the School Committee a decade earlier), made it unlikely he would give an ardent defense of the caste schools.

When the short hearing began on Tuesday, October 31, this proved to be just the case. Hillard, the man charged to defend segregation, admitted the practice was "unjust." He added that, whatever his own feelings on the issue might be, *Roberts* made it clear that the definition of race was clearly at the discretion of the School Committee.

Morris introduced evidence that demonstrated that William Pindall was, as Nell had speculated, white on both sides. Morris asserted that Pindall was actually of "Spanish blood." Hillard called forth two medical witnesses who had "examined" the boy. A Dr. Stedman thought Pindall was "one-sixth African," whereas Dr. Clark put the proportion of black parentage at one-eighth and ruled out that the boy was Spanish. Judge Perkins then informed the jury that in accordance with *Roberts,* the question rested only on the color issue, and not the validity of segregated education. With this said, Morris and Pindall promptly lost their case.

Compared to the grand moral declarations and hugely influential principles emerging from the *Roberts* case, this had been a thoroughly peculiar and even trifling hearing. Shaw's previous decision had so devastated any possible legal recourse for Morris that the only way he could envision getting a black child an equal education was trying to prove that the boy's slightly darker complexion was the result of his Spanish heritage.

Morris was beside himself. He found it difficult to accept this second defeat and immediately initiated an appeals hearing, feeling that the judge's instructions to the jury to decide the case on the evidence of color alone was wrong. A growing number of people around the city were appalled at the nature of the trial, and positive responses and support began to roll in. The *Boston Telegraph* at last maintained it was finally time to end segregation in schools. Nell composed some of his most passionate writings on the subject of segregation in the pages of the *Liberator,* asking whether the only way for a taxpayer to gain equal access to the "free institutions of Puritan New England" was to undergo a close skin examination and "estimation of a hair." He joked, "To this complexion of things has Boston come at last."

Injected with new urgency to end a system that made a boy like Edward Pindall go through such an experience, Nell proclaimed, "There is no such word as fail." Nell was moved to start a new petition drive for integration. The petition read, "The undersigned, inhabitants of _____, respectfully request the Legislature to provide, by due legislation, some efficient means to prevent the colored children of Boston from being deprived of the equal privileges of the common schools of that city."

Though Nell and Morris's relationship was still shaky, they continued to work together indirectly, at least by inspiring each other's efforts. Nell's book had motivated the effort for black militia representation, and now, Morris's lawsuit was the impetus for Nell's galvanizing the community around new pressure on the state legislature. They had, of course, tried legislative means before, to no avail, but now an insurgency was happening in Massachusetts politics leading people to believe things could be very different in the State House.

. . .

Imagine waking up after Election Day to find that almost every incumbent in your state government was thrown out of office, and those positions were now occupied by a party you had never heard of. All constitutional state officers, the whole congressional delegation, every state senator, and all 372 representatives (save three) were now men from what had been nothing more than a fringe party a few scant years earlier. This was the startling reality Massachusetts awoke to in 1854. Candidates calling themselves Know-Nothings seemed to have appeared out of nowhere, occupying almost every office in the state. Never in American history had there been such a dramatic combination of almost total political inexperience and nearly unchecked power because of such a vast majority. How could this have happened?

Shrouded in secrecy, Know-Nothings all across the state met in small lodges in nearly every town in Massachusetts. If the fraternal order of Masons became a political party overnight, it might look something like the Know-Nothings' culture, with rites, passwords, cryptic signs, elaborate ceremonies, and oaths. Their name came from the response members gave when asked questions about their party. They "knew nothing," which their opponents also construed as a comment on their political intelligence. Their secrecy meant that those not members of the party would have no idea that this grassroots, or "dark lantern," uprising was taking such a firm hold in Massachusetts.

The year 1854 was a peak one for foreign immigration to Massachusetts, and it was no coincidence that this would be the year of the rise and triumph of Know-Nothings. Anti-immigration, anti-Catholic, and anti-Irish attitudes all combined to fuel their sudden and surprising popularity. But there were other motivations driving people into the party. Aside from their nativist base, the Know-Nothings picked up dissatisfied Democrats, as well as disillusioned Whigs, as both parties were being split (the Whigs once and for all) by the Kansas-Nebraska Act, as well as gathering refugees from the faltering Free-Soilers. This coalition would be ephemeral but powerful when it coalesced. Today Know-Nothings are dismissed as intolerant and primitive by modern historians, if remembered at all. Still, as we will see, what united this revolt was also a populist cry for reform and change in the Brahmin-filled State House.

When the Irish arrived, they had been welcomed into the protecting arms of the proslavery Democrats, so it was natural that a party opposing the Irish Democrats would be influenced by antislavery forces that also needed a political home. Yet the common debate was: were the Know-Nothings antislavery? Since the party drew from so many influences, there was no one clear answer, and both sides of the debate would muster evidence for their views. The *Liberator* was hostile to the party, calling it "fanaticism," with "no principle of enduring vitality," and accurately predicting that it would be a short-lived phenomenon. Yet southerners were just as distrustful, with the *Atlanta Examiner* writing, "We are carefully informed that the negro population are manifesting strong sympathies with Know-Nothingism." The newspaper *Boston Know-Nothing* tried to explain their convoluted position on slavery with the puzzling statement "We are for justice to all parties—the slaveholder as well as the slave." They called slavery "unquestionably an evil," but then turned around to call abolitionists "insane." It seemed no one quite knew what to expect from this party, including many of its instant members.

One recently elected Know-Nothing member saw the possibilities in this situation and decided to make the most of his opportunity. Charles Slack was a liberal reformer at heart and viewed the Know-Nothings simply as an imperfect but convenient vehicle for his own advancement to the State House. The thirty-year-old had a focused gaze behind small spectacles and a long and wiry beard. It was not surprising that he was a friend of Nell, both excelling in Boston public schools (Slack received his Franklin medal, which Nell was denied), both entering the world of journalism. Ultimately, both would end up with valuable government appointments.

Slack's father had been a newspaperman for the *Boston Post.* Following his father's path, Slack learned his craft at the *Boston Journal* from the age of fifteen. After studying printing and journalism, he and five friends started a newspaper called *Excelsior,* devoted to the advancement of the many reform movements captivating young minds. This pursuit reaped him little financial security, as he struggled to support a wife and child on $5 a week.

With his newspaper's future highly uncertain, Slack searched for a new way to see his convictions realized. He turned to politics, although his party of choice, the Free-Soilers, was falling apart. Instead of going down with that ship, Slack astutely and pragmatically recognized the clandestine momentum building in the Know-Nothing party and decided this would be the party to cast his lot with. In doing so, he hoped he might move them to a more enlightened position on racial issues. He was never totally enthusiastic about the party, as he would not use their eccentric name, more optimistically calling them Know-Somethings.

Slack's political gamble was correct; the party was overwhelmingly swept into office in 1854. Now a state representative from Boston, Slack realized that almost none of his counterparts had legislative experience. Having none himself, he decided to reach high, and for his effort was nearly elected Speaker of the House. His near victory allowed him to become chairman of the Joint Committee on Education, which for the long-frustrated integrationists would be a crucial development.

Aside from noticing how great an authority he could have because of the inexperience of so many fellow members of the House, Slack also realized how many antislavery men like himself had made the same realistic calculations he had made about joining this upstart party. Indeed, there were many practical abolitionists for whom the Know-Nothings were a temporary political home, between the downfall of the Free-Soilers and the emergence of the Republicans. During his first days on Beacon Hill Slack was amazed by how it was a "very singular and somewhat unexpected thing to find so many anti-slavery men."

He did not know if it was "the providence of God or the accident of politics," but he would take advantage of it. For all he knew, "they might never get there again." He remembered resolving with some like-minded colleagues that however they could use this prospect for positive change, they would do it. In time, these men would remove a sitting judge for returning a fugitive to slavery, as well as pass the Personal Liberty Bill—both actions going a long way toward making the Fugitive Slave Law ineffective in Massachusetts.

These were remarkable achievements, but Slack was looking for something more. He could not put his finger on it, but he knew he wanted to press for something that had a "direct connection with the colored race." While he searched for a cause, William Nell was hard at work creating just the reform that Slack would need.

· · ·

Wendell Phillips once jokingly remarked that he wanted segregated schools to end just so William Cooper Nell would stop bothering him with his petitions. In the wake of the Pindall controversy, it was nearly impossible to run into the energetic Nell without seeing petitions proudly in his grasp. Nell was a man on a mission. It seemed like 1849 again. Back then, the great promise of the *Roberts* case had infused many with energy and hope. After a painful five years, the community was finally back to having regular meetings on equal school rights.

Nell told the crowds that he was sending his petitions far and wide in the Commonwealth and finding the responses encouraging. These petitions were sent back to Boston with dozens of names from such towns as Nantucket, Lynn, East Bridgewater, Lexington, Bolton, Haverhill, Charlestown, and Salem. These towns already had integrated schools and now wanted Boston to enjoy the same privileges. Nell put ads in the *Liberator* to make sure all readers knew of the massive push for names. The petitions are still preserved in the state archives. When you open them, the old blue documents unfurl, one section carefully glued to the next section, with their precious voters' signatures still bold. They tell a hard-won story. Before Nell knew it, he had more than fifteen hundred names.

It was time to take the petitions to the State House. As spring arrived in Boston in 1855, Nell packed his petitions, walked out of his house directly across from the Smith School, and climbed up Beacon Hill to the State House. He went directly to the office of Charles Slack, who could hardly believe the "huge budget of papers" Nell presented to him. The cause Slack was looking for had just fallen into his lap. He later recalled:

> It was as if an enterprising builder should bring his timber and bricks and mortar into the street, and then, calling in his master-workman, should say to him—"Here, I have got all the material and implements easy, and will furnish the capital needed; now go on and erect the building."

Slack was glad to erect the building and cover it with the "fair fabric of equality in the education of the colored youth of this Commonwealth." Perhaps not realizing he had been a mere fifteen-year-old when the first petition had been brought to the legislature

—also signed by Nell—the young legislator thought to himself, "It would be an easy matter to do."

He set to work preparing a report on behalf of his education committee in favor of integration, inspired by the petition drive. Although Sumner's argument had never convinced Judge Shaw in the *Roberts* case, Garrison had predicted that "the comprehensive view of Mr. Sumner will long be a treasure-house for other laborers to draw from." Five years on, this was at last coming true. Sumner's words on behalf of Sarah seemed alive again, firmly echoed in the writing of the House Report intended to finally bring down segregation. On March 17, 1855, Slack presented his work to his committee.

Sumner asked, "Can any discrimination of color or race, be made, under the Constitution and Laws of Massachusetts, among the children entitled to the benefit of our common schools?" Hardly changing any of Sumner's ideas, Slack now asked whether "any discrimination... can be made under the constitution and laws of Massachusetts, among the children entitled to those benefits." He used arguments straight from the *Roberts* case, mentioning the "practical inconvenience" for the minority children forced to travel great distances. Driving home Sumner's themes, he used similar language, such as "equal before the law" and "caste." Slack acknowledged Shaw's weighty opinion but cited numerous respectable Bostonians, from Supreme Court Justice Richard Fletcher to City Solicitor George Hillard, expressing their belief that blacks were entitled to an integrated education.

The City Council's report was also cited as more evidence for the changing views of segregated education. Slack studied years of School Committee reports on the Smith School and was convinced that they knew full well, and willfully disregarded, the fact that the school was in inferior condition, thus making Shaw's "Separate but equal" logic fallacious and disingenuous. He quoted an 1849 report, where it was written, "We have no hesitance in saying that as it is, and has been, the Smith School is an encumbrance upon the finances of the city and upon the patience of the school committee."

Where was the "equality before the law" in this kind of blatant racism?

A day of reckoning had come for a callous School Committee that had overlooked the "saddening thoughts" in these reports. Slack assured Bostonians that fears over the introduction of black children to their schools were unfounded, as proved by the success of integration all over the state.

Slack emphasized, *"Not a single complaint has been made to the committee thus far from any teacher"* from anywhere in the state concerning integration. In fact, he possessed just the opposite testimony. A teacher from New Bedford wrote, "I have had no instance of any difficulty arising from the admission of colored children." He had "noticed no difference in the aptitude to learn between them and the whites." Even more compelling was the Worcester instructor who had seen black children in both segregated and integrated education and found, "The older colored children in the separate school have always compared unfavorably with colored children of the same age in the other school." Sumner had previously asserted this point, but he had not laid forth the evidence that Slack now did.

Though not possessing Sumner's eloquence, Slack had effectively fused the grandness of that speech with evidence from School Committee reports and testimony from all over the state into a short document. After hearing Slack's report, the committee recommended that a law be passed, stating: "In determining the qualification of scholars to be admitted into any public school in this Commonwealth, no distinction shall be made on account of the race, color or religious opinion, of the applicant or scholar."

If a child, such as Sarah Roberts, was now denied access to the school closest to her house, she was entitled to collect damages. The committee wanted the law to be in effect by September.

# FIFTEEN

# September 3, 1855

With his powerful report, Slack convinced his Committee on Education. His bill was now bound for the larger legislative bodies. It took two months for the topic of desegregation to make its way to the House floor, where John Andrew introduced it. On April 3 Slack began the debate by saying there was actually no reason for debate. The precocious representative declared that the merits of such an amendment to the education laws "commend themselves to the propriety, justice and humanity of the House without argument." He also made it known that the superintendent of the city schools had been told to make arrangements for the integration of black children into the larger system by September, something that Slack was assured would happen.

Slack's opening remarks were filled with brimming self-assurance, but other legislators were not as confident and wondered how voting for such a bill might affect their careers. The push for the bill to go through without a fight was a fantasy. One after another a new state legislator rose to offer questions, problems, and possible postponements.

Slack's sure victory was very much in jeopardy. The Universalist clergyman John Prince stood up to bring a stop to the growing opposition. He reminded the Boston politicians how far behind the rest of the state they would be if they maintained this illiberality; integration was a simple norm everywhere else in the state. Of course, he was ignoring the uncomfortable fact that nowhere else had such a statute been passed, and that no other large city in America was even contemplating opening its schools to black children. Salem's Eben Kinball seconded the reverend's points, speaking about the harmonious relations of his city's black and white students, who knew no other reality but integration.

After much debate, the momentum began to swing back to the integrationists. Their opponents called again for indefinite postponement, but it was too late. Slack's passion overwhelmed the vote for a delay. The bill was ordered to a third reading without amendment. Fifteen years of struggle on Beacon Hill hung in the balance.

When the votes were called, a *Boston Evening Telegraph* reporter heard an "affirmative shout." Only six legislators opposed the bill. With such a resounding victory in the House, the bill moved through the Senate and onto the governor's desk with little more drama or delay. On April 28, 1855, Know-Nothing governor Henry Gardner signed his name to the act. Come September, Sarah Roberts could attend the school closest to her house.

. . .

Robert Morris rejoiced at what he called "a great blessing." Benjamin Roberts was even more emphatic, calling this act "the greatest *boon* ever bestowed upon our people." His children would never again feel like "*inferiors* and *outcasts*," as he himself had felt "a thousand times while passing a school-house." Word of this bold and unprecedented development spread much farther than Beacon Hill. Much of the country, in this unexpectedly frantic age of the telegraph, instantly heard of the Boston victory. Douglass's paper in Rochester spoke of the "glorious news, not only to us here, but to all who are battling against the proscriptions which have doomed us to occupy an inferior position." Douglass proudly declared that "the last vestige of caste in public schools has been abolished."

Others were not as pleased. The *New York Herald* sounded a bell of alarm. "The North is to be Africanized. Amalgamation has commenced. New England heads the column." The writer envisioned that "the blood of the Winthrops, the Otises, the Lymans, the Endicots, and the Eliots, is in a fairway to be amalgamated with the Sambos, the Catos and the Pompeys." The urgency was driven home with images of "the woolliest head and the thickest lips" having an equal chance for education with "the whitest skin and strongest Saxon peculiarities." The outrage boiled down to the fact that "now the niggers are really just as good as white folks." With this statement, minus the racial slur, Boston blacks could not have agreed more.

Perhaps the most gratifying aspect of this turn of events was that school segregation ended in a fully democratic vote. Abolitionists would have welcomed a favorable verdict from Judge Shaw, but the manner by which desegregation was achieved was, surprisingly, a consensus among representatives from all over the state. Despite fears of many officials that supporting integration would hurt their careers, this punishment from voters in fact never materialized. White voters did not target and punish those who promoted integration. The overwhelming cascade of national events highlighting differences between North and South had gone a long way toward making Massachusetts citizens more open to full equality. Slavery had once been a far-off institution, an almost abstract concept, until Boston had been forced to watch human beings forcibly removed from free lives and returned to bondage. The extreme results of this brutal legal racism helped the integrationists.

However, the black community had known disappointment before. There was a sense during the late spring and early summer of 1855 of postponing any celebration of the victory until they could see the long-promised integration actually happen.

The last day of legally segregated schools in Boston was not a jubilant one, but one acknowledged with muted emotions. Schoolmaster Thomas Paul well understood that this new law was a death knell for his school and his livelihood. Nell publicly criticized how this bitterness seemed to have prevented Paul from giving the departing students even "a shadow at least of encouragement for their pursuit of knowledge." For Paul, the end of an era of community self-reliance, begun under his illustrious father, had come to a sad end. Parents began withdrawing their children from the Smith

School immediately after the new law passed, though the children would not formally be admitted to white schools until the fall. The School Committee reported that the school was "rapidly running down." A concert had been planned and rehearsed with the music teacher and the children to mark the end of the school year, but Paul curtly called off these ceremonies. No medals were given to exceptional students. When it came to the final days of the school, Nell saw a depressed man, totally devoid "of his zeal."

The *Telegraph* wrote it was appropriate to have no festivities, for it would be a "farce to present testimonials of scholarship to so inferiorly-educated pupils." Their reporter had seen segregated education up close, and reported "depressing results and the total lack of ambition and pride, which must ever follow a caste school." The writer saw no "competition, no rivalry," but only children "laboring under a load of bondage."

With the school year now over and a six-week break until a new one would begin, Nell was busy. He was working with the superintendent on various logistics to make sure there would be a peaceful transfer of the black children to their new schools. This "mission" included working with various black parents from around Beacon Hill to help them with the adjustment. In a letter to Wendell Phillips, he expressed the fatigue he was now experiencing, as his obsession with seeing desegregation succeed had greatly "taxed my time and money." The suspense of how the first day of school would pass was nearly unbearable to him. He informed a New York friend of how "Our School Right matter is so nearly triumphant (all but the test)."

This test brought him much stress. It had taken so much toil to get to this point, and Nell could hardly believe integrated schools would soon be a reality. He kept reminding himself that "eternal vigilance is the price of liberty," and wrote to numerous friends of plots he thought were being hatched to disrupt the planned desegregation.

One final mass meeting was held in late August. Rev. Grimes, after being introduced to Boston during the 1849 school ordeal, was now a fixture of the community, having proved his fearlessness during the fugitive slave cases. Now he opened his Southac Street church's vestry to a meeting of anxious parents, discussing their newfound rights and "duties" under desegregation. Nell strongly bade the parents to see to it that the children were at school punctually, "neat in their dress," and ready to aid their instructors. According to Nell, this could be the parents' way of showing gratitude for the legislature's action. Nell prepared a comprehensive document with information on every school in the city, as well as more advice for parents. At 10 p.m. the participants filed out of the church and scattered over Beacon Hill ready for the anticipated day.

. . .

When Boston children left home for the first day of school on Monday, September 3, 1855, it was a brisk, chilly morning—a reminder that summer was over and fall was here. The temperature hung around fifty degrees. Clouds covered the sky, and fog, lifted from the harbor, was suspended above Beacon Hill. Throughout the neighborhood eager faces pressed against and hung out of windows to watch black children go off to school with white children. Many black Beacon Hill residents had waited a generation for this historic moment. Others poured into the streets anticipating trouble. It was only six years earlier that opening day had brought a near riot in front of the Smith School as integrationists tried to block the entrance. But today, no one would be blocking the way into any schools.

Boston papers covered the integration, but there seemed to be no story. The *Traveler* remarked on the "sensation" created when black children walked into their classroom but stated that nowhere in Boston were there any "violent manifestations of dislike." The paper had never seen children "happier" to go to school. The *Boston Bee* was impressed by the twenty-five black students new to one school, who displayed a "neatness" in their appearance and "correctness of deportment." The *Telegraph*'s reporter heard a white boy say, while walking down Myrtle Street on Beacon Hill, "Hurray! We

"Free to All," an illustration from *Harper's Weekly*. *(Courtesy of the Library of Congress)*

are to have the darkies to-day, and I'm going to have one right side of me."

Nell, always concerned that his dream might be deferred, assembled a committee of mothers who traveled from school to school to make sure the black children were received "in good faith." Everywhere they went, Nell saw children who had reached "the long-promised land." He personally had no children but always felt that through this struggle, he had "adopted" all the children of Beacon Hill. The memories of angry humiliation in his childhood were being washed away. He again felt the more innocent "heart of a child." Nevertheless, despite the revolutionary change that was occurring, it seemed so normal on that September morning that Nell was reminded, "The State House on Beacon Hill, and old Faneuil Hall, remain as firm in their bases as ever."

It was not a perfect day. Some white boys at the Phillips School, which because of its location on Beacon Hill absorbed many black students, started making fun of one new student. Principal Hovey asked the boys, "Is that your politeness to strangers?" Some similar banter was heard at another Beacon Hill institution, the Bowdoin School, between a group of girls, though this was also ended quickly with kind words.

By afternoon the cold had drifted away, along with many Bostonians' apprehensions about integration, and the *Telegraph* called the seventy-degree day "clean, cool and fine."

One place in the city that was not cheerful was the Smith School.

Thomas Paul came to work as though it were any other day, hoping that the children he had labored for over the last half decade would, in the end, choose to come back to their old school. He found a completely empty building. By the end of the following week, the School Committee officially abolished the now "unnecessary and inexpedient" institution. Paul lost not only the school he loved but also his job. The School Committee had no interest in introducing a black teacher into any of the other schools. He was given a small severance to cover, in the words of the School Committee, "the disappointment of being thrown out of employment." This was the twentieth anniversary of the proud afternoon on which the Smith School was dedicated, but notions of equality in the neighborhood had changed dramatically in the ensuing two decades. Paul was left to digest this reality in a noticeably silent building.

Paul was not the only Bostonian displeased with the new arrangements. The *Boston Gazette* expressed fury at the sight of black children "rushing into [the schools] in manifold flocks." The paper of the Irish, the *Boston Pilot*, conceded that there had been no violence, but warned, "There may be serious trouble yet." However, one *Pilot* editorial shared a prophetic insight belying the gruff racism on the surface of the writing. In October the paper wrote of the difference in race relations between the North and the South. The author noted that while in the South there was brutal racism, "in New England a deep repugnance to any thing like social intercourse with the blacks" held strong. More, it was felt that these Protestant reformers were hypocrites who were aware who would bear the brunt of this integration—the Irish, who now constituted most of the white students in the Boston school system. The editorial warned that wealthier whites might begin leaving Boston and putting their children in private schools.

This editorial looked straight ahead to Boston's painful and dismaying 1970s busing crisis. Fortunately, these sentiments were not true then; nor was there violence when black children arrived at their new schools in 1855.

With the day of desegregation passing more peaceably than anyone could have predicted, the only thing left to do was to celebrate. A year earlier, Morris and Hayden were publicly reviling Nell, but this unexpected success had gone a long way toward settling old disputes. A few days before the community celebration, Nell eagerly reported to a confidant that while walking down the street Hayden shocked him by cheerfully stopping and asking, "How do you do Mr. Nell!" Nell was overcome by "his civility without reference to the past."

As for Morris, his actions elicited more than a street greeting. In the celebration of Nell's magnificent push for equal school rights, Morris agreed to serve as vice president. Returning the favor, during his speech, Nell highlighted Morris's role in the Roberts case, calling him "a living protest against all exclusive colored institutions."

The words spoken that night were printed in a celebratory pamphlet, and so it is possible today to recapture the overwhelming joy and surging sense of stunned fulfillment coursing through the community on that night. This toughened and patient community knew their challenges were really just beginning. With nine in ten blacks still owned by another American, no one knew whether any act, either some violent cataclysm or a mighty deed of total moral suasion, could possibly alter this reality. However, this free black community took hope where they could. Now was that astonishing moment, so long dreamed of. Nell was hailed by the crowd as the great "Champion of Equal School Rights."

One minister compared Nell to Moses, and other members of the community presented him with flowers, an elegant gold watch, and a copy of Harriet Beecher Stowe's *Uncle Tom's Cabin,* autographed in tribute to him. Nell remembered it as "the proudest moment of my life" as members of the community, some who had known him since boyhood, beamed in front of him. He rose to speak, and once more recounted his story of the denied Franklin medal, how that angry night in the so-called Cradle of Liberty had set him on this course.

Now the struggle was completed, the boycott over. Nell heard a city councilman remark, "The colored people had in effect abolished the [Smith] school themselves." True, there had been key white allies at various points in the struggle: Sumner, Phillips, Slack, Garrison, but from start to finish, it had been Nell, Morris, and dozens of nameless members of the community who had held up hope. Nell then made sure to emphasize that it was the community's women who had really been the unwavering backbone of the struggle. Nell thought there were times when most men had become "lukewarm and indifferent," whereas the women of the Hill managed to "keep the flame alive," weaving "bright visions for the future."

Charles Slack then spoke about the process in the legislature that had brought about this "evening of jubilee." Garrison and Charles Lenox Remond followed, giving energetic addresses. Then Wendell Phillips summed up an era in their lives: "Men were always asking—what has the anti-slavery agitation done? Now they could say, 'It has opened the schools!' "

At one moment noted in the night's program, young children came forward presenting flowers of honor. One wonders if one of these children was Sarah Roberts. Her name and the name of her father were conspicuously missing from the pamphlet's program of speakers, though Benjamin Roberts is briefly mentioned in passing. It was Nell's night, not his.

The weight of this historic moment threatens to obscure the real children who were forced to endure and persevere through this transformation. Leaving the only school they had ever known, they stepped into places that offered a higher quality of education, but also the very real potential for painful and daily racism. However, ever since the days when Susan Paul's students sang their song "Mr. Prejudice," the black children of the community have always been aware of their vital part in the struggle for equality.

A story suggests that at least one of these children understood this and viewed integration with great excitement. On September 2, 1855, the morning before the first day of school, Nell watched a group of black boys in the street between Nell's house and the Smith School. Nell knew one of the boys, a student at the Smith

School. As the group walked away, the boy turned around and gazed up at the old school.

With his friends watching, the boy began to wave. Then he exclaimed just loud enough for Nell to hear, *"Good bye for ever, colored school! To-morrow we are like other Boston boys."*

# SIXTEEN

# Rock the Cradle of Liberty

Today Robert Morris is virtually unknown, even in his home of Boston, despite his being the first black lawyer to win a jury case in America. Part of this neglect is, of course, the fact that historians have only of late acknowledged a richer and more complex picture of white and black abolitionism and the reform movements of which Morris was fully a part.

Garrison remains a great and vital figure, but Boston's compelling saga of freedom and equality in this period was hardly the extended shadow of one man. Indeed, the more we learn, the plainer it appears that Garrison's powerful influence could have been possible only in Boston's particular environment, which was supported by a vital and vibrant free black community propelling and offering essential support at every step forward.

This is not revisionism; it simply reflects the facts of the case.

The other reason that Morris—as well as Lewis Hayden, William Cooper Nell, John Hilton, Benjamin Roberts, David Walker, Maria Stewart, and the innumerable other figures we have seen move across this timescape—is so obscure is more mundane and dispiriting. With the exception of Frederick Douglass, little was preserved of these free black leaders. We do not have, unlike famed figures such as Garrison and Phillips, the copious raw materials out of which to reconstruct their lives—no diaries, only a few personal letters, and few contemporary descriptions of their actions, movements, loves, failures, and personal triumphs. Much material exists, of course, which we have tried to highlight and uncover: community reports, newspaper articles, court transcripts, funeral orations, advertisements, tax and birth and housing and wedding records, census forms—these women and men are not lost to us. But these few facts have had to bear such intense scrutiny that it is hardly surprising their stories have not been told as thoroughly, and as compellingly, as they clearly deserve.

A few years ago, a small cache of Robert Morris letters and legal documents were discovered and bought by the Boston Athenaeum. They have only recently been catalogued and opened to scholars, to join the limited Morris documents that had already been collected for the massive Black Abolitionist Project. Though there are interesting papers in this small collection, it is daunting to reflect, as one goes through the bank checks, legal papers, and business letters from long-forgotten legal cases (which, after all, constituted the bulk of his lifetime's work), what a closed, constricted world of material exists on this man. It is, sadly, hardly a shock that a black man from the antebellum period would leave so little behind, and it could be said that we are astonishingly lucky to have even as much preserved information as we have; so much documentation of the daily lives of African Americans is lost and unrecoverable.

So little of his real voice survives. Of Robert Morris's speeches not lost to history, one stands without compare, giving us a stirring sense of what it must have been like to hear him, even in a reporter's hurried transcription. In August 1858, Morris addressed a convention gathering in New Bedford marking the anniversary of the British West India Emancipation Celebration. Exactly nine years earlier, he had been the only other black speaker sharing the stage of this great festivity with three of the greatest luminaries of the era, Emerson, Garrison, and Parker, demonstrating the promise seen in an untested twenty-six-year-old. Morris was now thirty-five, his achievements in the decade between these two speeches constituting full validation of that early promised potential.

His beloved Ellis Gray Loring had died unexpectedly from palsy only two months earlier. The first time Morris spoke there, he had been only two years out of his apprenticeship with Loring, who took him from his life as a servant to make him a Boston attorney. He had long since found his own voice, and Morris eloquently and forcefully presented the struggles abolitionists faced.

Looking out into New Bedford's City Hall, packed with reformers from all over New England, Morris began with the recent *Dred Scott* decision of the United States Supreme Court. They should, he cried, "trample" this pronouncement as they had done with the Fugitive Slave Law. This recent 1857 Supreme Court verdict had been met with absolute shock in Boston, the judgment not only maintaining that slavery ultimately had no restricting boundaries to its expansion but that *blacks were not even full citizens of the republic.*

This decision was an affront to everything Morris stood for. Thus, he, Nell, and Hayden, feuding adversaries only a few years earlier, demonstrated a renewed partnership by testifying in front of the legislature's Committee on Federal Relations on this decision's lack of applicability to Massachusetts's blacks. Nell also organized a celebration in honor of Crispus Attucks, as a reminder of their people's contribution to the freedom of the nation. Although this was a grand event for black Boston, it did not substantively alter white Americans' ideas of black citizenship. This would not change until slavery itself was overthrown. Morris, showing an increasing radicalism, told the audience, "Slavery is not to be abolished by peaceable means."

Morris's radical speech continued with his claim that neither prayer nor even helping escaped slaves could really change America: now, only "the strong arm" could prevail. This view helps to explain his passion for black representation in the militia. War was coming, and Morris would not allow blacks to be excluded. He discussed how they were still being barred from the militia in Massachusetts. He had been commander of the Massasoit Guards, a company that raised enough money to order uniforms and weapons. Other members of the body were Benjamin Roberts, Lewis Hayden, and William Pindall. In his New Bedford speech, Morris acknowledged that despite their noble appearance, this troop was training against the law. Morris had flaunted the law once in the Minkins rescue and was reluctant to be associated with riots again. The struggle to see black soldiers obtain legal legitimacy would continue, culminating not until well into the Civil War.

Morris wanted to point out what could be learned from the battles that had already been waged, going on to remind his audience of all that had been learned during the "school question." Now his language was increasingly animated. "When we wanted our children to go to the Public Schools in Boston, they offered them schools, and white teachers, but no, we wouldn't have them. Then they offered to give us colored teachers; no, we wouldn't stand that neither. Then the School Committee said—'Well, if you won't be satisfied either way, you shall have them as we choose.'" He was now more preacher than lawyer.

"So we decided on a desperate step, but it turned out to be a successful one." Recounting how they "went round to every parent in the city," Morris boasted about a boycott that removed so many children from the "caste" Smith School that it was almost unable to function. It was only so long until segregated schools were brought down. To Morris, the audacious move of maintaining a boycott was indicative of "the way we always should act."

He implored:

Let us be bold, and they'll have to yield to us. Let us be bold, if any man flies from slavery, and comes among us. When he's reached us, we'll say, he's gone far enough. If any man comes here to New Bedford, and they try to take him away, you telegraph to us in Boston, and we'll come down three hundred strong, and stay with you; and we won't go until he's safe. If he goes back to the south, we'll go with him. And if any man runs away, and comes to Boston, we'll send to you, if necessary, and you may come up to us three hundred strong, if you can—come men, and women, too.

When the Civil War broke out in 1861, Morris was nearly beside himself with urgency to see black soldiers enlisted. To thundering applause, he asserted at an 1861 community meeting, "There was not a [black] man who would not leap to his knapsack and musket, and they would make it intolerably hot for Old Virginia." Cries such as these went unheard by the war powers, despite the best efforts of legislators such as Charles Slack and constant petitions from Morris and Nell.

However, Massachusetts's governor John Andrew shared their sentiments. He was the man who had introduced the school desegregation legislation six years earlier, and he was now pressing President Lincoln to allow his black citizens to fight. While the hapless Union army suffered defeat after defeat in Virginia during the summer of 1862, Governor Andrew finally put out a call for a black militia. By the beginning of 1863, things were even worse for the Army of the Potomac, which lost thousands on the bloody slopes of Fredericksburg, Virginia. Men were needed. In February the War Department gave Governor Andrew the long-sought-after permission to raise a separate company of black soldiers.

This should have been a crowning moment for Morris, having initiated the militia struggle a decade before, but he found it unacceptable that there were to be no black officers. He visited the State House to protest, but Governor Andrew, having taken enough of a political gamble in endorsing any kind of black regiment at all, would not allow this further request, though he privately sympathized. The outraged Morris said he would "not lift a finger for that Regiment," nor "ask any to enlist in it." He was being forced to decide between his desire to fight for the end of slavery and the principles of equality he lived by and championed.

Governor Andrew went to a community meeting at the Twelfth Baptist Church to try to convince blacks that this new regiment would be a success. The evening soon turned into a debate between him and Morris. The fact that a sitting governor had come to their meeting was a considerable matter, but Morris would not back down from his stance. When Andrew pointed out that the state constitution forbade a black man to command such an outfit, Morris pleaded for the removal of the word *white* from the constitution.

A white abolitionist jumped in to support the governor in the hope and belief that black troops would be treated fairly. As he continued, he referred to "Brother Morris." As soon as these words left his lips, Morris was on his feet. A spectator was startled when Morris, "in a stronger, clearer voice than I ever heard," shot back with deep-seated anger at this patronizing tone. Morris pronounced, "Don't you call me 'brother' until you have taken the word 'white' out of the Constitution!"

In the wake of the formation of the popular Fifty-fourth Regiment of Massachusetts, despite initial hesitancy on the part of blacks, it was decided that the black regiment would be commanded by Robert Gould Shaw, a young, white colonel who had been raised on Beacon Street.

Shaw led his party of black volunteers out of Boston during a gloriously pristine day in May 1863. Hundreds came out to see these black men parade through the streets past the State House and along the Common. It was perhaps the proudest moment in the history of Boston's black community. Morris's stubbornness over the issue of black officers may have been a worthy, principled stand, yet one hopes he allowed himself a moment to look out with some pride upon these parading soldiers. Indeed, these men were heavily indebted to his years of fighting for their representation first within the militia, then in the Union army itself.

This march out of Boston with flags flying seemed to symbolize so many years of struggle. It was the culmination of the struggle to open the theaters, the railroads, and the schools and to eliminate the ban on interracial marriage. What had been learned at one step had been systematically applied to the next, and though this activist process may not have been clear to most citizens of the Commonwealth, it had been clear to the organizers.

Despite that glorious day, discrimination had not ended for the black troops. Though eventually some blacks became noncommissioned officers, only whites, although clearly selected for their abolitionist leanings, rose to leadership. Even more galling was the simple fact that the black soldiers were paid less than the white ones. In reaction, black soldiers refused their paychecks, an act in which Col. Shaw had the grace and instinctive leadership to join.

In the end, about 40 percent of military-age black Boston men enlisted. These men were the children of black Beacon Hill who had passed through the Smith School and grown up with constant activism in the community. Now they carried the fight into the heart of slave territory and fought bravely until the end of the war. Black servicemen comprised more than 10 percent of Union forces by the end of the war. Their losses were felt keenly on Beacon Hill, especially after the battle of Fort Wagner, where the idealistic and courageous Col. Shaw lost his life along with nearly a quarter of the men of the Fifty-fourth. Lewis Hayden had lost one child to slavery; he would lose another in the struggle to end the institution.

After the war, Morris's legal career continued to flourish. By 1882, he was earning an annual income of more than $3,000. Nevertheless, residential segregation and prejudice continued to be a problem for Morris, despite his growing wealth. In 1868 he purchased a Chelsea mansion, but unfortunately, Morris was never to live in this vast estate. He was candid with the seller, telling him that a black man living there would depreciate the value of the real estate. Morris was told his "money was as good as any man's." Morris was ecstatic at the good character of this dealer.

But when neighbors got wind of the proposed sale, a commotion arose, ending in threats that they would all leave the neighborhood if the Morris family moved in. The directors of the Cary Improvement Company refused to give the deed to Morris. Not understanding Morris's relentless quest for integration, they asked him why he would push himself into the vicinity of those who did not want him as a neighbor. Morris later wrote of the incident, calling the experience "prejudice against color to its extreme extent," but he would never be allowed to buy the house.

Even so, Morris was still a popular man in Chelsea. Nevertheless, the town disappointed him again in 1866, when he lost an election for mayor. Even in defeat, the impact of his having run in such a race was considerable. As far away as New Orleans, a paper reported that "those who believe that a black man is only fit for slavery and the lash, will probably be again shocked by the announcement that the citizens of Chelsea of Massachusetts have run Robert Morris, a Negro lawyer for mayor of that city."

After his defeat he decided to move back to Boston. He obtained a spacious brick house on West Newton Street, situated in the affluent neighborhood of the South End.

Morris was pleased with his progress in the law, but he was even prouder of the fact that his son, Robert Morris Jr., was now the first second-generation black lawyer. Morris was able to give his son the kind of background and privilege he himself never had. Robert Jr. had been educated in France, sent off to escape the segregated schools of Boston before they were overthrown. When Robert Jr. graduated from the Montpellier School in Paris, there were accounts of his achievement in newspapers from Boston to New York. Ellen Craft, the fugitive whom Loring had helped after her escape from the South, was in Savannah teaching former slaves when she heard of the younger Morris's distinctions. After Robert Jr. passed an examination at the Imperial College in France, she sent his father a note mentioning her "delight" at Robert Jr.'s triumphs. Eventually Robert Jr. would return to Massachusetts to attend Harvard Law School. After passing the bar, he would share the "Robert Morris & Son" practice on Washington Street.

By the end of the 1870s, Morris's energy was diminishing. His mother, Mercy, lived to the age of eighty-six, finally passing away in 1878. By 1881, though, the little man who once seemed larger than life with his infectious energy appeared "shriveled and emaciated." One old friend nearly did not recognize him when passing him on the street. He saw "a physical wreck of what was once robust manhood."

Morris was a lover of the law until the end. Even when he could no longer be a champion of the great questions of the day in the courtroom, he could still be found in the back of many a courtroom. Silently he would observe and perhaps reminisce about the days when he stood with Sumner for Sarah Roberts or helped free Shadrach Minkins from a certain return to slavery. Those were days when Morris had felt "like a giant."

On a winter morning in December 1882, the sixty-one-year-old Morris woke and called for his wife and son. They conversed "pleasantly" for a few minutes, and he reassured them he was all right. Then he fell silent. His family thought they had lost him, but he re-

Robert Morris near the end of his life. (*Joseph A. Willard Photograph Collection; courtesy of the Social Law Library, Boston*)

gained consciousness with a smile. His son felt Morris's lips, already cold. Morris said quietly, "Beautiful, beautiful," and then reassured them, "I will speak a good word for you when I get there." The grandson of an African slave, the son of a servant, and the soul of a movement for equality pressed the hands of his family and then was gone.

Sadness became tragedy when the often-sick Robert Jr., to whom Morris had given so much and invested such hopes in, passed away two weeks later. Catherine Morris had the inexpressibly sad task of burying her husband of thirty-six years and her son within the same month.

Morris was given a Catholic funeral in the Church of the Immaculate Conception in Boston. Among his pallbearers were Lewis Hayden and soon-to-be mayor Patrick Collins, the Irish boy Morris had taught to be a lawyer. One of those attending the Suffolk bar meeting in honor of Morris was none other than John C. Park, the domineering opposing counsel who had nearly caused Morris to abort his career before it began. Morris had won over even his respect.

. . .

On the eve of the Civil War, Morris had sent a letter to his old co-counselor Charles Sumner, thanking him for his "boldness, honesty, and sincerity" in the Senate. He could not help but recount the results of their efforts together on behalf of Sarah. Now, "the doors of the Common School in our beloved City have been thrown open to the colored children." Morris told him his gratitude had never wavered after the help Sumner gave after Morris's loss in the Court of Common Pleas. Today the senator still challenged "the bitterest opponents—the most severe hater of the colored race to point to any intellectual inequality on the part of the colored children here." Their defeat in front of Shaw had been redeemed.

Sumner needed no reminder of the *Roberts* case, for the principles propelling his argument were still guiding his political life. He had used the concept of "equality before the law" during the Kansas-Nebraska debates, when introducing the Hungarian freedom fighter Louis Kossuth to Congress, and at numerous times during Senate debates after the Civil War. As for the *Roberts* argument, in 1868 he wrote to a friend asking whether it could be reprinted as a "cheap pamphlet" to be distributed throughout the South. He thought the idea that he had introduced in that speech, "Equality before the law," was "precisely applicable" to the South. Much to his satisfaction, it was distributed throughout the country to provide aid to new campaigns against segregation.

Still, being such an outspoken voice for black people had its risks. Early in his Senate time in 1856, Sumner delivered his most biting speech on slavery, in the process personally insulting several southern politicians. Congressman Preston Brooks of South Carolina vowed to have revenge on the insolent abolitionist and went to him on the floor of the Senate, where Sumner was hard at work writing letters at his desk. Brooks stated his grievances, and before Sumner could respond, Brooks took his gold-headed cane and swung it on Sumner's head. Sumner could not see, as more blows rained down furiously. With blood flowing down his face, he rose frantically, pulling his desk out from the screws in the floor before collapsing. A group of southern politicians calmly watched Sumner writhing on the floor.

This savage beating made it clear that when congressmen were prepared to nearly murder each other, war could only be just around the corner. This view was confirmed by the approval many southerners offered for the assault. Brooks was sent canes from all over the South as a tribute to his reprisal. But if Brooks became an icon of southern fortitude, Sumner also assured his place in the North as an abolitionist hero and near martyr. His attack woke many to the impending harsh and threatening realities of the state of the nation. Bloody conflict in Kansas had shown the violence that slavery could provoke, but few would imagine this brutality could spill unto the most decorous halls of the nation. Emerson said, "We must get rid of slavery, or we must get rid of freedom."

For even moderate and conservative northerners, the South had gone too far. Peleg Chandler had been an opponent of all things abolitionist, arguing against integrated schools in the *Roberts* case. Yet regardless of political affiliation, Sumner had been his friend. Now Chandler rose to speak at a Faneuil Hall meeting honoring their senator, sounding like a thoroughly converted abolitionist. He cried out, "Every drop of blood shed by him in this disgraceful affair has raised up ten thousand men."

When Sumner was brought back to Boston to recover, he was greeted with one of the largest gatherings the city had ever witnessed. He would spend three and a half years incapacitated, often lapsing into fevers, torturous head pains, and insomnia. One of his many visitors during these difficult days was an odd farmer named John Brown. The intense fellow asked to see the coat Sumner was wearing during the attack. Sumner limped to his closet, pulled out the bloody coat, and handed it to Brown. Brown held the coat without speaking; "his lips were compressed, and his eyes shone like polished steel." Sumner was watching a man with a fierce prophetic anger that would lead him to a fateful raid at Harpers Ferry, an act that would do much to hasten the outbreak of the war.

Though never quite the same again, Sumner eventually returned to the Senate. Still helping Morris's causes, during the war Sumner advocated for the use of black troops. Sumner was responsible for allowing blacks to become mail carriers, to serve on juries in Washington, D.C., and to be allowed to watch Congress in session from the galleries. Furthermore, he saw to it that segregation was legally ended in the District of Columbia and that discrimination against witnesses in federal courts became illegal.

His contributions to our nation after the war were even more significant. Slightly altering the phrase "equality before the law," Sumner introduced the phrase "equal protection of the laws" into our Constitution by way of the passage of the Fourteenth Amendment. He also helped drive through the Fifteenth Amendment, which was supposed to settle the issue of black enfranchisement forever. This set him up for a final legislative ambition, the ultimate tribute to the *Roberts* case. In 1870 he introduced a civil rights bill intended to ensure blacks widespread equality, from schools to any other public institution supported by law. Sumner's words rang out with the passion and themes he had spoken of in a cold Boston courtroom in 1849, when he believed segregation was an "ill-disguised violation of the principle of equality" and segregated public schools were a "misnomer and mockery. It is not a school for whites or a school for blacks, but a school for all; in other words a common school for all."

A vote on his bill was put off in 1870. Sumner introduced it again in 1871. During a speech in South Carolina, he again addressed the idea of "separate but equal," which was gaining popularity in a post-slavery era. Sumner had faced down this idea ever since it emerged from Judge Shaw's prodigious and agile legal mind, and he continued to find it a fraud. He said, "It is not enough to provide separate accommodations for colored citizens, even if in all respects as good as those of other persons. Equality is not found in any pretended equivalent, but only in equality."

Sumner's bill was unpopular, but he was persistent even as his health failed again. On the night of May 21, 1872, while Sumner was out of the Senate, his bill was passed, but without any mention of schools and other vital components of the law. With his body getting weaker every day, Sumner would not acquiesce in his crusade for this bill, so clearly harkening back to his days on the *Roberts* case. He told a friend, "If my works were completed, and my Civil-Rights Bill passed, no visitor could enter that door that would be more welcome than death."

He introduced the measure again in 1873, written as it was supposed to have been the first time. However, Sumner would not live to see any of it enacted, though he worked until the last day of his life to see a comprehensive assurance of black equality in American law. A bill passed months after he was gone, giving equal rights to all in public inns, public conveyances, theaters, and juries, but any mention of school desegregation had been gutted. Furthermore, it would not be long before the Supreme Court nullified the whole bill.

Though Sumner did not leave behind a lasting civil rights bill, he left words, arguments, and ideas that would help bring down segregation. He also died a world-famous figure, lionized as one of most influential figures in the overthrow of American slavery.

. . .

Back on Beacon Hill, much had changed since the desegregation of the schools in 1855. For one thing, the members of the great equal rights generation were dying. Morris, Nell, Roberts, and others passed away in the 1870s and 1880s, but they did so after watching desegregation work astoundingly well for more than twenty years.

It had not taken Boston long to adjust to integrated schools. Already in 1856, the *Christian Examiner* decided these black children were "not by half so objectionable as the Patricks, Michaels, and Bridgets," and desegregation was in "everyway successful." On the sixth anniversary of school desegregation, legislative hero Charles Slack proudly stepped before the Boston School Committee, telling them of the many achievements of black children over the past six years. Slack was gratified to see that "a new generation of colored youth has risen to receive the great boon of impartial school education."

Of school-age Beacon Hill black children, the percentage attending school went from 75 percent during segregation to 91 percent after integration. Among black children who were of school age after integration, 8 percent were more likely to be literate than those children who had been of school age during segregated times. By 1860 the black literacy rate in Boston ran about the same as that of white Virginians. Blacks attended Boston high schools and, to William Nell's particular delight, won Franklin medals and City medals. Abolitionists were elated in 1863 when the top scholar at the heralded Boston Latin School was black.

There were numerous cases of parents moving from nearby states so their children could attend the integrated schools of Boston, the only major city with desegregated schools. It was in Massachusetts alone that the wall of segregated schools was completely shattered before the Civil War. Thus the spread of Boston's new system proved most instrumental. A western New York paper wrote in 1863 of surprise at seeing black children in a Boston schoolhouse, finding them "well dressed and behaved well." Similarly, in an 1859 *Anglo American Magazine* article, a writer asserted, "With the experience of Boston...there is no sound reason why colored children shall be excluded from any of the common schools." That same year, the *Christian Examiner* challenged anyone to "go into the schools, and see if the colored children who sit by the side of the white children are any less intelligent, well-behaved or neat in person and attire."

Boston was held up not just as a model of desegregated schools but as a prototype for how to advocate for those rights. The petitions, boycotts, and patient organizing became a prototype for those looking for similar results. However, school desegregation was not a concern in places where efforts were concentrated on more basic rights. In the "free" states in 1860, blacks were still not enfranchised in Connecticut, New Jersey, Indiana, Illinois, Iowa, Wisconsin, Minnesota, California, and Oregon. In New York, Ohio, and Michigan blacks had limited voting rights. Most states had isolated municipalities with some integrated education, but in major northern cities, such as New York, New Haven, Hartford, Philadelphia, Providence, and Cincinnati, the battle for integrated schools did not really begin until after the Civil War. This battle was won at various times, with desegregation in Hartford coming as early as 1868, and New York City having to wait until 1884 to have desegregated schools.

It took less than a year for word of Boston's progress to spread to the other end of the country. Black citizens in Sacramento, California, in January 1856, asked, "Why should we in California be behind our brethren of other states?" and cited "Massachusetts—that cradle of liberty." A friend wrote to Nell from Sacramento, lamenting, "The school question still remains in status quo, and is likely to be for the present."

Bostonians would lend their efforts anywhere that educational progress could be made. Most of the money that would start schools for the fourteen thousand black children of Washington, D.C., came from Boston. Pennsylvania, which from 1790 to 1830 had clearly been the most egalitarian state, had greatly regressed since then, robbing blacks of their voting rights and segregating transportation. A meeting of blacks in Philadelphia during the Civil War commended Massachusetts for being "first in opening her public schools to colored youth." Nell understood their predicament, because where no "citizen can approach the ballot-box, equal school rights are of course not immediately expected." Nonetheless, a young Massachusetts woman began teaching in Bucks County outside Philadelphia and, to the amazement of Nell and many others, integrated her small school. This was a start.

Yet Boston could not rest. While it was lamented in 1864 that community meetings seemed to happen less frequently (primarily because so many black leaders had moved to the suburbs), the final victory for this remarkable generation came in 1865, with the legislature passing a law "forbidding unjust discrimination on account of color or race" in "any place of public amusement, public conveyance, or public meeting." Anyone resisting the decree would be fined up to $50. This extraordinary piece of legislation foreshadowed Sumner's ill-fated bill and the ultimately successful Civil Rights Bill of 1964.

The transformation of Boston's laws and customs that this remarkable and inventive generation created bears many similarities to the modern civil rights movement. These activists ended legalized segregation in every sphere of Boston life, but there were two crucial blind spots in their work. As was the case in the 1960s, the law books were certainly changed, but economics and residential patterns never altered as much as leaders would have liked. In 1860 Dr. John Rock bitterly remarked, "Colored men in business here receive more respect and less patronage than in any other place I know of." Jobs were still hard to come by for Boston laborers. Also, Rock found it vastly more difficult to get a house in a "good location" of Boston than in the otherwise more racist Philadelphia. It was these problems in residential segregation that would sow the seeds for a new battle over educational segregation and equality, one that would be ignobly fought before the eyes of the nation by a different generation of Bostonians.

. . .

For William Cooper Nell, after all his fights on behalf of his community, it was time at last to have a family. The mysterious "singleness" of the handsome Nell came to an end when he met a New Hampshire woman half his age and was married in the town of Nashua. His wife, Frances, would bear him two sons, William and Frank, but the eldest boy was only four when Nell died unexpectedly of "paralysis of the brain" on May 25, 1874. Before his death, he had given up journalism so that he could accept the honor of being the first black to be appointed to a federal post, as a postal clerk in the Boston Postal Office.

A week after his death, people poured into the African Meeting House for his funeral, the exact place where Nell had first seen Garrison create the New England Anti-Slavery Society on that snowy night, and where years later he had been pelted with rocks for advocating integration. Across the street from the church stood the house where Nell had lived and looked over at the segregated school he deplored and vowed to end. But this time it was not mobilization bringing the community together but a farewell to a leader who had served them as well as he could and for as long as most could remember.

· · ·

The man who initiated the lawsuit that crystallized the whole struggle for equality also lived a quiet life once that battle was over. Benjamin Roberts constantly moved around Boston (often at least once a year) and its surrounding towns, continuing to work as a printer. When he was not printing and instructing young men in the manual arts, he loved to perform as a singer. In 1858 he sang at the famed Faneuil Hall. He also continued writing. Though never again attempting to start his own publication, he published multiple pieces in Frederick Douglass's son's short-lived Washington, D.C., paper, the *New National Era*.

One of the events he covered for that paper was the celebration of the Fourteenth Amendment in Boston in 1870. Roberts reported that a procession of three thousand blacks, which he believed to be "the largest that the colored people ever had in this part of the country," marched from the Public Garden to Faneuil Hall, where Morris was among the speakers. An era had dawned where "*Sympathy*, after this, for anybody on account of color, will be a thing of the past." As for the celebration of the Fifteenth Amendment at Faneuil Hall, for this day Roberts predicted, "The 'Old Cradle of Liberty' would be rocked on that as it was never rocked before."

Near the end of his life, Benjamin Roberts wrote an article called

"Our Progress in the Old Bay State," recounting the struggles of his family, from his grandfather to the present. Roberts remained proud of the court case he had begun more than twenty years earlier and was still grateful to Charles Sumner, whom he called "the great vindicator of impartial justice, and the champion of the great national reformation in the nineteenth century." After desegregation, Roberts saw that "new ideas are opened," and more children were learning trades, all of which he felt would eventually bring more blacks into Boston's professional class. Looking back at their struggles, Roberts felt "the deepest and most profound astonishment of our people." He closed by writing:

> Who among us can refrain from giving vent to his feelings in the highest exultation over these remarkable events? But amid all this we have important duties to perform. We must be true to each other. We must encourage each other. We must devote our energies, if we mean success, to the acquirement of *education*, which is power, and the accumulation of *money*, which will add all that will be necessary to our elevation.

Roberts died of epilepsy in 1881. His career, judging by the episodic quality of his writings and sporadic efforts in public to create change—often separated by long years of silence—was obviously a frustrating and often humbling experience. He never received the kind of affection given to Nell or the honor of being a civic hero, as was true of Morris. He seems to have been too prickly, too independent, too sensitive to stay at the forefront of the black community's efforts for long. Yet in the end, his brief partnership with Morris was to produce the most important element of this generation's contribution to our history when the *Roberts* case began its curious legal trail to the very steps of the United States Supreme Court in 1954.

And what of his daughter, the mysterious center of our story? Information on Sarah has been excruciatingly hard to come by. In the end, we have only glints and glimmers of a woman who in some sense represents the thousands upon thousands of those lost to our inspection and analysis, children of the African American journey.

They are the unknown souls who lived and died leaving behind little or no record; yet live they did, and like Sarah, it is impossible to understand ourselves without reckoning with them.

Her siblings are easier to find and track than she is. Like Robert Morris, Benjamin Roberts had a son follow him into his profession, as Benjamin Jr. was a printer in Boston until near the beginning of the twentieth century. Another of his sons, William, married the granddaughter of community leader John Hilton and worked as a bookbinder until his death in Cambridge, Massachusetts, in 1931. Charles Sumner Roberts, a letter carrier, also married into the Hilton family.

As for Sarah, after the lawsuit that made her name known all over the country, she attended schools in Cambridge. By seventeen she had moved in with her grandfather, the servant and writer Robert Roberts, in Charlestown. They seemed to have had an exceptional relationship, as she was the only grandchild he included in his will. By twenty-three she had moved back to Boston and was living on her own.

During the next two years she met and was courted by a man named John Casneau. Casneau was the son of Haitian immigrants and had served in the Union navy during the Civil War. After the war he stayed on the sea as a ship's steward. They were both twenty-three when they were married in 1867. His naval career soon came to an end, and he worked in Boston as a janitor. From there Sarah becomes very hard to trace. She seems to have divorced the sailor and married twice more. Unlike her siblings, she left the Boston area, and the last record of her life shows her living in New Haven, Connecticut, near the turn of the century, as Sarah Dyer.

No photograph or etching seems to exist of her or of any member of the family. There survives no written description of her. Sarah was and remains a historical tabula rasa. Even in the time of Sumner's argument, Sarah was already a symbol of a child forced to persevere in unjust circumstances. She could have been any black person living through daily indignities. Perhaps it was simply luck or fate that her name has entered American history. Yet this does not make Sarah Roberts any less deserving of grateful remembrance.

Descendents of the Roberts family continue to live in the Boston area. They are currently working to find Sarah's burial place and hope to finally write the Roberts family's long history.

Popular histories vie with one another with grandiloquent labels like "the greatest generation." No such claims are needed here, since this is a story about a remarkable generation of activists who, with little wealth, social standing, and political influence (indeed, with many in the community living in fear of being returned to slavery), changed our nation.

They did not create a Utopia. They did not alter basic patterns of racism. Yet it is hard to think of any other single group, especially one possessing so little social capital, that forced so much change in so little time. They did so without well-known leaders, though they had inventive and determined leaders, an ever-shifting and loose assemblage of men and women who rose up on the north slope of Beacon Hill to demand their dignity, acknowledged by law, and simple respect.

## *Brown* and Beyond

After that December day in 1849 when the *Roberts* case was heard, no one realized that the stage was being set for a protracted one-hundred-year war between two competing ideas: "Separate but Equal" and "Equality before the Law."

The advent of 1954 seemed to signal the possible stunning victory for the latter, but as we will see, Judge Lemuel Shaw's brainchild had a dangerous, and deceivingly adaptive, staying power.

The United States Supreme Court was not yet ready to decide the issue in 1952, calling a halt to the *Brown v. Board of Education* case to send both sides scurrying back to their history books and old yellowed newspaper files. Whether or not the framers of the Fourteenth Amendment a century earlier intended its extension of full equality to apply to integrated schools has been the subject of much debate, but none was so fierce as in the period between the first argument of *Brown* and the period when the Supreme Court asked the litigants to thoroughly research the amendment's meaning before coming back to the court for resolution.

Since Judge Shaw denied Sarah access to the school closest to her home while claiming to accept Sumner's general ideas of equality, he crafted an argument useful for all those who did not want to integrate schools but were forced, after the passage of the Fourteenth Amendment, to provide at least a facade of equality.

For twenty-five years after the adoption of the Fourteenth

Amendment, Shaw's reasoning seemed to crop up every time there was a school integration case. The first was in Nevada in 1872, where justices ruled the state had to provide schools for black children but, citing *Roberts*, did not have to integrate them. A black San Francisco parent sued for his child's rights in 1874, but Shaw was quoted at length to fend off the integrationist lawsuit. The California judge made the odd assertion that the Shaw decision was as weighty as the Fourteenth Amendment, a compliment even Shaw could not responsibly have accepted.

At the other end of the country, the New York Supreme Court rejected the plea for the admittance of a black girl into a white Brooklyn school in 1883, again citing Shaw. Courts in Arkansas, Missouri, Louisiana, Kansas, Oklahoma, South Carolina, Oregon, and West Virginia all made similar decisions, mentioning the *Roberts* case. A bright spot came in Michigan in 1890, when the state's Supreme Court accurately assessed that Roberts was "a reminder of the injustice and prejudice of the time in which it was delivered" and thus "it cannot now serve as a precedent." Unfortunately, judging by the reasoning of other state courts, it most certainly was being used that way.

Still, it was not until 1896 that the full force of Shaw's influence was realized. More than five decades after Frederick Douglass refused to move from the whites-only train carriage, a "seven-eighths" white man named Homer Plessy used this same tactic and was arrested. When it came time for the U.S. Supreme Court's ruling, the man chosen to write the opinion was Massachusetts native Henry Brown. Judge Brown's decision was deeply rooted in *Roberts*. Brown quoted Shaw prominently and went to great lengths in his text to highlight *Roberts*.

So infatuated was the Justice with the idea of "separate but equal" that Brown totally ignored the fact that Shaw's *Roberts* decision was written twenty years before a constitutional amendment mandating equality and, further, was a decision overruled by the Massachusetts legislature six years later. It is for this and other reasons that the *Plessy* decision has been called "a compound of bad logic, bad history, bad sociology, and bad constitutional law."

The only silver lining to the disaster for black America came in

*Plessy*'s one-person dissent of Justice John Harlan. In Harlan's lonely, yet forceful dissent, Sumner's declaration that *"all men, without distinction of color or race, are equal before the law"* (emphasis added) was strongly echoed. Harlan acknowledged that when it came to power, education, and wealth, whites may at the moment be the dominant race, but this could not change the fact that "in the view of the Constitution, in the eye of the law, there is in this country no superior, dominant, ruling class of citizens. There is no caste here. Our constitution is color-blind, and neither knows nor tolerates classes among its citizens. In respect of civil rights, all citizens are equal before the law."

Harlan had written beautifully, but to no avail. America now had racism legitimized in its constitutional law under the guise of egalitarianism.

. . .

Like Robert Morris before him, Thurgood Marshall's father was a proud waiter who raised his son to believe he was the equal of any man. Morris had Loring to impart to him the law's vast potential for changing society, and Marshall had Charles Houston, who created an environment at Howard University Law School emphasizing both excellence and the potential of law for social change.

Morris initiated the first school-desegregation suit, and a hundred years on, Marshall worked doggedly for more than a decade for just one case that could end segregation forever. The Jim Crow years were a time of devastation for black America. Lynching rates skyrocketed, the Ku Klux Klan grew, and educational opportunities for black youth refused to improve. For years during this discouraging period in the late 1940s, Marshall traveled through the darkest corners of the country, assisting as many as he could. Morris and Marshall both knew the importance of white allies, but at times they became quite frustrated with the firm entrenchment of white racism. Morris once reprimanded a white ally for calling him brother during a debate. Marshall, exhausted one night during his travels in the South, sadly told a friend, "I'm tired, tired of trying to save the white man's soul."

*Brown v. Board of Education* bears the name of Oliver Brown of

Topeka, Kansas, by a quirk of court procedure. Brown, although not an activist like Benjamin Roberts, was nevertheless tired of watching his seven-year-old daughter Linda walk every day to a school noticeably inferior to a nearby white school. Topeka's schools had been segregated since the *Reynolds v. the Board of Education of Topeka* decision of 1903, consisting almost entirely of lengthy quotations from *Roberts*. When Benjamin Roberts and Oliver Brown had had enough of what their daughters were forced to endure, they each walked their girls to the closest white school and tried to enroll them.

The segregated white school Brown walked Linda to, on that September 1950 morning, was named after none other than Charles Sumner. When Brown's daughter was turned away from the Sumner School, Linda remembered him being "quite upset." He never told her that she was part of a lawsuit, though she remembered in church hearing an NAACP member ask the audience, "Why should this child be forced to travel so far to school each day?" Linda was never in the courtroom while her father testified about her daily walk.

The three other states from which *Brown* cases emerged were South Carolina, Virginia, and Delaware, as well as Washington, D.C. Another suit with key similarities to *Roberts* was one from Prince Edward County, Virginia, though for different reasons from Kansas's *Brown*.

Like *Roberts*, this was a case with a boycott of the segregated black school behind it. What is most surprising about this boycott was that it was created and led not by older community leaders but by a sixteen-year-old girl. Barbara Johns was simply a student at Robert R. Moton High School in rural southern Virginia who had become obsessed with the quality differences between the white schools and Moton. Though a quiet girl, she was also the niece of the fiery reverend Vernon Johns, who at the time was preaching hugely controversial sermons on the immorality of segregation in Alabama. Barbara acted on these ideals when she led 450 students in a strike and contacted two NAACP lawyers in Richmond, Oliver Hill and Spottswood Robinson.

With Morris and the *Roberts* case in mind, we asked Oliver Hill, now in his nineties, how taking a case with a boycott behind it made it unique. He spoke of the infectious energy and momentum this gave the case. Hill also remarked that he had no choice but to fight especially hard, because he "didn't have the heart to break their spirit." As a teenager, Hill had gone to the Congressional Library to read *Plessy* and decided "to take another case to the Supreme Court and convince them *Plessy* was wrong." He and Marshall attended Howard Law School together, and eventually Hill was responsible for guiding one of the five cases before the Supreme Court.

As for Barbara Johns, once her now-famous boycott ended, she was sent to live with her forthright uncle, Rev. Johns. By the time the case was decided by the Supreme Court in 1954, Rev. Johns had been fired from the Dexter Avenue Church and replaced by an untested minister named Martin Luther King Jr.

·  ·  ·

Behind closed doors, the venerable court in 1953 was divided as to whether there was a constitutional basis to overturn segregation. The NAACP's constitutional case rested on the Fourteenth Amendment's assurance of equal protection before the law, which was not being met under segregation. The questions dealt with the framers of the Fourteenth Amendment's intentions and opinions on its relevance to school desegregation. The memory of *Roberts* would be unavoidable. The NAACP legal team's brief saw Sumner and Morris's Boston suit as a legal tool to achieve genuine equality for all citizens. This, they claimed, was Charles Sumner's "outstanding contribution to American Law." Quoting extensively from *Roberts*, they called his argument in *Roberts* "one of the landmarks in the crystallization of the egalitarian concept."

It was not just Sumner who made it into this crucial *Brown* brief. The whole black Beacon Hill community's struggle to see schools desegregated, after the defeat in *Roberts*, was summarized. Morris, Nell, and others were never mentioned by name, but the effect of their community's activism was incorporated as the NAACP lawyers wrote of the clear shift from abolitionism to "the status and rights of the free Negros" happening in this era.

Both sides wrote on the implications of Sumner's outspoken advocacy of integrated schools. The NAACP stated that his argument had been read throughout the nation in the years leading up to the Civil War. The fact that Sumner then became a major player in the writing of the Fourteenth Amendment also showed that at least one senator was interpreting the amendment as encapsulating equal school rights.

However, Sumner did lose the *Roberts* case, as well as his battles on behalf of his civil rights bills in the 1870s. To the NAACP's legal opponents, this showed that those writing the amendment found no favor for integrated schools. In the appeals brief, they conceded that Sumner had indeed been "brilliant," but then turned to his defeats as proof he failed to make his point. Thurgood Marshall's adversary, the stately former presidential nominee John Davis, referred to Sumner and the *Roberts* case in front of the court as an example of how Sumner "never missed an opportunity to bring the question forward, and never succeeded." However, Davis could not ignore the community activism that brought about legislation to end segregated schools in 1855, and he conceded this fact.

These were the answers both sides came back to the court with in their return argument before the court, but something more important than their research had happened in the meantime. Chief Justice Fred Vinson, highly skeptical of the NAACP's case, died suddenly. In speaking of *Brown*'s prospects, Frankfurter said of his chief's death: "It was the first time I ever saw convincing evidence for God."

The man chosen by President Eisenhower to replace Vinson was California governor Earl Warren. Warren had been at the bench for only a year when it came time to decide a case that would change the course of American history. During the time he was mulling over his decision, he decided to visit nearby Civil War battlefields to meditate on the decision at hand. After a comfortable night at a Virginia hotel, he casually asked his chauffeur how he had spent the night. To Warren's chagrin, the black driver told him he had no place to stay because of his color.

The Justice recalled, "I was embarrassed, I was ashamed. We turned back immediately."

On May 17, 1954, with no hint of the long-awaited decision being near, reporters told one another, "It will be a quiet day at the court." Instead, at 12:42 p.m., Chief Justice Earl Warren began to read the momentous decision. Opposing counsels Thurgood Marshall and John W. Davis had been warned to be there, and both were present, each confident he had made a good case—though Marshall was aware that a narrowly split decision for them, especially in the South, might be almost as bad as outright defeat. The faces of the Justices betrayed nothing, and neither did the first fifteen minutes of Warren's reading as the Chief Justice proceeded to set the historical context for the ruling to come, one that had been in the making for a century or more.

Newsrooms across the nation were now alerted, waiting for the verdict, which finally became clear when Warren reached the crucial words: "Does segregation of children in public schools solely on the basis of race, even though the physical facilities and other tangible factors may be equal, deprive the children of a minority group of equal educational opportunities? We believe it does."

Warren had no intention of revisiting the myriad cases that upheld "separate but equal." He concluded, "We cannot turn the clock back." He saw this decision as based not on old legal precedents but on a changing America. However, *Roberts* was one of the few specific legal cases cited, as he indicated this had been the birth of the "separate but equal" doctrine.

A far greater tribute to the *Roberts* case came in the similarities of Warren's and Sumner's language. Sumner stressed, "The separate school is not an equivalent," and Warren wrote, "Separate educational facilities are inherently unequal." As to the effect of the schools, Sumner saw black children deprived of "those healthful, animating influences which would come from participation in the studies of their white brethren. It adds to their discouragement. It widens their separation from the community." Warren confirmed that separate schools generated "a feeling of inferiority as to their status in the community that may affect their hearts and minds in a way unlikely to be undone."

Marshall recalled later, "I was so happy, I was numb." Exiting the courtroom, he spotted Joe Greenhill, a white Texas lawyer on vacation who by coincidence had brought his family to the court that day. Greenhill recalled that Marshall "picked up our son Bill and put him on his shoulders and ran down the corridors of the Supreme Court. He was having a good time, and we were having a good time, and to hell with dignity. He just won a biggie."

*Roberts* was now part of a decision marking the end of Jim Crow's legal backing. Finally, all Americans had the constitutional guarantee of equality that had been sought for so long. Furthermore, many agree with author J. Harvie Wilkinson III when he describes *Brown* as the "catalyst that shook up Congress and culminated in the two major Civil Rights acts of the century." If this is an overstatement, Wilkinson is not off by much. It is difficult to imagine the modern civil rights movement without the possibility for change so momentously supported in *Brown*.

However, the lofty promise of *Brown* fifty years ago has made the process of implementation all the more protracted, problematic, and painful. The decision was historic and powerful, but never has the phrase "with all deliberate speed" been so easily translated into "deliberate sloth." Nowhere has this been truer than in the very city where the "separate but equal" doctrine first emerged and where school integration in a major American city first became a reality.

. . .

After the historic desegregation of 1855, Boston schools remained truly integrated for about twenty years. Between 1865 and 1875 the black population increased by 400 percent, and the north slope of Beacon Hill became more intensely segregated. By 1880, however, the Phillips School on the Hill had gone from being all white to predominately black. Eventually demographic patterns changed, and blacks moved away from Beacon Hill. One of the factors in this alteration was the reemergence of dissatisfaction with these now all-black schools. Black middle-class families relocated to Cambridge and the South End, and poorer families moved to Lower Roxbury.

By the time of *Brown* in 1954, the Boston schools were thoroughly segregated again. In the aftermath of the U.S. Supreme Court decision, Boston's NAACP brought legal challenges to Boston's segregated schools. June 18, 1963, was declared "Stay out for Freedom Day." The protest of the segregated public schools resulted in "freedom schools" being set up in churches and other community agencies, so the children of Boston could still be taught. To close observers of Boston history, the parallel to the past was not lost.

One hundred and seventeen years later, the boycott was back. In antebellum days, the boycott was never observed by more than two hundred children. During another "Freedom Day" in 1964, twenty thousand students would not enter their school.

Of course, the busing debacle that followed is most painfully remembered as revealing the depth of northern racism. Only a few hundred yards from where Robert Morris's law offices stood and Crispus Attucks died, another black lawyer, Theodore Landsmark, was walking to City Hall when suddenly a group of young white men tried to spear him with the sharp end of an American flagstaff. His effort to avoid being impaled by our national symbol of freedom was captured in a Pulitzer Prize–winning photograph, epitomizing how vitriolic the desegregation issue had become on the streets of Boston.

As unforgettable as this image is, what truly speaks of the legacy, and failure, of modern desegregation attempts in Boston are the statistics. *Morgan v. Hennigan,* the case that triggered the busing edict, was filed in 1970, when there were fifty-nine thousand white students in Boston schools. Twenty years later, that number had dropped by 76 percent, to only fourteen thousand. Almost half of white children in Boston now attend private (usually parochial) schools.

According to a new study by the Harvard Civil Rights Project, Boston-area elementary school students are more segregated than the national metropolitan average. Minority students are vastly more likely to be attending school in places where there are higher concentrations of poverty. Within Boston, years of desegregation efforts have made the racial balance more favorable than many cities, yet this percentage has been slipping in the last decade.

Around the nation, of the twenty-five largest central city school districts, all of which are in metropolitan areas with white majorities, eighteen have a student population that is less than 20 percent white. The average white child in America attends school with a student body that is 80 percent white. One-third of black children attend a school that is more than 90 percent black. Seventy percent of all black children attend a school where racial minorities are in fact the majority at that school. The desegregation of black students is now at its lowest level in three decades. There is no avoiding the truth that we live in an era of "resegregation."

This was not inevitable even after "white flight." There have been a long string of Supreme Court decisions choking efforts to desegregate our schools. Judicial discouragement of desegregation efforts continues today from the Supreme Court down. Today, politicians talk of improving American education but no longer of desegregating it, as if tacitly accepting a new "separate but equal" reality. There are, however, solutions at hand for making our children less separated by race, including charter and magnet schools, educational choice programs, or actively changing residential segregation patterns with housing mobility programs and affordable housing in suburban districts. Gary Orfield, head of the Harvard Project of School Desegregation says, "If you really believe in *Brown,* you can't celebrate it right now. But the potential is there."

A contemporary reader might confront these dismal statistics with despair, concluding that nothing can be done. If so, this fatalism is curious. The assumption would seem to be that citizens in this generation somehow have less power and agency than black Bostonians in the 1850s, though those citizens were burdened by poverty and political disenfranchisement and even the ongoing threat of being legally defined as mere property. They did this by not letting hopelessness overwhelm them. When William Nell looked out on the group of black children who would be the first to integrate into Boston's schools, he told them those public schools were "the gateways to the pursuits of honor and usefulness, and if rightly improved by you, the imagination almost wearies as future prospects dawn upon its vision." His message speaks through the years, directly to us.

These characters were not unrealistic about the slow pace of equality and how this would affect the gains they made. One of the last letters William Lloyd Garrison ever wrote was to Robert Morris. The year was 1879, and reports were coming from the South of increasing brutality and brutal economic exploitation that emancipation and the Reconstruction era were supposed to end. Morris organized a public meeting at Faneuil Hall with regard to the messages coming with refugees from the South. A weary Garrison wrote to Morris regretting that he would be unable to attend. Garrison had shut down the *Liberator* after the Civil War, but now, despite the lofty legislation that had come during Reconstruction, the old system had regenerated.

The old warrior acknowledged, "It is clear, therefore, that the battle of liberty and equal rights is to be fought over again." But in the end, this was not reason for despondence—it was cause for action. The old man implored Morris, "Once again for Freedom's sake, rock your father's hall!"

In writing this book, we have had to face these present realities; indeed, we live them every day as Boston residents. It is tempting to simply conclude the story in the past and present the triumph of the generation of 1850. Triumph it was, as an inspiring object lesson.

However, it is equally tempting to succumb to a defeatist despair, to conclude that, in the end, their heroic work could never survive, or if it did, only as a glimmering moral relic.

There is, thankfully, a middle way here. We can be as realistic as they were, aware that not only is this kind of change a generation-long project but it is likely to be many generations long—and more, that any gains will *always* have to be painstakingly recaptured over and over again, and so we might as well get on with it. To simply despair is somehow a romantic notion and hardly worthy of the grit and nerve of a Robert Morris. The power of racism is vast and deep-rooted, and it is impossible to "win" except by the constant application of repeated failures that take us, inch by inch, toward a little decency in our common life. One way or another, giving up is only surrender in a cynical guise, a pretense that we ever cared to effect change in the first place.

Like it or not, we *are* engaged, we must respond to the realities of our time (and doing nothing is a response much appreciated by those who would prefer things as they are). Emerson said it well: "It is impossible to extricate oneself from the questions in which your age is involved. You can no more keep out of politics than you can keep out of the frost." And it is cold out there.

If one chooses to say that the gains of this generation of free blacks were, in fact, noble failures, since our generation has so steadily retreated from their vision, then we ask that you consider the way historian E. P. Thompson, who studied the Luddites, views those movements in the past that we easily label as disappointments: it is in fact important to recover their vision, and most of all, to release them from an "enormous condescension of posterity.... Our only criterion of judgement should not be whether or not a man's actions are justified in the light of subsequent evolution. After all, we are not at the end of social evolution ourselves. In some of the lost causes of the people...we may discover insight into social evils we have yet to cure."

No, the problems faced by Nell, Roberts, Garrison, Morris, Douglass, and Sumner have not been solved. Yes, American schools are still obstinately black and white. Yet it is crucial to realize that racism, powerful as it is, is not an unchanging current, somehow frozen into stasis. Racial separation still warps and ruins lives, but it is also true that race, a social concept, can change and undergo subtle shifts and alterations before our eyes.

They hoped; we can do no better. We have no right to do less.

In the end, the story of Sarah's long walk is more a promising gesture to the future than a paean to the past. It is an unabashed evocation of certain core American values. In the 1855 celebration for Crispus Attucks arranged by William Nell, the free blacks of Boston wisely called their school desegregation victory "partial, hopeful, and prospective." What the citizens of Beacon Hill achieved before the Civil War is a remarkable American story, in its own way as impressive as any victory in our history on the battlefield or triumph at the ballot box.

It is also important to recognize the promising things happening in Boston schools every day. In 2002 a group of Roxbury fourth-graders from Emerson Elementary School, along with the Boston Cantata Singers, gave a resounding tribute to Sarah Roberts's memory. They sang a piece written by Donald Sur and T. J. Anderson (with the input of about two hundred talented Boston students). The choral piece was subsequently performed at the African Meeting House and at Boston's venerated Symphony Hall. In the 1830s Susan Paul wrote "Mr. Prejudice" for children to sing; today the children sing a new song:

> Sarah Roberts,
> Born black and smart.
> Ev'ry school she went to
> She felt lonely.
> Eighteen fifty-five
> Eighteen fifty-five
> There was a new law
> And a fair one, too.
> Sarah Roberts,
> Sarah Roberts,
> Born black and smart.

For these children, there was no doubt who is at the center of the story: a little girl not much younger than themselves.

> Sarah Roberts, proud to be an American
> Her father fought for her rights.
> Two lawyers, one black, one white,
> Fought and won against unfairness.
> They didn't give up.
> They didn't give up.

# NOTES

## ABBREVIATIONS FOR FREQUENTLY CITED TITLES AND COLLECTIONS

BA        Benjamin Quarles, *Black Abolitionists* (New York: Oxford University Press, 1969)

BAP       Peter Ripley, ed., *The Black Abolitionist Papers* (Chapel Hill: University of North Carolina Press, 1991)

BB        James Oliver Horton and Lois Horton, *Black Bostonians* (New York: Holmes and Meier Publishers, 1979)

BM        Carleton Mabee, "Negro Boycott to Integrate Boston Schools," *New England Quarterly* 41 (September 1968): 351–61

BNRC      Donald Martin Jacobs, "A History of the Boston Negro from the Revolution to the Civil War" (Ph.D. diss., Boston University, 1968)

BPL       Boston Public Library, Boston, Massachusetts

BSC       Boston School Committee

BSCP      Boston School Committee Papers, BPL

CBC       Andrew Kull, *The Color-Blind Constitution* (Cambridge, MA: Harvard University Press, 1992)

CF        Stanley K. Schultz, *The Culture Factory: Boston Public Schools, 1798–1860* (New York: Oxford University Press, 1973)

CSP       Charles Sumner Papers, Houghton Library, Harvard University

DD        Gerald Nelson Davis, "Massachusetts Blacks and the Quest for Education: 1638 to 1860" (Ph.D. diss., University of Massachusetts, 1977)

EBL     J. Clay Smith, *Emancipation: The Making of the Black Lawyer, 1844–1944* (Philadelphia: University of Pennsylvania Press, 1993)

EGLP     Ellis Gray Loring Family Papers, Arthur and Elizabeth Schlesinger Library on the History of Women, Radcliffe Institute for Advanced Study, Harvard University

FRM     Michael Friedman, "Robert Morris" (unpublished paper, Boston College)

FD     John W. Blassingame, ed., *The Frederick Douglass Papers, Series One, Speeches, Debates, and Interviews*, 3 vols. (New Haven: Yale University Press, 1979)

HHL     Houghton Library, Harvard University

JMN     William Gilman, ed., *Journals and Miscellaneous Notebooks* (Cambridge, MA: Harvard University Press, 1960–1982)

LeBB     George August Levesque, *Black Boston: African-American Life and Culture in Urban America, 1750–1860* (New York: Garland, 1994)

*Lib.*     The *Liberator*

RMM     *Robert Morris, Sr., in Memoriam*, 1882, Massachusetts Historical Society

RMP     Robert Morris Papers, Boston Athenaeum, Boston, Massachusetts

SBE     Leonard W. Levy and Douglass L. Jones, eds., *Jim Crow in Boston: The Origin of the Separate but Equal Doctrine* (New York: DeCapo Press, 1974)

SER     J. Morgan Kousser, "The Supremacy of Equal Rights: The Struggle against Racial Discrimination in Antebellum Massachusetts and the Foundation of the Fourteenth Amendment," *Northwestern University Law Review* 82 (1988): 941–1010

SJ     Richard Kluger, *Simple Justice: The History of Brown v. Board of Education and Black America's Struggle for Equality* (New York: Random House, 1975)

SP     Charles Slack Papers, Kent State University Special Collections and Archives

SM     Gary Collison, *Shadrach Minkins* (Cambridge, MA: Harvard University Press, 1997)

TAB     Albert J. Von Frank, *The Trails of Anthony Burns* (Cambridge, MA: Harvard University Press, 1998)

TESR     *Triumph of Equal School Rights in Boston, Proceedings of the Presentation Meeting Held in Boston, December 17, 1855* (Boston, 1856)

WCN     Dorothy Porter Wesley and Constance Porter Uzlac, *William Cooper Nell: Nineteenth-Century African-American Abolitionist, Historian, Integrationist: Selected Writings from 1832–1874* (Baltimore, MD: Black Classic Press, 2002)

WD      Arthur O. White, "Blacks and Education in Antebellum Massachusetts" (Ph.D. diss., State University of New York at Buffalo, 1971)

WLG     Henry Mayer, *All on Fire: William Lloyd Garrison and Abolition of Slavery* (New York: St. Martin's Griffin, 1998)

YCS     Ann-Marie Taylor, *Young Charles Sumner and the Legacy of the American Enlightenment, 1811–1851* (Amherst: University of Massachusetts Press, 2001)

## FRONTISPIECE

**Well, race**/ Ken Burns and Geoffrey Ward, *Jazz* (New York: Knopf, 2000), 118. **This town**/ *Complete Works of Emerson* (Boston: Houghton Mifflin, 1900), 12:188.

## INTRODUCTION *Brown* and Before

**P. xiii Frankfurter was**/ Juan Williams, *Thurgood Marshall* (New York: Times Books, 1998), 217. **P. xiv blue eyed**/ Mark Tushnet, ed., *Thurgood Marshall: His Speeches, Writings and Arguments* (Chicago: Lawrence Hill Books, 2001), 26. **P. xix brain of negro**/ Louis Menard, *The Metaphysical Club* (New York: Farrar, Strauss, Giroux, 2001), 109. **P. xix separate but**/ J. Anthony Lukas, *Common Ground* (New York: Vintage, 1986), 55. **P. xxi On one side**/ Sumner argument. **P. xxii How does**/ Alfred Young, *The Shoemaker and the Tea Party* (Boston: Houghton Mifflin Company, 1999), vii. **P. xxii dumb masses**/ Peter Knights, *The Plain People of Boston* (New York: Oxford University Press, 1971), foreword. **P. xxii citizen who**/ Tushnet, *Thurgood Marshall*, 224. **P. xxiii Let us be bold**/ *Lib.*, 8/13/58. **P. 1 Peculiar one**/ WCN, 318.

## ONE The Lawyer

**P. 3 Long years after**/ RMM. **P. 3 First Blood**/ *Lib.*, 10/10/62. **P. 4 Robert E. Davis**/ SBE, xvii. **P. 4 Sat down**/ RMP. **P. 4 Though Morris**/ William Wells Brown, *The Black Man: His Antecedents, His Genius and His Achievements* (New York: T. Hamilton, 1863), 240; *Lib.*, 1/28/48. **P. 5 Roughly nine**/ EBL, 5, 615–16; U.S. Census Bureau, *Negro Population in the United States, 1790–1915* (1918). **P. 6 Allen**/ EBL, 162. **P. 6 Exclusion**/ *Lib.*, 6/27/45. **P. 6 Jay**/ Macon B. Allen to John Jay, 11/26/1845, BAP. **P. 6 Jury trial**/ RMM. **P. 9 Quomono**/ *The Ipswich Chronicle*, 12/23/1882; FRM, 1–2; WD, 28; Eleanor Broadhead, "A Brief History of the Negro in Salem," Salem Committee on Racial Understanding, 1969, 1; Arthur White, "Salem's Antebellum Black Community: Seedbed of the School Integration Community," Essex Institute Historical Collections, 99; *Vital Records of Ipswich, Massachusetts to the End of the Year 1849, Volume II of III: Marriages and Deaths*, 472, 635, 720; *Vital Records of Ipswich, Massachusetts to the End of the Year 1849, Volume VI of VI: Deaths*, 360. **P. 10 York**/ White, "Salem," 101–3; William Piersen, *Black Yankees: The Development of an Afro-American Subculture in Eighteenth-Century New England* (Amherst: University of Massachusetts Press, 1988), 74–75; *Vital Records of Salem, Massachusetts to the End of the Year 1849, Volume IV of IV: Marriages*, 517. **P. 11 Judge**/ Leverett Saltonstall, *Reminis-*

*cences of Salem* (Salem, 1945), Essex Institute Historical Collections, 71:62. **P. 11 Salem/** Broadhead, "Brief History," 2; White, "Salem," 107–9; Joanne Pope Melish, *Disowning Slavery: Gradual Emancipation and "Race" in New England, 1780–1860* (Ithaca: Cornell University Press, 1998), 45–47. **P. 12 Last election/** *Salem Gazette,* 10/10/34; *Lib.,* 6/5/63; RMM. **P. 12 King/** *Salem Gazette,* 9/9/84; *Salem Register,* 9/27/80. **P. 13 Loring/** Mary Caroline Crawford, *Famous Families of Massachusetts* (Boston: Little, Brown 1930), 264; *Loring Genealogy* (Cambridge, MA, 1917); *Lib.,* 6/4/58. **P. 13 Family/** *Lib.,* 10/15/36. **P. 14 Altogether odious/** Len Gougeon and Joel Myerson, eds., *Emerson's Anti-slavery Writings* (New Haven: Yale University Press, 1995); JMN 9:120. **P. 14 Nothing/** Ellis Gray Loring (EGL) to Palfey 12/27/42, EGLP; Susan King to EGL, 1851, EGLP. **P. 14 Med/** *Lib.,* 9/3/1836; John Quincy Adams to EGL, 11/14/39, EGLP. **P. 16 Servant/** BB, 60. **P. 16 Boston/** *Lib.,* 1/23/36, 9/23/42; TAB, 175; William Wells Brown, *Black Man,* 228–30. **P. 18 All I claim/** Jane Holtz Kay, *Lost Boston* (Boston: Houghton Mifflin, 1999), 136. **P. 19 Study/** Pauline E. Hopkins, "Famous Men of the Negro Race: Robert Morris," *Colored American Magazine* 3 (September 1901): 337–42. **P. 19 Study law/** RMM, 29. **P. 19 White man/** *Lib.,* 10/10/62, 6/4/58. **P. 19 Morris and Loring/** *Lib.,* 5/1/46. **P. 19 Pretense/** RMM, 18. **P. 20 Withdrawal/** B.A. Gould to Louisa Loring, 7/3/58, EGLP. **P. 20 Service/** *Lib.,* 6/4/58; EBL, 96–97. **P. 20 Work/** *Lib.,* 10/10/62.

## T W O  The Slopes of Beacon Hill

**P. 21 Jobs/** WD, 52; P.S. Foner, *The Life and Writings of Frederick Douglass: Early Years, 1817–1849* (New York: International Publishers, 1950), 333. **P. 22 Drawing/** Robert Morris, *Speech of Robert Morris, Esq. before the Committee on the Militia, March 3d, 1853,* RMP. **P. 22 Beacon Hill/** Barbara W. Moore and Gail Weesner, *Beacon Hill: A Living Portrait* (Boston: Centry Hill Press, 1992), 22; Oscar Handlin, *Boston's Immigrants, 1790–1865* (Cambridge, MA: Belknap Press of Harvard University Press, 1959), 96; LeBB, 34–37. **P. 23 Corner of Beacon/** Shawn O'Connell, *Imaging Boston* (Boston: Beacon Press, 1990), 182. **P. 23 Colonial Days/** LeBB, 33, 129; CF, 220. **P. 23 Residential/** BB, 21. **P. 23 Constrained/** Deborah Pickman Clifford, *Crusader for Freedom* (Boston: Beacon Press, 1992), 63. **P. 24 We are barely/** O'Connell, *Imaging Boston,* 282. **P. 25 Family/** BB, ix, 16; Lois E. Horton, "Community Organization and Social Activism: Black Boston and the Antislavery Movement," *Sociological Inquiry* 55, no. 2 (Spring 1985): 186–87. **P. 25 Northern slope/** LeBB, 440; WD, 59, 59. **P. 26 Prostitution/** LeBB, 382; James Horton, "Black Activism in Boston, 1830–1860" (Ph.D. diss., Brandeis University, 1973), 33; *Lib.,* 1/4/31; WD, 61, quoted in CF, 164. **P. 26 It consists/** *Report of Reverend James Davis, 1817,* quoted in Walter Muir Whitehill, *Boston: A Topographical History* (Cambridge, MA, 1959), 71. **P. 27 Child/** Lois Brown, ed., *Memoir of James Jackson: The Attentive and Obedient Scholar, Who Died in Boston, October 31, 1833, Aged Six Years and Eleven Months, By his Teacher, Miss Susan Paul* (Cambridge, MA: Harvard University Press, 2000), 72. **P. 27 Hall/** Prince Hall, "[Extract from] a Charge Delivered at Menotomy, Massachusetts," 98–99. **P. 28 Molestation/** William C. Nell, *Colored Patriots of the American Revolution* (Boston: R.F. Wallcut, 1855), 26–27; Kathryn Grover and Janine V. da Silva, *Historic Resource Study: Boston*

*African-American National History Site* (Boston: National Park Service, 2002), 75. **P. 28 Two ways**/ Irving Bartlett, *Wendell Phillips* (Boston: Beacon Press, 1961), 5. **P. 29 Generation**/ Lois E. Horton, "From Class to Race in Early America: Northern Post-Emancipation Racial Reconstruction," in *Race and the Early Republic: Racial Consciousness and Nation-Building in the Early Republic,* ed. Michael A. Morrison and James Brewer Stewart (Oxford: Rowman & Littlefield, 2002), 55; BB, 85. **P. 29 Slavery**/ Frederick Douglass, "Slavery Takes Refugee in the Church in the United States," *London Tavern,* 3/30/47; BB, 52; Lois E. Horton, "From," 67; *Freedom's Journal,* 6/8/27. **P. 29 Course, grinning**/ Edward Renehan, *The Secret Six* (Columbia: University of South Carolina Press, 1997), 43. **P. 30 Social structures**/ BB, 38, 35; Morrison and Stewart, *Race,* 35. **P. 31 Church**/ George T. Downing, *To the Friends of Equal Rights in Rhode Island* (Providence, RI, 1859); Grover and da Silva, *Historic Resource Study,* 78; Beth Anne Bower and Byron Rushing, *"The African Meeting House": Archeological Perspectives on Ethnicity in America,* vol. 1 (New York, 1980), 69. **P. 31 Paul**/ Lois Brown, *Memoir,* 6–9; BB, 42. **P. 33 Strong web**/ Lois E. Horton, "Community Organization and Social Activism," 182–99. **P. 33 David Walker**/ Peter P. Hinks, *To Awaken My Afflicted Brethren: David Walker and the Problem of Antebellum Slave Resistance* (University Park: Pennsylvania State University Press, 1996); David Walker, *David Walker's Appeal: To the Colored Citizens of the World,* ed. Peter Hinks (University Park: Pennsylvania State University Press, 2000); Hinks, *To Awaken.* **P. 34 Humanity**/ Walker, *Appeal,* 25, 29. **P. 35 Paine**/ Hinks, *To Awaken,* xiv, xxxix–xl. **P. 36 Difference**/ *Boston Evening Transcript,* 3/28/30. **P. 37 Maria Stewart**/ Marilyn Richardson, ed., *Maria W. Stewart: America's First Black Woman Political Writer* (Bloomington: Indiana University Press, 1981), xiii. **P. 37 Tell us**/ Maria Stewart, *Lecture Delivered at the Franklin Hall* (Boston, 1832). **P. 38 Protest**/ quoted in *Lib.,* 1/7/37; quoted in BNRC, 112. **P. 38 Daughters**/ Maria Stewart, *Religion and the Pure Principles of Morality.* **P. 39 Sons**/ Maria Stewart, *An Address Delivered at the African Masonic Hall* (Boston, 1833). **P. 39 Contempt**/ Maria Stewart, "Mrs. Stewart's Farewell Address to Her Friends in the City of Boston. Delivered September 21, 1833."

## THREE Through the Vestry Window

**P. 41 January night**/ Nell, *Colored Patriots,* 344. **P. 41 Friends, we**/ WLG, 131. **P. 43 Puritan**/ WLG, 67. **P. 43 Emerson**/ James M. McPherson, *The Struggle for Equality: Abolitionists and the Negro in the Civil War and Reconstruction* (Princeton: Princeton University Press, 1964), 355. **P. 44 Maryland**/ WLG, 71, 79. **P. 44 White man**/ Paul Goodman, *Of One Blood: Abolitionism and the Origins of Racial Equality* (Berkeley: University of California Press, 2002), 55. **P. 45 Paul**/ WLG, 109. **P. 45 Black support**/ William S. McFreely, *Frederick Douglass* (New York: Touchstone, 1991), 83; Douglass, "Slavery," 213–14; FD, 4:508–9. **P. 45 Smith**/ BA, 18. **P. 45 Your moral**/ *Lib.,* 1/1/31. **P. 46 Glimpse**/ Lawrence J. Friedman, *Gregarious Saints: Self and Community in American Abolitionism, 1830–1870* (Cambridge, MA: Harvard University Press, 1982), 162. **P. 46 No tyrannical**/ *Lib.,* 4/30/31. **P. 46 Aliens**/ *Lib.,* 1/15/31. **P. 46 Auxiliary**/ *Lib.,* 2/8/50. **P. 47 Referred**/ *Lib.,* 4/3/40, 11/1/39. **P. 47 Everything around**/ Allen Nevins, *The Ordeal of the Union,* vol. 1 (New York: Scribners, 1947), 137. **P. 48 Somebody**/ Patrick T. J. Browne, " 'To Defend Mr. Garrison.' William Copper Nell and the Personal Politics of Antislavers," *New England Quarterly* 70:417. **P. 48 stroll**/ Nell, *Colored Patriots*, 10. **P. 48 Slim**/ William Wells Brown, *Black Man*, 240. **P. 48 Moving**/ William Wells Brown, *The Rising Sun; or The Antecedents and Advancement of the Colored Race* (Boston: A. G. Brown, 1874), 486. **P. 48 No white lad**/ *Emancipator and Journal of Public Morals*, 4/1/34, reprinted from *The New England Telegraph.* **P. 49 Self-help**/ BA, 100. **P. 49 Colorphobia**/ Nell to Post, 7/3/50, WCN. **P. 49 Notes**/ William Wells Brown, *Black Man*, 241. **P. 49 Journalist**/ McFreely, *Frederick Douglass*, 152. **P. 49 Seldom**/ WCN, 14. **P. 49 Lecturer**/ *Lib.*, 2/5/47. **P. 49 Topics**/ *Lib.*, 11/24/43, 4/1/42, 2/21/40, 12/27/39. **P. 49 Political views**/ *Lib.*, 12/25/40, 2/3/43, 1/13/43, 11/17/43, 12/13/44, 1/10/40, 1/15/41. **P. 50 Promising**/ *Lib.*, 12/12/45. **P. 50 Friend**/ Nell to Phillips, 4/15/41,WCN. **P. 50 far more rooted**/ BB, 63. **P. 50 Gloves**/ RMM, 36. **P. 51 Romance**/ Nell to Jeremiah Burke Sanderson, 1/4/41, WCN. **P. 51 slight him**/ Nell to Robert Morris, 3/17/41, WCN. **P. 51 Success**/ Nell to Phillips, 8/28/43, WCN. **P. 51 Hilton**/ Elizabeth Bethel, *The Roots of African American Identity* (New York: St. Martin's, 1997), 2.

## FOUR  First Class

**P. 53 Douglass**/ McFreely, *Frederick Douglass*, 93. **P. 55 Old universe**/ Kay, *Lost Boston*, 129. **P. 55 Society is**/ Margaret Christman, *1846* (Washington, DC: Smithsonian Institution, 1996), 4. **P. 56 Campaign**/ TAB, 42. **P. 56 Civil rights**/ BA, 48; Anne W. Weston to Deborah Weston, 2/4/42, Weston Papers, BPL; BB, 103; Friedman, *Gregarious Saints*, 164. **P. 57 shock the feelings**/ *4th Annual Report of the Board of Managers of the Massachusetts Anti-Slavery Society*, 1/2/36, quoted in "The Abolitionist Dilemma: The Antislavery Movement and the Northern Negro," by Leon Litwack, *New England Quarterly* 24, no. 1 (March 1961): 52. **P. 57 Garrison**/ Louis Ruchames, "Race and Education in Massachusetts," *Negro History Bulletin* 13, nos. 53–59:251; *Lib.*, 8/13/31. **P. 58 Privilege of**/ *Boston Post*, 1/12/39, in *Lib.*, 2/8/39; *Boston Gazette and Centennial*, 3/5/38, in *Lib.*, 3/9/38. **P. 58 Bradburn**/ *Lib.*, 2/15/39; *Boston Daily Evening Transcript*, in *Lib.*, 2/7/40; *Boston Phoenix*, in *Lib.*, 2/7/40. **P. 59 Railroad industry**/ Michael B. Katz, *The Irony of Early School Reform: Educational Innovation in Mid-Nineteenth Century Massachusetts* (Cambridge, MA: Harvard University Press, 1968), 223; Nell to Phillips, 8/31/40, WCN; *Lib.*, 9/6/41; Louis Ruchames, "Jim Crow Railroads in Massachusetts," *American Quarterly* (July 1956): 62–68. **P. 60 Morris**/ Hopkins, "Famous Men of the Negro Race," 5, 341. **P. 61 Traveler's Directory**/ *Lib.*, 4/2/42, among others. **P. 61 Eastern Railroad**/ *Lib.*, 4/29/42, 4/13/42. **P. 61 Bradburn**/ Ruchames, "Jim Crow Railroads"; *Lib.*, 12/10/41. **P. 62 Phillips**/ *Lib.*, 2/8/42. **P. 62 Remond**/ William Wells Brown, *Black Man*, 247; *Lib.*, 2/5/41. **P. 63 Broad Principle**/ *Lib.*, 2/25/42; LeBB, 151. **P. 63 Puzzlement**/ *Washington Globe*, in *Lib.*, 6/17/42. **P. 63 Marriage bill**/ *Lib.*, 2/25/42, 2/10/43. **P. 64 1843**/ *Lib.*, 2/10/43, 4/19/39; SER, 958; Morris, *Speech*, RMP; BB, 131. **P. 65 Where ever they**/ Knights, *Plain People*, 29. **P. 65 We don't allow**/ Philip Foner, ed., *Frederick Douglass—Selected Writings* (Chicago: Lawrence Hill Books, 1994), 19. **P. 66 Indian and Negro**/ Louis Masur, *1831* (New York: Hill and Wang, 2002), 45.

## FIVE "Mr. Prejudice"

**P. 67 Franklin medal**/ *Lib.*, 12/28/55. **P. 69 Change**/ CF, 68; James Fraser, Henry Allen, and Sam Barnes, *From Common Schools to Magnet School: Selected Essays in the History of Boston's Schools* (Boston: Trustees of the Public Library of the City of Boston, 1979), 29. **P. 69 Mann**/ CF, 270. **P. 70 Foreign people**/ CF, 230, 7–9; Katz, *Irony of Early School Reform*, 120. **P. 70 Discovery**/ Horace Mann, *Ninth Annual Report* (Boston, 1846), 64. **P. 70 Resisted**/ 1846 report; V. P. Mayer, ed., *Alexis de Tocqueville: Journey to America* (New Haven: Yale University Press, 1962), 224–25. **P. 70 worse than**/ Hosea Easton, *A Treatise on the Intellectual Character and Condition of the Colored People of the United States* (Boston: I. Knapp, 1837), 40–41. **P. 71 Primus Hall**/ Grover and da Silva, *Boston*, 86. Some historians have asserted that this school was on George and May Streets, but Grover based her placement of the house on Michael Terranova's extensive research of Boston tax records; Nell, *Colored Patriots*, 32. **P. 71 African Meeting House**/ William Parsons and Margaret A. Drew, *The African Meeting House in Boston: A Source Book* (Boston: Museum of Afro American History, 1988), 380; LeBB, 167–69. **P. 72 Basement**/ David Childs, "The African School House, October 11, 1833," in *Boston School Committee Minutes, 1815–1836*. **P. 73 Childs**/ CF, 181; David Lee Child, Committee Report on the Memorial for Joseph Woodson," BSCP. **P. 74 Crandell**/ BA, 124–29. **P. 75 Free States**/ U.S. Bureau of the Census, *The Seventh Census of the United States: 1850* (Washington, DC, 1853); EBL, 5. **P. 76 Smith**/ William Minot, *Address at the Dedication of the Smith School, 1835*, BPL; Barbara Yocum, *The African Meeting House Historic Structure Report* (Boston: National Park Service, 1994), 17–20. Lois Brown, *Memoir*, 96. **P. 77 "Mr. Prejudice"**/ *Lib.*, 5/31/34; Lois Brown, *Memoir*, 68. **P. 78 Inferior**/ WD, 159. BSCP, BPL; *Lib.*, 9/3/36. **P. 80 Woodson**/ DD, 154–55. **P. 80 Forbes**/ Garrison to Henry C. Wright, 7/13/69, Anti-Slavery Papers, BPL; *Lib.*, 4/5/34; *School Committee Report, 1841*, BSCP; *Sub-Committee Report*, 5/5/40, BSCP. **P. 81 Labors**/ WD, 144, 200; *School Committee Report*, 1841, BSCP; *Lib.*, 11/24/37. **P. 81 Vagrant**/ *School Committee Semi-Annual Report*, 1843, BSCP; Abner Forbes to Dr. Winslow Lewis, Chairman of the Sub-Committee of the Smith School, 8/2/45, BSCP; Abner Forbes and J. W. Greene, *The Rich Men of Massachusetts* (Boston, 1851), 40. **P. 81 Meetings**/ *Petition on Separate Schools to the Boston School Committee*, BSCP; WD, 211; *Boston Atlas*, 7/25/44. **P. 83 Skeptical**/ *Boston Courier*, in *Lib.*, 7/5/44. **P. 84 Emerson**/ BNRC, 233; *Lib.*, 6/28/44. **P. 84 Sargent**/ David Pettee, "John Turner Sargent," http://www.uua .org/uuhs/duub/articles/johnturnersargent.html (2003); *North Star*, 3/17/48. **P. 84 colored parents**/ *Lib.*, 6/28/44; *Boston Atlas*, quoted in DD, 157. **P. 84 Drastic**/ *Lib.*, 6/28/44; *Boston Olive Branch*, in *Lib.*, 7/19/44; SER, 964; BM, 347; Forbes to Lewis, 8/2/45, BSCP. **P. 85 1845**/ WD, 156. **P. 86 Nell**/ Nell to WP, 5/18/45, WCN; Charlotte Forten, *Journal of Charlotte Forten* (New York: Dryden Press, 1953), 213. **P. 86 Phillips**/ *Boston Olive Branch*, in *Lib.*, 8/8/45. **P. 88 Damp, dark cellar** *Lib.*, 12/24/47, 4/15/53, 1/21/45. **P. 88 Minority**/ Henry I. Bowditch and James Tolman, *Minority Report on Abolishing Separate Colored Schools* (Boston, 1845). **P. 88 Morris**/ *Boston Courier*, in *Lib.*, 9/5/45. **P. 88 Nell**/ *Lib.*, 9/4/46. **P. 88 Physical conditions**/ *Smith School Quarterly Report*, August 1846; *City of Boston School Committee Reports, 1846, 1847*, BSCP; CF, 196. **P. 88 Frustrated**/ *Report to the Primary School Committee, June 15, 1846, on the Petition of Sundry Colored Persons,* *for the Abolition of the Schools for Colored Children. With the City Solicitor's Opinion* (Boston, 1846), BSCP; *Lib.,* 7/10/46. **P. 88 Minority**/ *Report of the Minority of the Committee of the Primary School Board, on the Caste Schools of the City of Boston; With Some Remarks on the City Solicitor's Opinion (Boston, 1846),* SER, 983; *Lib.,* 3/7/45, 7/10/46, quoted in WD, 210, minutes 1846. **P. 89 Chandler**/ *City of Boston School Committee Reports, 1846,* BSCP, 37. **P. 89 Mann**/ Jonathan Messerli, *Horace Mann: A Biography* (New York: Random House, 1972), 370. **P. 90 Phillips**/ *Lib.,* 8/28/46. **P. 90 Minority**/ *Report of the Minority of the Committee...*, *1846; Lib.,* 7/10/46. **P. 90 Other Massachusetts towns**/ *Lib.,* 2/20/46; Barbara Linebaugh White, *The African School and the Integration of Nantucket Public Schools, 1825–1847* (Boston: African American Studies Center of Boston University, 1978). **P. 90 Fletcher**/ DD, 187; Richard Fletcher, *The Hon. R. Fletcher's Opinion as to whether the school committee can lawfully exclude colored children from the public free schools established exclusively for them,* BPL. **P. 91 Armed camps**/ LeBB, 196. **P. 91 Divided**/ *Boston Olive Branch,* in *Lib.,* 8/28/46; *Boston Chronotype,* 8/8/46. **P. 91 1846**/ *Address of the Committee Appointed by a Public Meeting, Held at Faneuil Hall, September 24, 1846, for the Purpose of Considering the Recent Case of Kidnapping from Our Soil, and of Taking Measures to Prevent the Recurrence of Similar Outrages* (Boston, 1846). **P. 92 Wedding**/ WLG, 352; *Lib.,* 5/1/46. **P. 95 Clients**/ Richard Newman, *The Transformation of American Abolitionism* (Chapel Hill: University of North Carolina Press, 2002), 60.

# SIX The Client

**P. 97 Benjamin**/ Benjamin Roberts, *Report of the Colored People of the City of Boston, on the Subject of Exclusive Schools* (Boston, 1850); *New National Era,* 3/31/70; *Lib.,* 4/4/51. **P. 99 Removed**/ *Boston Herald,* 12/5/49. **P. 99 Grandfather**/ An excellent source of information on the early Roberts family is George R. Price and James Brewer Stewart's "The Roberts Case, the Easton Family, and the Dynamics of the Abolitionist Movement in Massachusetts, 1776–1870," *Massachusetts Historical Review* 4 (2002): 88–115. George R. Price and James Brewer Stewart, eds., *To Heal the Scourge of Prejudice: The Life and Writings of Hosea Easton* (Amherst: University of Massachusetts Press, 1999), 90–98; Nell, *Colored Patriots,* 33. **P. 101 Immense value**/ *Lib.,* 4/4/51. **P. 101 Enterprising**/ *New National Era,* 3/31/70. **P. 101 Failure**/ Price and Stewart, *To Heal,* 110–11. **P. 101 Robert**/ Grover and da Silva, *Boston African-American Site,* 52; Robert Roberts, *The House Servant's Directory, or A Monitor for Private Families: Comprising Hints on the Arrangement and Performance of Servants' Work* (Armonk, NY: M. E. Sharpe, 1998); Price and Stewart, "The Roberts Case," 88–115. **P. 103 dark skin**/ *Lib.,* 12/6/34. **P. 103 Garrison**/ Friedman, *Gregarious Saints,* 165; BB, 91. **P. 104 Black newspapers**/ James Horton and Lois E. Horton, *In Hope of Liberty: Culture, Community, and Protest among Northern Free Blacks, 1700–1860* (New York: Oxford University Press, 1998), 207; BA, 85–87. **P. 104 Phelps**/ Amos A. Phelps, To Whom It May Concern, 16 May 1838, Anti-Slavery Collection, BPL; Benjamin F. Roberts to Amos A, Phelps, 6/19/38, BAP, vol. 3. **P. 106 Enterprises**/ *Lib.,* 3/26/31. **P. 106 Douglass**/ Frederick Douglass, *The Life and Times of Frederick Douglass* (New York: Collier, 1962), 269–70; *North Star,* January 1848. **P. 106 Travel**/ *Lib.,* 10/12/38. **P. 107 Nell**/ BNRC, 201; *Lib.,* 6/7/39. **P. 107 Directory**/ Grover, *Boston African-American National His-*

*tory Site*, 52, 53. **P. 107 Printing**/ BB, 82. **P. 108 Family**/ *Lib.*, 6/3/42; Price and Stewart, "The Roberts Case," 88–115. **P. 108 Experiment**/ *Lib.*, 4/4/51; *New National Era*, 3/31/71; *Lib.*, 3/8/34. **P. 109 Constitution**/ *Lib.*, 4/4/51. **P. 109 Redress**/ BSR, 1846, 4. **P. 109 Triumph**/ *Lib.*, 1/28/48; EBL, 96. **P. 109 Income**/ RMP. **P. 109 Business**/ *Lib.*, 1/28/48. **P. 110 Irish**/ CF, 193; RMM. **P. 110 Adlow**/ Elijah Adlow, *The Genius of Lemuel Shaw: Expounder of the Common Law* (Boston: Court Square Press, 1960), 53; Paul Finkel- man, "Not Only the Judges' Robes Were Black: African-American Lawyers as Social Engineers," *Stanford L. Rev.* 47 (1994): 178. **P. 111 cause of equal**/ *Lib.*, 4/4/51. **P. 111 Chandler**/ SER, 968; *Meeting of the Suffolk Bar, Held at Boston, June 7, 1889. In Memory of Peleg Whitman Chandler,* Boston Social Law Library; *Lib.*, 8/28/46. **P. 113 initial hearing**/ #976, *Roberts v. City of Boston,* Court of Common Pleas, Suffolk County, 1848 October term. **P. 114 Library**/ BSCP, #22, 3/31/48. **P. 115 Fletcher**/ WD, 258.

## SEVEN A Gathering Tempest

**P. 117 Nell**/ WCN, 21–22. **P. 118 Morris's excellence**/ *North Star,* 1/28/48. **P. 119 Threat**/ BM, 349; Thomas P. Smith, *An Address Before the Colored Citizens of Boston in Oppo- sition to the Abolition of Colored Schools* (Boston, 1849); DD, 176; Alexander Crummele, *Africa and America* (Springfield, 1891). **P. 120 Floundering**/ *Lib.*, 9/17/41, 12/15/37; BB, 79; *Lib.*, 5/12/43; WD, 204. **P. 121 Petition**/ DD, 177. **P. 122 Meeting**/ BSCP, #33–36, 1848, BPL; WD, 266; *Lib.*, 8/18/48. **P. 123 Invitation**/ LeBB, 284; Horton, *Black Bostoni- ans,* 51; BSCP, #37, 1848, BPL. **P. 125 Cholera**/ Handlin, *Boston's Immigrants,* 114; Simon Schama, *Dead Certainties: Unwarranted Speculations* (New York: Knopf, 1991), 287; *North Star,* 8/24/49. **P. 125 City Hall**/ *Lib.*, 8/14/49. **P. 127 Integrationists**/ *Majority Report of a Special Committee of the Grammar School Board, August 29, 1849* (Boston City Doc. No. 42, 1849); SER, 996. **P. 127 Smith took**/ *Semi-Weekly Republic,* 8/22/49. **P. 127 Two days**/ *Lib.*, 9/7/49; CF, 197; BSC, *Majority,* 26; BSC, *Report of the Minority of the Committee upon the Petition of John T. Hilton and Others, Colored Citizens of Boston, Praying for the Abolition of the Smith School and that colored children may be permitted to attend the other schools of the City; Doc- ument of the City of Boston for the Year 1849* (Boston, 1849), 4; BSC, *Minority,* 4–5, 8. **P. 129 however much**/ *Lib.*, 9/14/49. **P. 129 Nell and Roberts**/ *Lib.*, 9/14/49; LeBB, 206. **P. 130 McCune Smith**/ *Boston Chronotype,* 12/27/49. **P. 131 Emancipation**/ *Lib.*, 7/27/49, 8/3/49, 9/17/49.

## EIGHT No Neutrals

**P. 132 Assailed**/ *Lib.*, 9/21/49; BM, 349; John Daniels, *In Freedom's Birthplace: A Study of the Boston Negros* (Boston: Houghton Mifflin, 1914), 448. **P. 133 Evening**/ *Boston Daily Journal,* 9/18/49; *Lib.*, 9/21/49. **P. 135 patrolling**/ BM, 349; *Lib.*, 10/5/49; White, "An- tebellum," 214; Pastor E. A. Stockman, Jos. P. Smith, Will Cohmes, Tom Blakemore, and Henry Frenley, *To the School Committee of Boston,* 1849, BPL; BSCP, 12/5/49. **P. 136 Hilton**/ WD, 297–98. **P. 136 our battle**/*Lib.*, 10/5/49. **P. 136 ambivalence**/ DD, 175. **P. 137 $76**/ WD, 228. **P. 137 Paul**/ BM, 347, 352; *Report on the Subject of Uniting Immediate School for Colored Children with Smith School,* 11/15/48. **P. 137 Law**/ *Boston Post,* quoted in

*Lib.*, 11/16/49; White, "Antebellum," 206. **P. 138 Morris and Smith**/ *Lib.*, 10/5/49.
**P. 138 Meetings**/ *Lib.*, 4/26/50, 12/28/55; White, "Antebellum," 212; Horton and Horton, *In Hope of Liberty*, 228–29; BA, 61. **P. 139 War**/ *Lib.*, 11/9/49. **P. 139 Garrison**/ *Lib.*, 12/14/49. **P. 139 Celebration**/ *Lib.*, 11/23/49. **P. 139 Conceded**/ *Daily Advertiser*, 8/17/49. **P. 140 10 percent**/ Horton, "Black Activism," 110. **P. 140 Caesar**/ "Report of Special Committees of Grammar School Board," 1849, 16, BPL.

## NINE A Brahmin of Black Beacon Hill

**P. 141 Lincoln**/ David Donald, *Charles Sumner and the Rights of Man* (New York: Knopf, 1970), 59. **P. 141 without payment**/ David Donald, *Charles Sumner and the Coming of the Civil War* (New York: Knopf, 1960), 180. **P. 142 Douglass**/ FD, 371. **P. 142 Sumner grew**/ Grover, *Boston African-American National History Site*, 21; YCS, 17, 22, 27, 74; Jeremiah J. D. Chaplin, *Life of Charles Sumner* (Boston: D. Lothrop, 1874), 28; *Lib.*, 11/27/46; BB, 35. **P. 143 Sumner perplexed**/ Donald, *Coming*, 147; Richard Henry Dana, *The Journal*, ed. Robert F. Lucid (Cambridge, MA: Belknap Press of Harvard University Press, 1968), 1:59; Donald, *Coming*, 218. **P. 144 Harvard**/ Archibald H. Grimke, *The Life of Charles Sumner: The Scholar in Politics* (New York: Funk and Wagnalls, 1892), 22; YCS, 6, 53; CS to Jonathan F. Stearns, Cambridge, 9/25/1831; CS to Charlemagne Tower, Law School–Divinity Hall No. 10–19, September 1831, CSP. **P. 144 Slavery**/ Hayes, CS, 100; CS to Cornelius Felton, 4/9/50; CS to Wendell Phillips, 2/4/45, CSP; CS to Robert C. Winthrop, 2/9/43, CSP. **P. 145 Paris**/ CS, *Travel Journal*, 1/20/38, quoted in YCS, 251. **P. 145 Education**/ Charles Sumner, *The True Grandeur of Nations* (Boston: William D. Ticknor, 1845). **P. 146 July Fourth**/ YCS, 184; Donald, *Coming*, 111. **P. 146 Morals**/ Donald, *Coming*, 168. **P. 147 Horace**/ Elias Nason, *The Life and Times of Charles Sumner: His Boyhood, Education, and Public Career* (Boston, 1874), 137; YCS, 299. **P. 147 Webster**/ Schama, *Dead Certainties*, 142, 152, 172, 187–88, 186, 290; George Bemis, *Report of the Case of John W. Webster* (Boston, 1850). **P. 149 Shaw**/ Leonard W. Levy, *The Law of the Commonwealth and Chief Justice Shaw* (New York: Oxford University Press, 1994), 1, 26; Frederic Hathaway Chase, *Lemuel Shaw: Chief Justice of the Supreme Judicial Court of Massachusetts, 1830–1860* (Boston: Houghton Mifflin, 1918), 136, 275; Adlow, *Genius*, 3–13; Chase, *Lemuel Shaw*, 133. **P. 151 Shaw and Slavery**/ Levy, *Law of the Commonwealth*, 60, 80–81. **P. 152 Chandler and Sumner**/ "Meeting of the Suffolk Bar, Held at Boston, June 7, 1889. In Memory of Peleg Whitman Chandler," *Lib.*, 8/28/46; PWC to CS, 6/24/45, 6/23/44, 8/1/44, 8/15/45, CSP.

## TEN The Argument

All quotations from Sumner's argument come from *Argument of Charles Sumner, Esq., against the Constitutionality of Separate Schools in the Case of Sarah C. Roberts v. the City of Boston. Before the Supreme Court of Massachusetts* (Boston: B. F. Roberts, 1849). **P. 153 The day**/ *Boston Post*, 12/4/49; *Boston Courier*, 12/5/49; BB, 15; *Boston Herald*, 12/4/49; *Boston Daily Atlas*, 12/4/49. **P. 153 Walking together**/ Grimke, *Life of Charles Sumner*, 42, Gary Gillerman, "Sarah Roberts, Charles Sumner and the Idea of Equality," *Boston Bar Journal* 31 (1987): 41; RMM, 36; Grimke, *Life of Charles Sumner*, 98; RMM, 18. **P. 154 Thronged**/ BM, 351. **P. 155 Toad**/ Schama, *Dead Certainties*, 198. **P. 155 Other judges**/ Schama, *Dead*

*Certainties,* 198; WD, 258, 313–14; SER, 988. **P. 157 Morris tried**/ RMM, 18; Leonard W. Levy and Harlan B. Phillips, "The *Roberts* Case: Source of the 'Separate but Equal' Doctrine," *American Historical Review* 56 (1951): 513. **P. 158 Sumner's argument**/ All quotations from Shaw's notes are preserved in the Boston Social Law Library. **P. 159 Weakened**/ CS to George Sumner, 12/10/49, CSP. **P. 161 Jay**/ CS to John Jay, 5/13/50, CSP. **P. 162 American legal instrument**/ Arthur Darling, "Prior to Little Rock in American Education: The *Roberts* Case," *Proceedings of the Massachusetts Historical Society* 72:126–42. **P. 162 Loring**/ *Lib.,* 3/4/42. **P. 167 Kull**/ CBC, 28–29. **P. 167 Charter**/ C. Edwards Lester, *Life and Public Services of Charles Sumner* (New York: United States Publishing Company, 1874), 75–76. **P. 169 Uneasy**/ CS to George Sumner, 12/10/49, CSP. **P. 169 Chandler's argument**/ *Daily Evening Traveler,* 12/4/49; *Boston Courier,* 12/5/49. **P. 170 Nell**/ *Lib.,* 12/10/52.

## ELEVEN  A Doctrine Is Born

**P. 172 Traveler**/ *Daily Evening Traveler,* 12/10/49. **P. 172 luminous and profound**/ *Lib.,* 12/7/49. **P. 173 Sumner's friends**/ John Gorham Palfrey to CS 12/12/49, WCN to CS, 1/12/50, Salmon P. Chase to CS, 12/14/49, CSP. **P. 173 ten days after**/ *Lib.,* 12/14/49; SBE, xxi. **P. 173 Smith**/ *Lib.,* 2/15/50. **P. 174 Hayden**/ *Age,* 4/10/89; Harriet Beecher Stowe, *A Key to "Uncle Tom's Cabin," Presenting the Original Facts and Documents Upon Which the Story is Founded* (Boston: John P. Jewett, 1853); Joel Strangis, *Lewis Hayden and the War against Slavery* (North Haven: Linnet Books, 1999), 14; *Lib.,* 4/1/53, 9/6/49; Stanley J. and Anita W. Robboy, "Lewis Hayden: From Fugitive Slave to Statesman," *The New England Quarterly* 46, no. 4 (December 1973): 592. **P. 176 Unanimous decision**/ *Lib.,* 4/26/50; George Dargo, "The *Sarah Roberts* Case in Historical Perspective," *Massachusetts Legal History* 3 (1997): 42. All quotations from Shaw's decision come from *Roberts v. City of Boston* (1894), 5 Cush. 198. **P. 176 Accept equality**/ Gillerman, "Sarah Roberts," 44; SER, 986. **P. 177 *Animal Farm***/ George Orwell, *Animal Farm* (New York: Signet, 2004), 112; Levy and Phillips, "The *Roberts* Case," 516. **P. 177 Classification**/ CBC, 50. **P. 178 Progenitor**/ Roderick T. Baltimore and Robert F. Williams, "The State Constitutional Roots of the 'Separate but Equal' Doctrine: *Roberts v. City of Boston,*" *Rutgers Law Journal* 17, no. 8 (1986): 538; Charles Miller, "Constitution Law and the Rhetoric of Race," *Persp. Am. Hist.* 5 (1971): 147, 171. **P. 178 Influential**/ Dargo, "The Sarah Roberts Case," 44; CBC, 202. **P. 179 Sumner**/ CS to John Jay, 5/13/50, CSP. **P. 179 Most**/ *New Englander,* in *Lib.,* 5/3/50. **P. 179 Dejected**/ *Lib.,* 4/26/50. **P. 180 Roberts**/ *Lib.,* 5/31/50, 4/4/51, 5/31/50; Henry Box Brown, *Narrative of the Life of Henry Box Brown,* ed. Richard Newman (Oxford: Oxford University Press, 2002), xv, ix, xxvii; *Lib.,* 5/31/50, 8/16/50; Roberts, *Report.* **P. 182 In June**/ Nell, *Colored Patriots,* 327.

## TWELVE  Vigilance

**P. 185 Minkins**/ *Boston Daily Times,* 2/17/51; *Commonwealth,* 11/7/51. **P. 186 Union hung**/ *Lib.,* 6/8/55; William H. Gilman, ed., *The Journals and Miscellaneous Notebooks of Ralph Waldo Emerson,* 16 vols. (Cambridge, MA: Harvard University Press, 1960–1982), 11 (1848–1851): 346; *Lib.,* 9/27/50; BA, 198; Kenneth O'Reilly, *Nixon's Piano: Presidents and*

*Racial Politics from Washington to Clinton* (New York: Free Press, 1995), 38; Leon F. Litwack, *North of Slavery* (Chicago: University of Chicago Press, 1961), 24. **P. 187 Effect/** Martin Delany, *The Condition, Elevation, Emigration, and Destiny of the Colored People of the United States* (Philadelphia: privately printed, 1852), 155; BB, 126; *Lib.*, 4/11/51; Robert Hayden, *The African Meeting House in Boston* (Boston: Companion Press, 1987), 40; Wilbur H. Siebert, "The Vigilance Committee of Boston," The Bostonian Society (Boston, 1953), 2, 17; BB, 59; Grover, *Boston African-American National History Site*, 107; BB, 69, 110; Siebert, "Vigilance," 246; TAB, 37; BA, 200; WD, 66. **P. 188 Mobilizing/** *Lib.*, 10/4/50, 10/11/50. **P. 189 not just organized/** Siebert, "Vigilance," 3; BA, 150; TAB, 43; Gary Collison, "The Boston Vigilance Committee: A Reconsideration," *Historical Journal of Massachusetts* 12 (June 1984): 112. **P. 189 Pride/** Siebert, "Vigilance," 38; Charles Francis Adams, *Richard Henry Dana: A Biography* (Boston: Houghton Mifflin, 1890), 2:178; SM, 86; *Baltimore Sun*, 11/1/50. **P. 189 Douglass/** FD, 8/20/52. **P. 190 Crafts/** William Craft, *Running a Thousand Miles for Freedom; or, The Escape of William and Ellen Craft from Slavery* (London, 1860; reprint, New York: Arno, 1969); *Pennsylvania Freeman*, 10/31/50; BNRC, 273–74; BB, 113; SM, 93–99;Gamaliel Baily to Charles Sumner, 11/15/50, CSP. **P. 192 some time/** Richard Henry Dana, *The Journal of Richard Henry Dana*, ed. Robert F. Lucid (Cambridge, MA: Harvard University Press, 1968), 411–13; *Commonwealth*, 11/7/51. **P. 192 Curtis/** SM, 117, 119; Dana, *Journal*, 412; *Commonwealth*, 5/13/51. **P. 193 Dana left/** Dana, *Journal*, 411–12; SM, 122–23. **P. 193 Fifteen minutes/** *Commonwealth*, 11/7/51, 11/6/51. **P. 193 Violently/** RMM, 13; BB, 115; SM, 126; *Boston Courier*, 2/17/51; Dana, *Journal*, 412. **P. 194 Witness/** *Commonwealth*, 11/6/51; *Daily Globe*, 4/8/89; SM, 127, 130; *Daily Globe*, 4/8/89. **P. 195 talked about/** EBL, 98; Levy, *Law of the Commonwealth*, 89; *Congressional Globe*, 31st Cong., 2d sess., 96–97; quoted in *The Papers of Henry Clay*, ed. Melba Porter Hay (Lexington: University of Kentucky Press, 1991), 10:863; quoted in *Hayden*, by Strangis, 77. **P. 195 Papers/** *New York Herald*, 2/18/51, quoted in SM, 138; *Savannah Republican*, quoted in *Lib.*, 4/11/51; *Boston Courier*, 2/17/51; *Boston Daily Times*, 2/18/51; *Daily Commonwealth*, 2/20/51. **P. 196 Arrested/** SM, 147–48; *Final Record Book*, vol. 32, U.S. District Court, Boston, March 1851. **P. 196 Sims/** BNRC, 280; Levy, *Law of the Commonwealth*, 102, 61 Mass. 285 (1851); Strangis, *Hayden*, 80–82; TAB, 26–29. **P. 198 November/** *Lib.*, 8/15/51. **P. 199 federal treason/** Benjamin Robbins Curtis, *A Memoir of Benjamin Robbins Curtis, LL. D.: With some of his professional and miscellaneous writings / edited by his son, Benjamin R. Curtis* (Boston: Little, Brown, 1879), 161; *Lib.*, 11/3/54; Strangis, *Hayden*, 87. **P. 199 Hale/** Richard H. Sewell, *John P. Hale and the Politics of Abolition* (Cambridge, MA: Harvard University Press, 1965), 73, 9. **P. 199 presiding judge/** TAB, 21. **P. 200 encouragement/** *Commonwealth*, 6/7/51, 6/11/51, 6/13/51; SM, 193–95. **P. 201 Trial/** *Commonwealth*, 11/6/51, 11/7/51. **P. 203 Grateful/** Morris to Hale, 1/1/52, in *National Anti-Slavery Standard*, 2/5/52, in BAP; Hale to Morris, 1/18/52, BAP. **P. 203 Lunt/** *Commonwealth*, 11/10/51. **P. 203 Jury/** TAB, 117; *Commonwealth*, 11/13/51.

## THIRTEEN New Alliances, New Divisions

**P. 205 The Minkins trials/** *Commonwealth*, 11/14/51, quoted in *Lib.*, 11/21/51. **P. 205 Hayden, Morris/** BB, 61–63. **P. 206 growing reputation/** RMM, 13; EBL, 99. **P. 206 era**

of change/ *Lib.*, 12/10/52; Nell, *Colored Patriots*, 113; BM, 353. **P. 206 Spiritual gulf**/
RMM, 31. **P. 207 Conversion**/ *Boston Pilot*, 12/31/59; Noel Ignatiev, *How the Irish Became
White* (New York: Routledge, 1995), 162; BNRC, 333; RMM, 8–9. **P. 207 Collins**/ FRM,
30; RMM, 22–23; M. P. Curran, *Life of Patrick A. Collins* (Norwood, MA, 1906), 8–17.
**P. 207 Relationship**/ BB, 61; RMM, 14, 12. **P. 208 Garrison and Douglass**/ Philip Foner,
*History of Black Americans* (Westport: Greenwood Press, 1983), 140–41; Tyrone Tillery,
"The Inevitability of the Douglass-Garrison Conflict," *Phylon* 37, no. 2 (June 1976): 145;
*North Star,* January 1848, July 1848, January 1848; *Lib.*, 9/3/47. **P. 211 early as 1848**/ *Lib.*,
8/25/48. **P. 211 later account**/ *Frederick Douglass's Paper,* 8/12/53. **P. 211 Nell's chagrin**/
*Lib.*, 8/12/53, 12/16/53, 11/18/53; Foner, *History,* 145, 147. **P. 212 Patriots**/ quoted in
WCN, 34; Elizabeth Rauh Bethel, *The Roots of African-American Identity: Memory and History in Antebellum Free Communities* (New York: St. Martin's Press, 1999), 13; *Lib.*, 12/17/52.
**P. 212 Morris and Remond**/ Nell, *Colored Patriots*, 11, 101–4, RMP. **P. 213 Morris testimony**/ Robert Morris, *Speech of Robert Morris, Esq. before the Committee on the Militia, March
3d, 1853,* RMP; Nell, *Colored Patriots*, 11; *Boston Herald*, 4/22/53, in *Lib.*, 5/13/53. **P. 214
Nell was hurt**/ Nell to Post, 8/12/53, WCN. **P. 214 Roberts**/ BNRC, 270, RMP; Henry
Box Brown, *Narrative*, xxviii, xxix; *Lib.*, 4/1/53, 4/1/53. **P. 215 Sumner**/ *Lib.*, 4/1/53,
5/2/51; *Richmond Whig*, quoted in *Lib.*, 5/16/51; Nason, *Life and Times of Charles Sumner*,
132; *Lib.*, 11/12/52, 9/17/52. **P. 215 not forgotten Morris**/ Nell, *Colored Patriots*, 327;
*Lib.*, 12/8/54. **P. 216 Convention**/ *Lib.*, 12/8/54, 8/5/53.

F O U R T E E N  So Close to Passing

**P. 217 Pindall**/ *Lib.*, 11/10/54; Nell to Jeremiah Burke Sanderson, 7/1/57, WCN. **P. 219
almost forgotten**/ BM, 352, 356; *Lib.*, 3/19/52, 1/27/54; Nell to Post, 3/25/53, WCN.
**P. 220 City Council**/ *Lib.*, 3/3/54; City of Boston, *Report of Committee on Public Instruction,
On Case of a Child Excluded From a Public School of This City,* City Document No. 54,
5/22/1854; *Lib.*, 8/18/54. **P. 221 Burns**/ *Washington Union*, quoted in *Lib.*, 6/9/54; TAB.
**P. 221 Court of Common Pleas**/ *Lib.*, 9/8/54; SER, 940; *Boston Post*, 11/1/54. **P. 221
Hillard**/ YCS, 60. **P. 223 Nell**/ *Lib.*, 11/10/54. **P. 223 Know-Nothings**/ George H.
Haynes, "A Know Nothing Legislature," *American Historical Association*, 1896, vol. 1; Ignatiev, *How the Irish*, 85, 162; *Lib.*, 11/10/54; *Atlanta Examiner,* in *Lib.*, 11/24/54; *Boston
Know-Nothing*, in *Lib.*, 11/17/54; Dale Baum, *The Civil War Party System: The Case of Massachusetts, 1848–1876* (Chapel Hill: University of North Carolina Press, 1984); John R.
Mulkern, *The Know-Nothing Party of Massachusetts: The Rise and Fall of a People's Movement* (Boston: Northeastern University Press, 1997), 92. **P. 225 Slack**/ *Boston Commonwealth*, 5/2/85, 4/18/85; *State*, 1/16/86; TESR. **P. 226 his petitions**/ TESR. **P. 228
House report**/ Committee on Education, *Report*, March 17, 1855, Massachusetts State
Archives.

F I F T E E N  September 3, 1855

**P. 230 Bill**/ Arthur Burr Darling, "Prior to Little Rock in American Education: The *Roberts*
Case of 1849–1850," *Proceedings of the Massachusetts Historical Society* 72 (1963): 141; *Boston*

*Post,* 4/4/55; *Lib.,* 4/6/55, *Boston Evening Telegraph,* in *Lib.,* 4/6/55; *Boston Bee,* 4/4/55. **P. 230 Legislators**/ Massachusetts House Special Collections. **P. 231 Morris rejoiced**/ Morris to Sumner, 6/11/60, CSP; *New National Era,* 3/31/70; *Frederick Douglass's Paper,* 5/18/55; FD, 5/13/1855, 57. **P. 231 Others**/ *New York Herald,* quoted in *Lib.,* 5/4/55. **P. 232 most gratifying**/ SER, 1005. **P. 232 Paul**/ *Lib.,* 8/17/55. **P. 232 Nell**/ Nell to Phillips, 7/8/55, WCN; *Lib.,* 8/17/55; Nell to Post, 8/14/55, WCN; *Lib.,* 8/31/55. **P. 234 First day**/ *Boston Evening Telegraph,* 9/4/55, 9/7/55; *Lib.,* 9/7/55; *Boston Bee,* 9/5/55; SCP, 9/11/55; TESR. **P. 236 Displeased**/ *Boston Gazette,* 9/15/55; *Boston Pilot,* 10/6/55. **P. 237 Celebrate**/ BB, 81–82; Nell to Post, 11/30/55, WCN; TESR.

## S I X T E E N  Rock the Cradle of Liberty

**P. 241 Morris's speech**/ *Lib.,* 8/13/58. **P. 242 Committee**/ *Lib.,* 8/28/57. **P. 242 Massasoit Guards**/ RMP; *Boston Herald,* in *Lib.,* 11/27/57; *Boston Bee,* in *Lib.,* 9/10/58, 8/13/58; BNRC, 338–39. **P. 243 Old Virginia**/ *Lib.,* 4/26/61. **P. 244 Outraged Morris**/ *Lib.,* 6/5/63. **P. 244 "Brother"**/ RMM, 38–39. **P. 246 Chelsea mansion**/ *Chelsea Telegraph and Pioneer,* in *Lib.,* 9/24/58. **P. 246 Mayor**/ quoted in EBL, 99. **P. 247 energy was slowing**/ RMM, 42, 46. **P. 249 sent a letter**/ RM to CS, 6/11/60, CSP. **P. 249 Equality**/ Nason, *Life and Times of Charles Sumner,* 149, 208; CS to Edward L. Pierce, 9/11/68, CSP; Louis Ruchames, "Race and Education in Massachusetts," *Negro History Bulletin* 13 (53–59): 55. **P. 250 Preston Brooks**/ Alan Nevins, *The Ordeal of the Union: A House Divided, 1852–1857* (New York: Collier Books, 1992), 444; *Lib.,* 6/13/56, 6/6/56; Nason, *Life and Times of Charles Sumner,* 226; *Lib.,* 11/7/56; Nason, *Life and Times of Charles Sumner,* 250. **P. 251 Sumner advocated**/ McPherson, *Struggle for Equality,* 103; *Congressional Globe,* 42d Cong., 2d sess. 244 (1871), quoted in "Charles Sumner and the Rights of the Negro," by Carl M. Frasure, *Journal of Negro History* 13, no. 2 (April 1928): 146. **P. 252 Death**/ Nason, *Life and Times of Charles Sumner,* 329. **P. 252 Boston**/ *Christian Examiner,* January 1856; *Lib.,* 12/13/61; DD, 231; WD, 378; Horton, "Community Organization," 189; Samuel May and James M. Smith, "The 'Separate but Equal' Doctrine: An Abolitionist Discusses Racial Segregation and Educational Policy during the Civil War," *Journal of Negro History* 41, no. 2 (April 1956): 145; BA, 11; *Lib.,* 6/7/61; *Lockport Daily Journal,* 4/28/63; *Anglo American Magazine,* July 1859, quoted in White, *Antebellum,* 377; *Christian Examiner,* March 1859, quoted in *Lib.,* 3/18/59. **P. 253 nearby states**/ Paul Finkelman, "Prelude to the 14th Amendment: Black Legal Right in the Antebellum North," *Rutgers Law Journal* 17 (Spring/Summer 1986): 425. **P. 254 Boston's progress**/ *Lib.,* 1/11/56, 1/25/56, 6/5/57, 4/17/63, 2/20/65. **P. 255 Community meeting**/ *Lib.,* 8/5/64, 6/9/65, 3/16/60. **P. 255 Nell**/ WCN, 47; Robert P. Smith, "William Cooper Nell: Crusading Black Abolitionist," *Journal of Negro History* 55 (July 1970): 194. **P. 256 Roberts**/ *Lib.,* 3/5/58; *New National Era,* 3/17/70, 3/31/70. **P. 258 her siblings**/ Franklin A. Dorman, *Twenty Families of Color in Massachusetts, 1742–1998* (Massachusetts: New England Historic Genealogical Society, 1998), 120–39. **P. 258 Sarah**/ U.S. Census, Massachusetts Veterans Records, *Massachusetts Marriage Records,* 1867, 201:25; Robert Underwood, *Preliminary Report: The Descendents and Heirs of Robert Roberts, Author of "The House Servant's Directory,"* Gore Place Society, Research Paper No. 5, January 1998.

## EPILOGUE *Brown* and Beyond

**P. 262 twenty-five years**/ Levy and Phillips, "The *Roberts* Case," 517–18; Douglas J. Ficker, "From *Roberts* to *Plessy*: Educational Segregation and the 'Separate but Equal' Doctrine," *The Journal of Negro History* 84, no. 4 (1999): 306–12. **P. 262 Compound**/ Robert Harris, *The Quest for Equality: The Constitution, Congress and the Court* (Westport, CT: Greenwood Publishing Group, 1977), 101. **P. 263 Marshall and Morris**/ RMM, 14; Michael D. Davis and Hunter R. Clark, *Thurgood Marshall: Warrior at the Bar, Rebel on the Bench* (New York: Citadel Trade, 1992); RMM, 40. **P. 263 Tired**/ Williams, *Thurgood Marshall*, 199. **P. 264 Linda**/ Peter Irons, *Jim Crow's Children* (New York: Viking, 2002), 118–19; SJ, 408–9. **P. 264 Johns**/ SJ, 479. **P. 264 NAACP**/ Brief for Appellants in Nos. 1, 2, and 4 and for respondents in No. 10 on Reargument, Appendix to the Supplemental Brief for the United States in Reargument. **P. 265 Hill**/ Interview with Oliver Hill, Richmond, VA, 10/12/03. **P. 265 legal team's brief**/ *Argument: The Oral Argument before the Supreme Court in* Brown v. Board of Education of Topeka, *1952–1955* (New York: Chelsea House Publishing, 1983). **P. 267 Sumner and Warren**/ Gillerman, "Sarah Roberts," 45–46. **P. 268 won a biggie**/ Williams, *Thurgood Marshall*, 227. **P. 268 Catalyst**/ J. Harvie Wilkinson III, *From Brown to Bakke: The Supreme Court and School Integration, 1954–1978* (New York: Oxford University Press, 1979), 49. **P. 269 Freedom day**/ James Fraser, ed., *From Common School to Magnet School: Selected Essays in the History of Boston's Schools* (Boston: Boston Public Library, 1979), 103. **P. 270 Around the nation**/ Irons, *Jim Crow's Children*, 289; Erica Frankenberg, Chungmei Lee, and Gary Orfield, *A Multiracial Society with Segregated Schools: Are We Losing the Dream?* (Cambridge, MA: Harvard Civil Rights Project, 2003). **P. 270 Orfield**/ Adam Cohen, "The Supreme Struggle," *New York Times*, 1/18/2004, 22. **P. 271 Gateways**/ TESR. **P. 271 Garrison**/ Garrison to Morris, 4/22/79, Garrison Papers, Houghton Library, Harvard University. **P. 272 extricate oneself**/ Irwin Howe, *The American Newness* (Cambridge, MA: Harvard University Press, 1986), intro. **P. 272 Luddites**/ James Fraser, *The History of Hope* (New York: Palgrave MacMillian, 2004), xiv. **P. 272 Partial, hopeful**/ SER.

# ACKNOWLEDGMENTS

Our first thank you goes to the hundreds of people who daringly built their homes atop the towering Trimountain now called Beacon Hill, and to the long generations of householders and all in the community—servants to students to workers—who lovingly preserved this extraordinary neighborhood for the future. Every night, as we walked along these brick sidewalks and passed under glowing gas lamps, we could not escape a haunting, evocative sense of what this neighborhood was like in 1849. This historical resonance and beauty inspired and sustained us all along the way.

Yet bricks and cobblestones go only a small way to tell the tale of the women and men who lived on both sides of the Hill, and so we have many people to thank who have worked equally hard to preserve both the story of what happened here and why it matters. We want to thank the rangers (all historians in their own right) of the National Park Service who care for the African Meeting House and all the sites along the Black Heritage Trail in Boston, particularly Horace Seldon and Bernadette Williams. State representative Byron Rushing was helpful as well, but most of all we thank him and all those who helped preserve the heritage of the antebellum free black community through the creation of the Museum of Afro American History more than thirty years ago. Renovation, rebuilding, and new research are all actively underway along Smith Court, and if *Sarah's Long Walk* contributes in any way to the ongoing recovery of the work of this remarkable generation, we are pleased. We tried to make this place come alive in your thoughts, but we hope as well that this story encourages you to visit and take your own long walk through the neighborhood.

This book would not have been possible without the exceptional staff of the Boston Athenaeum, under the kind direction of researcher Stephen Nomack, who have been helpful beyond imagination. Unfailingly curious and courteous, they exemplify historical research assistance of the highest level. We are also indebted to the staffs of the Boston Social Law Library, the Massachusetts Historical Society (in particular Donald Yacovone and director William Fowler), the Gore Place, Massachusetts State Archives, the Bostonian Society, the Essex Institute of Salem, the rare book collection of Houghton Library of Harvard University, the rare book department of the Boston Public Library, as well as the libraries of Howard University, Bowdoin College, and Kent State University.

Individuals not affiliated with the aforementioned societies that we wish to thank include Libby Bouvier of the Supreme Judicial Court Archives; Jonathan Kozol; Lena Reddick and the Roberts family; Rev. Franklin Dorman, whose research into Massachusetts black genealogy is an exemplar of loving historical reconstruction; Professor James Horton, Paul's professor at George Washington University and an inspiration; Professor Donald Jacobs, whose illness in retirement has robbed us all of what promised to be the definitive history of black activism in Boston; Judge Julian Houston; Professor Hubie Jones; Professor James B. Stewart; Rev. Robert McKetchnie; Joy Lucas; Melissa Browne; indomitable local Beacon Hill researcher Michael Terranova; Rev. David Pettee; renowned Boston historian Professor Thomas H. O'Connor; Rev. Forrest Church; Professor Joseph Brodley; John and Mimi Kline; and Lindsay and Lynn Strachan. Having the pleasure to sit down with former NAACP lawyers and civil rights giants Oliver Hill and William Taylor was enough to make this book worth writing, and we also acknowledge Judge Robert Carter.

Stephen wishes to thank everyone associated with the First and Second Church of Boston, especially administrator Ellen Meyers. Paul thanks George Washington University's NAACP chapter and the Leadership Conference on Civil Rights. The support of friends

James Golden, Stephen Harris, Omar Woodard, Steve Puzzo, Joel Brooks, and "the Bens" has been immeasurable and invaluable.

Also located at the crest of Beacon Hill is a small but remarkable press that for 150 years has exemplified the highest liberal spirit in publishing: Beacon Press. If every editor displayed the encouragement and sustaining enthusiasm of Joanne Wyckoff, the nation's writers would be a happier and more fulfilled lot. We thank her and her patient assistant, Brian Halley, from the bottom of our hearts, and we look forward to future projects that will uphold a beleaguered yet absolutely vital tradition of activism and simple justice. And the person who has made all literary things possible, the warm and inventive agent Flip Brophy.

# INDEX

PLAN

of the

CITY of BOSTON.

Lat. N. 42° 21' Lon. E. from Washington 5° 54'

Population 120,000